LECTURES ON
THEORIES OF LEARNING

ALSO BY DENNIS FORD

Fiction

~ Red Star ~
~ Landsman ~
~ Things Don't Add Up ~
~ The Watchman ~

Humor

~ Thinking About Everything ~
~ Miles of Thoughts ~

Family History

~ Eight Generations ~
~ Genealogical Jaunts ~
~ Genealogical Musings ~

Psychology

~ Lectures on General Psychology ~ Volume One ~
~ Lectures on General Psychology ~ Volume Two ~

LECTURES ON THEORIES OF LEARNING

THEORIES OF

DENNIS FORD

LECTURES ON THEORIES OF LEARNING

iUniverse books may be ordered through booksellers or by contacting:

iUniverse
1663 Liberty Drive
Bloomington, IN 47403
www.iuniverse.com
1-800-Authors (1-800-288-4677)

Because of the dynamic nature of the Internet, any web addresses or links contained in this book may have changed since publication and may no longer be valid. The views expressed in this work are solely those of the author and do not necessarily reflect the views of the publisher, and the publisher hereby disclaims any responsibility for them.

Any people depicted in stock imagery provided by Getty Images are models, and such images are being used for illustrative purposes only.
Certain stock imagery © Getty Images.

ISBN: 978-1-5320-7706-7 (sc)
ISBN: 978-1-5320-7708-1 (hc)
ISBN: 978-1-5320-7707-4 (e)

Print information available on the last page.

iUniverse rev. date: 06/17/2019

To my students
and to the memory of Ken Graser

CONTENTS

PREFACE

For many years I taught the graduate Theories of Learning course (PSY 5320) at Kean University in Union, New Jersey. I wanted to create a more permanent record of the lectures in the style of my books on General Psychology. This book reflects that attempt with a few exceptions. In order to keep the size of the book manageable and to avoid a second volume, the lectures on Albert Bandura and on the "memory wars" of the 1980s and 1990s were excluded. Similarly, I excluded an overview of the methodological designs of the Applied Analysis of Behavior. A book does not guarantee that the lectures will avoid sailing into the overpopulated land of oblivion, but it provides a public record of what formerly existed as bullet points in an uncirculated outline.

In earlier years the psychology department was located in Hutchinson Hall on the Main Campus. (The school was Kean College in those years.) Hutchinson Hall was a ponderous user-unfriendly building. The elevator held two or three people at best and the staircases were concrete with handrails raised on concrete walls. Anyone who descended the staircases in inclement weather took their lives in their hands.

In later years the psychology department moved across Morris Ave. to the East Campus in the adjacent town of Hillside. (Kean became a university at this time.) The building had once housed the Pingry School, an upscale and fantastically expensive preparatory school founded in 1861. The interior of the building was rehabilitated and refurbished. The corridors were wood. The lighting was subdued, a mellow golden-brown in color. The spotless floor shone. So did the ceiling. The staircases were safe in any weather. The handrails were easily accessible.

The interior of the building was beautiful. It was also eerie. Theories of Learning was held at night. There were few other night courses in session.

Sometimes we were the only course in session on the entire second floor. I joked that the East Campus was the *Rose Red* of schoolhouses. As in the movie, classrooms mysteriously appeared and disappeared. An entire wing of classrooms appeared in my final semester. As I wandered the empty corridors I expected to encounter something paranormal—maybe the ghosts of former professors, maybe the ghosts of former students. This confuses Stephen King movies, but I expected the ghosts to blink into view with hatchets in their foreheads and caked blood on their uniforms. I told the students that if the lights started to flicker, class was over. I intended to bolt the building and not slow down till I arrived at the Cheesequake rest stop on the Garden State Parkway.

I've been retired for a number of years, but I remember many former students. As is the case in any course, I remember the brightest, most creative students. I suppose I remember the students who were trouble and troubling. I remember many of the faculty in the psychology department. These were the older faculty, nearly all of them retired. For most of my years at Kean I was never in the department in daylight, so I never met the younger faculty, who taught day classes and were never around at night.

The person I remember best was neither student nor teacher. Ken Graser was the maintenance man in Hutchinson Hall. Ken was a soft-spoken, round-faced man with an exceeding fondness for coffee. When we first met, he was in his late fifties. He was an army veteran and a widower. He lived at the time in Sewaren in Woodbridge. He was from a family large enough to field a baseball team with subs on the bench. He had seven brothers and five sisters.

As I usually arrived early for class, Ken and I had long conversations. They must have involved multiple topics, but the topic I most recall was professional baseball. Ken was a devote Baltimore Orioles fan. He had visited the new ballpark at Camden Yards on occasion. I was a tepid Detroit Tigers fan. I had never been to Tiger Stadium. Between the time I arrived and the time Ken checked out, we avidly compared stats and rosters for these teams. And we debated the performances of the various players.

Ken moved to Chelsea, Vermont, after he retired. He lived with a nephew. We never met or spoke again, but we exchanged letters for many years. Ken was a great lover of nature. I believe he was a member of the World Wildlife Fund. He regularly sent clippings and articles about animals and pictures of the Chelsea countryside—there always seemed to be snow on the ground. I sent clippings and articles about sports and about events at Kean and in New Jersey.

Ken died in March 2010. He was 81 years of age.

Note: The text we used for the course was *An Introduction to Theories of Learning* by B.R. Hergenhahn and, later, by Matthew Olson and B. R. Hergenhahn. The last edition used was the eighth, published in 2009 by Pearson Educational.

LECTURE ONE

Introduction to Learning

Most courses start with a definition. Ours is no exception. Edwin Guthrie, one of our theorists, defined learning as the "ability ... to respond differently to situations because of past experience." Gregory Kimble (1917 – 2007) provided the definition that is found in most introductory textbooks—*learning is the relatively permanent change in behavior potentiality that occurs as a result of reinforced practice and experience.*

Definitions are like life rafts dropped from the decks of steamships in storms. They break apart once they hit the water. Ours is no exception. Except for the verb and the articles, our definitions are flotsam in the surf.

Take "change in behavior." Change is what learning is all about. Change is what psychology is all about. Change is what life is all about. No one goes to bed praying, "Dear God, keep me exactly the way I am." We want to be different. We want to do and say different things. We want to be new and improved members of the human race.

Learning involves honest to goodness change. Learning is not the same as habitual action. If I tell you that Trenton is the capital of New Jersey, I'm demonstrating habitual action. I'm telling you what I know. You probably know the same. The moment I found out that Trenton was the capital of New Jersey and retained this information—that was the moment of learning. True learning. Learning is a lot like falling in love. It happens in a moment. We hate to think it, but most everything afterward becomes habitual action.

1

Change comes about through reinforced practice. Change also comes about in other ways. We change because of physical maturation. In peewee baseball leagues coaches put the ball on tees so the tots can hit it. In one- or two-years' time the coaches are pitching the ball and the not-so-little tots are drilling line drives over the shortstops' heads.

Change comes about through temporary physical states, such as fatigue and illness. I suppose I should add intoxication and hangovers to the list. I know how to catch a ball. Usually, I'm pretty good at catching balls. But if I'm sleepy or tired or tipsy, I'm likely to make an error. I haven't unlearned to catch. And I haven't learned anything knew. But my behavior has temporarily changed.

Change also comes about through the principles of persuasive communication. There is a huge literature on social influence coming out of social psychology that concerns the qualities of speakers and speeches. We encounter this literature in politics and in marketing. For example, speakers who argue against their professions—like doctors speaking out against the medical association or lawyers speaking out against the legal association—are perceived as especially trustworthy and believable.

Change comes about through reinforced practice. B. F. Skinner and the operant conditioning crowd would be happy to hear this. They would not be so happy to hear the term "behavior potentiality." For Skinner there is no "potentiality." There is only behavior. I might add that Skinner is the outlier and the exception throughout the course. The other theorists can be more or less lumped together in the theoretical stew. Throughout his long career Skinner was consistent in avoiding what we'll call in the next lecture "intervening variables." He refused to theorize about anything inside the organism, whether psychological or physiological.

Kimble included the term "potentiality" in the definition because learning is not always translated into immediate performance. Organisms do not always show what they've learned. In the 1920s Edward Tolman and his colleagues spoke about *latent learning*. Modern psychologists speak of *behavioral silence*. So a child hears his parents utter a word. The child doesn't rehearse the word. Sometime later, the child uses the word to the dismay of the second-grade teacher. A boy watches his father shave. Later, he plays at shaving, let's hope without a blade. A girl watches her mother put on mascara. Later, she applies the makeup. Let's hope she doesn't get any makeup in her eyes.

I had an experience with behavioral silence recently. I drove into a gas station in Virginia and waited for an attendant to pump the gas. No one came out. I waited, figuring this was the South where people, including gas jockeys, move a tad slower than we do in the North. I realized after a while that no one was coming out. Everyone pumps their own gas in Virginia. I had never pumped gas in my life, but I had seen enough attendants in New Jersey pump gas. I knew what to do, although I had never done it before. After a few dry runs, I filled the tank and drove back to a state where we don't have to exert ourselves in this demeaning way.

A last point about the definition. Skinner firmly believed that reinforcement is a vital component of learning. But not every theorist shared this view. Tolman, for example, believed that reinforcement affected performance and not learning. We perform what we have been reinforced to do, but we learn whether or not we receive reinforcement.

I'll like to introduce four orientations that you may find useful in conceptualizing learning. These orientations are product vs. process, behavioral analysis (the "ABCs" of learning), content vs. capacity, and the person-by-situation approach.

The first orientation is *product vs. process*. We can focus on the product or end result of learning or we can focus on how learning is achieved. Of course, we can focus on both. Most of the time we focus on one or the other. Usually, we focus on product. In this course I invite you to focus on process.

Every morning across our state big yellow buses drive up and the little darlings go off to school. Later in the day, the same buses deliver the darlings back to the corner where they were picked up. A child on the bus that stops at our corner has gotten an "A" in arithmetic. The parents are very proud. The "A" is all they care about. But there are many ways to a grade of "A," even in elementary school. Maybe the child studied long and hard—this is the right way to an "A." But maybe the child cheated and copied answers. Maybe the teacher helped the child take the test—it may be review time and the teacher expects a raise. Maybe the child made lucky guesses. Maybe the test was ridiculously easy.

The focus on product is universal. We want the car fixed. We're not interested in how the mechanic does it, so long the bill is reasonable. We want a steak on the table. We're not interested in how the cow gets from the pasture to the plate—we may turn vegetarian if we saw the process. We want to find out if our candidate won the election. We don't care how the votes are counted. It was only in the Bush – Gore presidential election that people became interested in the process of counting votes.

In this regard I'm reminded of a story about a particular Mafioso who owned the politicians in a Bergen County town. I'm not going to tell you the name of the town in case you live there. It seems in one election a reform candidate looked like the new mayor. Someone asked the Mafioso if he was worried about losing city hall. "Not at all," the mobster supposedly replied. "It's not important who votes, it's important who counts the votes." For the sake of democracy, I like to think the story is apocryphal.

The second orientation is a *behavioral analysis* of the learning situation. This involves unraveling the acronym "ABC." "A" stands for "antecedent." This is the place where learning occurs. Other terms are "situation," "environment," and "context." The items in this place are referred to as "stimuli."

"B" stands for "behavior." The older term, which emphasizes discrete events rather than an ongoing sequence of events, is "response."

"C" stands for "consequences" of the behavior. These consequences immediately follow a behavior (or response). Of course, we can focus on long-term consequences, but a behavioral analysis focuses on immediate consequences. The difference is between what happens in the here and now when we take a drag on a cigarette and what happens over the career of taking drags on cigarettes.

In a sense good behavioral analysis is similar to good journalism. In journalism school they teach reporters to state in the clearest, most precise, terms, "Who did what to whom, where, when and how." I invite you to take that approach with respect to an analysis of behavior—be as literal as possible. We're not in the clouds when we study learning. We're in the swamp and we're going to get dirty.

The third orientation asks us to consider *content vs. capacity*. *Content is what we are being asked to learn*—arithmetic in grade school, theories of learning in grad school. Presumably, content is what we will be quizzed on.

Capacity is the underlying ability to learn particular content. What abilities are required to learn arithmetic? What abilities are required to learn theories of learning? We can view capacity as the underlying *gifts and limitations* a person possesses in mastering particular content. We often think of gifts and limitations in biological terms, often in genetic terms. I suggest that we not overlook psychological gifts and limitations in our analyses. Motivational and emotional factors are important in learning situations. I know from long experience that some intellectually "gifted" students fail at learning content because of the personal baggage they carry into classrooms.

If you wanted to understand content vs. capacity as *nature vs. nurture*, you would not be far off the mark. But the more we learn about the relationship between nature and nurture the more complicated matters become. We live in a scientific period that places great stress on nature. This was not always the case. When I was in school in the 1970s nurture, understood as the environment, was dominant. There are social-cultural factors at play in science as there are in politics and in the media. Of course, neuroscience and genetics were not as developed then as they are now. The concept back then was—change the environment and behavior will change. It was a hopeful and optimistic strategy. And it didn't work out all that well. Currently, the concept is—change the brain and change the genes and behavior will change. It remains to be seen how well this will work out.

The pendulum is not going to shift back—there's too much known about the brain and about genetics—but the situation has, as I said, become complicated. One of the hottest research fields today is epigenetics. Chemical marks or markers sit atop genes, so to say. These marks consist of acetyl, which activates genes, and methyl, which suppresses genes. These chemicals do not change genes. Rather, they affect the activity of genes, turning them on and off and modulating the rate of genetic activity. The interesting thing is these marks are strongly affected by environmental events and by personal experiences.

Research has demonstrated that drugs like cocaine affect epigenetic processes in the reward center of the brain. This is a site called the nucleus accumbens. Since this involves reward, it is a site we would like to visit, frequently. Cocaine instigates acetyl to activate numerous genes at this site.

Complex research with rats found an intergenerational process involving the influence of methyl. Rat pups that were raised by nurturant mothers grew up to be less anxious—and they grew up to be more nurturant in their turns as mothers. Rat pups that were raised by mothers that were not nurturant showed increased methyl activity in a gene that regulates a protein that mediates the response to cortisol, a steroid secreted when stress occurs. The response to stress was intensified in these unfortunate rats. The key element to consider is that the genetic factor was affected by an environmental factor, in this case by non-nurturant mothers.

There are other processes in which environmental events affect neuronal processes. Depending on a person's experience, dendrites and axons proliferate and reconnect. Whenever we have new experiences or think new thoughts, the wiring in the brain at the synapses changes. The process is called *brain plasticity*—we teach this to undergraduates in the introductory course.

Myelin is a substance that speeds up nervous transmission. Myelin is produced not by neurons but by cells in the nervous system called glia (glial) cells. These cells monitor nervous transmission. They gravitate to brain sites that are consistently active. Different practices and occupations result in different brain sites becoming myelinated. The brain of a novelist is myelinated differently than the brain of a major league shortstop. The brain of a shortstop is myelinated differently than the brain of a composer. The key factors in this process are environmental practices and experiences.

I'll like to suggest that we might conceive of capacity (nature) as bestowing a *ceiling effect* or upper limit on characteristics. There are a number of characteristics we might consider—intelligence, longevity, and height, to name three. Let's consider height as prototypical. Nature (genetics) has bestowed an upper limit on an individual's height. There are a number of environmental factors that determine whether the ceiling effect involving height will be reached. Maybe I should say climbed. These factors include diet, health, and the presence or absence of stress in childhood. If we eat well, stay in good health, and avoid excessive stress in childhood, we can attain the God-and-Mendel-given height we were born to express. But no amount of good living is going to turn a person foreordained to be five-foot-ten to become six-foot-seven. If our diet is poor, if our health is poor, and if we suffered excessive stress in childhood, we may not reach the ceiling. A person foreordained to be five-foot-ten may reach five-foot-four. There's a medical condition called "deprivation dwarfism" in which children exposed to severe stress remain abnormally short. The operative factor that stunts growth is lack of sleep. If there's a lot of stress, children do not get adequate sleep. Children grow only in sleep. Lack of sleep results in lack of height. Take the children out of the stressful environment and they revert to growing properly.

The fourth orientation invites us to focus on the *interaction of person and situation* variables. *Students bring to the learning experience attributes that facilitate or hinder learning.* These attributes include capacity, motivation and past experiences in the same or similar environments. These attributes also include the history of reinforcements and punishments and whatever psychodynamic baggage the students haul into class. We all know students who are enthusiastic to learn—I could conquer the nation with a classroom of such students. And we all know troubled students who are anything but enthusiastic about learning.

Although it may sound odd to say, *situations also bring attributes to the learning experience that facilitate or hinder learning.* These attributes include content, the physical setting in which learning takes place, and the expertise of the teachers. We might recall the Russian educator Lev Vygotsky and his concept of the *zone of proximal distance*. This is the idea that educators have to find the right level of content for the groups of students they teach. This level can't be too difficult, else the inexperienced students get intimidated. And this level can't be too easy, else the experienced students get bored.

With respect to the physical setting, it's one thing to learn in a noisy, chaotic and hot environment. It's another thing to learn in a quiet, calm and air-conditioned environment. It's one thing to learn in a swanky building like the one we're in. It's another thing to learn in a dilapidated and distressed place. I'm thinking of some of the inner-city schools. I don't know if it's still in use, but there was a high school named Westside on South Orange Ave. in Newark. The building was built in 1926. It looked like it was built in 1926. It looked like a prison more than a school. None of the water fountains worked. There was no air conditioning. Nothing had been repaired in years. One side of the building overlooked a cemetery. Between assignments the students could watch caskets get lowered into the earth.

Historically, learning psychology emerged from philosophical associationism, which stressed the frequency, similarity and contiguity of ideas and which used introspection as the main method, and from biology (natural philosophy), which stressed the concepts of evolution and the unity of organisms.

The assumption is that we are uncovering the fundamental and universal laws of learning. This analogy is often given—regardless of the make of the vehicle (species) we inhabit, every vehicle on the road runs because of the principles of internal combustion. This is true of sedans and of vans and of race cars and of tractors and, in the case of the make of my car, of jalopies. The shape, color, weight and size of vehicles vary, but the principles that move them are the same. With respect to learning, the idea is that organisms and species differ, but the same principles apply across the road of evolution.

Not everyone agrees with the idea that we should search for the universal principles of learning. James Garcia, whose research on taste aversion we cover in the classical conditioning lecture, believed that psychologists should focus on what makes organisms different and unique.

It is not true that the learning psychologists we study in this course focused exclusively on lower organisms like rats and dogs and pigeons and cats. It is not true today and it was not true at the commencement of psychology. It is true that lower organisms were heavily experimented on. This was due, in part, to the idea I just mentioned—the fundamental principles applied across species. This was also due to issues of experimental control. And it was due to ethical constraints on using humans. Today, we are more sensitive to the welfare of animals. Unfortunately, ethical issues involving animals were of little interest in former years.

Say hello to Ralph the rat. I can control Ralph's environment completely. I can control Ralph's training completely. Nothing happens in Ralph's life that I don't direct. I can control heredity—I knew Ralph's great-great-grandpappy. Ralph does not have a personality that can get in the way of the experiment. Ralph can't purposely sabotage the experiment. Ralph can't deliberately go along and help the experimenter out. I don't need informed consent to proceed. I can sacrifice Ralph after the training and dissect his brain.

Now say hello to Ralph the college sophomore. He's participating in the experiment for a few course credits. I don't know this Ralph from the proverbial hole in the wall. I don't know his history. I don't know what occurred in his life. I don't know his capabilities. I don't know his heredity—I never met his great-great-grandpappy. I don't know his personality. I don't know if he wants to help or hurt the research. I require informed consent before proceeding, which he may or may not give. And I can't sacrifice Ralph after the experiment and dissect his brain.

I'll like to add two observations about the use of lower organisms. We've become squeamish about abusing animals in psychology, but animals are extensively used in medical and pharmaceutical research. Mice, rats and pigs are routinely bred to mimic human diseases and to model drug and other treatments. And I'll like to add that the term "lower organism" is on the pejorative side. Maybe we should drop the term "lower" or replace it with a term like "different." I wonder what these organisms call humans. Do they call us "higher organisms" or "upper organisms?" Maybe they refer to us as "taller organisms."

The study of learning was tied in with particular theorists and with what became known as *schools of psychology*. This was especially true in the period 1930 – 1960.

By "schools" I mean, literally, schools. These schools were, of course, psychology departments in universities. The departments were organized around famous psychologists and their theories and preferred research strategies. There was Hull at Yale, Tolman at Berkeley, and Skinner at Harvard. These psychologists were engaged in active research programs. These programs attracted graduate students. These students became proselytizers for the professors. Some students became prominent psychologists in their own right.

Schools of psychology developed because of the unique social and historical situation of the time. Psychology was a small endeavor at the time these schools flourished. The prominent psychologists were acquainted with one another—and they were in competition with one another. Theorists competed for students and for research grants and for publishing opportunities and, not incidentally, for the truth. There were intellectual battles between psychologists who favored classical conditioning as the fundamental process and psychologists who favored operant conditioning as the fundamental process. We might say this was a "cat and dog" fight and we wouldn't be far off the mark.

The search for victory in these battles was no idle quest. The question which learning process is fundamental is an important one. The losing side wouldn't vanish, but the terms and procedures involved would be subsumed by the winning side and be reinterpreted using the winning vocabulary. Skinner, for one, was fond of reinterpreting classical conditioning research in the vocabulary of operant conditioning. For example, he reinterpreted Watson and Rayner's famous experiment with Little Albert as demonstrating operant punishment rather than as anything Pavlovian.

The schools of psychology that we cover in this course demonstrate what I call *oracular psychology*. The psychologists who directed these schools were famous and important men. Their classes were well attended. Their books and papers were read and discussed. Their theories were debated, hotly. They were seen as occupying a higher level than the ordinary herd of psychologists. Oracular psychology became a hazard in personality psychology—consider the worshipful treatment of Freud, Jung and Adler—but it existed to a lesser degree in learning psychology. It's something we want to avoid in science, where evidence is supposed to decide matters, but psychologists are people and people can't help themselves. It's in our nature to seek out sages and celebrities. And it's in our nature to see ourselves as full of sagacity when people seek us out and ask us questions. All kinds of questions about all kinds of topics.

I'll like to introduce the concept of the *referent experiment*. Several of our theorists, notably Tolman and Skinner, had a preferred experimental arrangement. Tolman used mazes as his preferred methodology. Skinner used the operant conditioning chamber. Referent experiments provide the major units and concepts of the theories they originate. They serve as orientations that provide the vocabulary and the intellectual horizon of the theories. They are what the theorist comes back to in discussions. And in the case of Tolman and Skinner they became worldviews. Tolman saw the world as an immense "God-given maze." Skinner saw the world as an immense operant conditioning chamber amenable to the manipulations of crafty behavior analysts.

Experiments are crucial in learning psychology because we want to get to the causes of behavior. We want to discover how practice and experience change behavior—and we want to be sure that it is only practice and experience that change behavior and not something else. Discovering cause and effect relationships are possible only in experiments. It is not possible to discover cause and effect relationships using case studies, surveys, or naturalistic observation as our methods.

The strength of experimentation is its artificiality—artificiality is also the weakness of experiments. In experiments we attempt to control all factors that may obscure the relationships among the variables we study. This is not ordinarily possible in the "real world." Think of the difference in the control possible in an operant conditioning chamber and the lack of control in a playground.

The relationship among variables in experiments can be considered in terms of a *signal and noise* analysis. In experiments we control the noise in order to ascertain whether a signal exists—we're like the announcer in that old television series *The Outer Limits* in the sense that we adjust the horizontal and the vertical in the laboratory. If it exists, we expect the signal—the relationship—to appear once the noise is squelched.

Lest we grow overly fond of experiments as the be-all and end-all of research methods, we need to keep in mind that many important topics are not amenable to experimental control. Topics such as love and hate and creativity and all those indefinable quirks that go into personalities and into interpersonal relationships. With these topics we have to accept "natural experiments" and "accidents of nature" as the sources of data. And, of course, there are ethical constraints on what we can do in experiments. We'd all like to take Watson's "world to raise him in" and create our versions of men and women, but that's not possible. The fact that it's not possible is a good thing. Our versions of experimentally-created men and women may turn out to be modern versions of Frankenstein and his bride.

A few concluding issues.

In America classical and operant conditioning derived from a behaviorist or behavioral perspective. Learning psychology and behaviorism are not the same, however. Many behaviorists were learning psychologists, but we can certainly study learning without becoming behaviorists. We'll look closely at behaviorism when we review the careers of John Watson and B. F. Skinner. We'll see that behaviorism was very much a product of the scientific milieu that existed at the time of its origin.

The early behaviorists—the later ones, too—tended to work out of a biological orientation and to reject philosophical viewpoints. I suppose this reflects the pragmatic and extraverted character of American scientists. Behaviorists tended to reject theories that involved cognitive concepts. That is, they rejected the mind as the object of study. They were not intrigued by the irony that the mind was the subject studying behavior. Behaviorists rejected introspection as the method of study and they rejected instinct as a causal factor. As we'll see, the concept of instinct was badly utilized in the time period behaviorism arose. Finally, behaviorists held to a stridently environmental focus, which is also part of the American character.

The capability to learn produces a whole new level of adaptation and survivability. Many organisms are creatures of instinct. They are limited to the capabilities God and Darwin implanted in them. These capabilities work fine so long as the environmental niche they inhabit remains unchanged. If the niche changes—say a food source disappears or a new predator arrives on the scene—these organisms are in trouble. They have limited ability to change. Other organisms—organisms like us—have the capacity to change. We even have the capacity to change the niche. We have evolved the capabilities of abstract thought and social communication. We learn from practice and experience and we pass our learning onto our descendants.

NET airs a documentary every so often about events at a crocodile-infested river in Africa. (You don't want to watch this documentary at dinner time.) A herd of wildebeests needs to cross this river—the grass must be chewier on the other side. The first wildebeest enters the river and gets eaten. The second one goes in and gets eaten. The third one goes in and gets eaten. At this point the herd charges across. A few more get eaten, but the majority make it safely to the other side.

Consider what would happen if a group of humans arrived at this river. The first one goes in and gets eaten. The second one goes in and gets eaten. The third one goes in and gets eaten—this one must be from Bayonne. The rest of us are not charging across. We'll look for a different place to cross. And we'll likely put up a sign. "Danger! Crocodiles!" The next herd of wildebeests that arrive at the river are on their own, but the next group of humans has been warned.

And consider what happens in the complex where I live. Every summer a bright gull learns to tear open garbage bags in the dumpster and help itself to last night's dinner. There soon follow raucous fights in the parking lot over leftover scraps of food. I don't know, maybe a second bright gull learns the same behavior. These bright gulls can stay fed all season long, but they can never pass the information on. When they die, they take dumpster diving with them into the avian afterlife. Every summer, members of the flock have to learn this behavior anew. Humans can dumpster dive, too, if we want a free meal. And we can pass this behavior onto other people. "If you're broke and desperate for food, here's what you do—tear open a garbage bag in a dumpster and help yourself." When I die, the information stays behind. I like to think it helps people in need of a meal.

Sigmund Koch (1917 - 1996), the great psychologist and philosopher, suggested that a part of the learning process in science involves learning what to observe and pay attention to. (Koch, affectionally called the "other Sigmund," was a critic of learning theories, especially Hull's. He edited the six-volume series *Psychology: A Study of a Science* in the 1950s. The series was intended as a summary of psychological research as it stood in the middle of the twentieth century. The essays on learning appeared in *Volume Two*.) Koch believed that learning a particular science was a kind of *perceptual training*. Of course, we have to be sure we're looking for something that exists. This has not always been the case.

In this course we become sensitive to the arrangement of stimuli, as in classical conditioning, and to the immediate consequences of responses, as in operant conditioning. I'll like you to think as concretely and literally as possible. I'll like you to think in the present tense. And I'll like you to stop making the fundamental attribution error. The fundamental attribution error is a concept in social psychology in which we look for the causes of behavior inside people, as in the personality or in the mind, rather than in the social situations people find themselves in. I invite you to focus on social situations rather than on personalities or on minds, whether conscious or unconscious. In this course I want you to stop thinking mental.

Koch's suggestion that learning a science involves perceptual training applies to all areas of expertise. Forensic scientists are trained to look for the implications of clues at crime scenes. Meteorologists are trained to look for the implications of cloud formations. Anthropologists are trained to look for the implications of shards found in clay. Medical doctors are trained to look for implications of the sights and sounds found in bodies. My doctor listens to my heart and my breathing. He also squeezes my ankles. Either he's looking for something that could indicate a problem or he's a very weird man. I prefer to think it's the former.

Thank you.

LECTURE TWO

Operationism and Fallibilism

The early psychologists who were not radical behaviorists had a problem. A lot of research had been conducted with lower organisms, as we call them. The conclusions drawn from this research were then generalized to an organism called a "human being," who had a private interior life of thoughts and feelings. A rather large question loomed—how shall these private factors be included in theories based on animal research?

The idea developed that there is a class of unobservable variables called *intervening variables* that exist inside organisms and that presumably lie between observable independent and dependent variables. These intervening variables influence dependent variables (changes in behaviors), but they have to be inferred from behavior. For example, something called "motivation" may influence a student's performance in school. And something called "mood" may influence the interpretation of events. Motivation and mood seem to be important factors, but they are not as easily definable as conditioned responses or operant rates of response.

Early on, Edward Tolman and others introduced intervening variables into psychology via the concepts of *operationism* and *operational definitions*. Intervening variables could be introduced into theories if:

1. They were anchored to specific experimental manipulations.
2. They led to predictable behavioral outcomes.

The idea, which was borrowed from physics, was that an intervening variable was operationalized by the way it was defined or measured.

Intelligence was a score on a test. Anxiety was a score on a survey. Anger was a score on another survey.

Every student who does research faces the issue of operational definitions. How shall I define a particular variable? The usual way to proceed is to choose the survey that is most heavily used. That is, students generally rely on the consensus of experts in the selection of methods and surveys.

The hoary issue of operational definitions is still causing methodological grief. Researchers in brain imaging studies using the most sophisticated devices face the same problem psychologists struggled with a century ago. I can pinpoint the area of the brain that lights up when I study the concept of hope, but how shall I define hope in the behavioral sense and how shall I create procedures that result in participants feeling hopeful? I can pinpoint the area of the brain that lights up when I study the concept of love, but how shall I define love in the behavioral sense and how shall I create procedures that result in participants feeling love? The technical sides of these studies are straightforward, but the venerable issue of operationism is still very much with us when it comes to implementing procedures that lead to internal (brain) states.

In the 1930s and 1940s there was an avalanche of intervening variables in learning psychology, as we shall see when we get to Tolman and Hull. The situation is immeasurably worse in personality psychology. It became obvious that operationism in psychology was not the same as operationism in physics. In physics there is no surplus meaning when a variable is operationalized. The concept is exactly as defined. So temperature is—or once was—the level of mercury in a tube. Force is exactly mass times acceleration.

This is not how things are in psychology, although people who do research write as if it were. Intelligence is a score on a test—and it is a lot more. Anxiety is a score on a survey—and it is a lot more. Anger is a score on another survey—and it is a lot more.

The situation is complicated by the fact that each intervening variable can be assessed—inferred—in a number of ways. The different ways may not correlate strongly—let's hope the same area of the brain lights up. I can operationalize anger using a self-report survey, or as fantasies on a projective test, or as the number of angry responses in a word association test, or as the number of angry words spoken in a conversation, or as a pattern of nonverbal behavior (making threatening gestures or putting on the angry face). A person may be angry in one assessment, but not in another. Some psychologists believe it is possible to repress anger. And, of course, a person may conceal anger by pretending to be amicable, which is the essence of what an intervening variable is all about and the perfect example of the difficulties we encounter in psychology.

I'll like to add that we have in psychology a peculiar fixation with single numbers as indicators of complex processes. So I score 120 on an intelligence test, as if a number can capture something as complicated as intelligence. I suppose the idea is that the number allows us to rank order individuals, but words like "low" and "moderate" and "high" can serve without the pretense that a score of 120 is superior to a score of 115 and inferior to a score of 125.

In 1948 Paul Meehl and Kenneth MacCorquodale suggested that we should distinguish between measurable intervening variables and problematically measurable internal variables they called *hypothetical constructs*. The level of a particular hormone would serve as an intervening variable. Intelligence and anxiety and anger would serve as hypothetical constructs. These constructs exist, but they are infinitely more difficult to measure (operationalize) than the level of a hormone. Contrary to their sage advice, in this course we refer to all internal variables as intervening variables regardless how easy or difficult it is to assess them.

Tolman was sensitive to these issues. He stated that intervening variables are "… intermediating functional processes which interconnect between the initiating causes of behavior … and the final resulting behavior." He went on to state that intervening variables "… are more in the minds of psychologists than they are in reality."

Let me introduce a theory of learning that has intervening variables. This is the theory of O. Hobart Mowrer (1907 - 1982). According to Mowrer, there are four basic situations that produce emotional states. These states serve as intervening variables.

> When a safety signal turns on, an organism experiences *hope*.

When a safety signal turns off, an organism experiences *disappointment*.

When a danger signal turns on, an organism experiences *fear*.

When a danger signal turns off, an organism experiences *relief*.

It's pretty clear that experimental manipulations can lead to safety and danger signals turning on and off, so Mowrer's theory fulfills the first requirement of introducing intervening variables into our theories. The operative process involves classical conditioning. As we'll see in the lecture on avoidance learning, the relief that occurs when a danger signal turns off serves as a reinforcer that can increase the rate of a response. The operative process involves operant conditioning. The second requirement of introducing intervening variables into our theories is also fulfilled.

Hobart Mowrer was a prolific experimenter and theorist in the area of learning from the late 1930s to 1960, when he abruptly changed directions and became one of the founders of small group psychotherapy. His major works on learning are *Learning Theory and Behavior* and *Learning Theory and the Symbolic Process*. I was a huge fan of Mowrer back when I was in college. I think he deserves a chapter in the text all to himself.

Mowrer self-disclosed that he led a "double life"—a successful and proper public life and a secretive private life of torment. He self-disclosed that he suffered from periodical mood disorders. The story goes that he crashed into major depression on the way to becoming president of the American Psychological Association. In developing his clinical views Mowrer became a severe critic of Freud—in this, he was not alone. He believed that Freud had things in reverse. The id is not repressed. The superego is repressed. The id achieves gratification in a selfish life style that is secretive and immoral.

Treatment to right this reversal occurred in small groups modelled after Alcoholics Anonymous. The groups were called "integrity groups." The troubled person had to come clean and acknowledge his or her secrets in a public confession and the person had to make amends for the sins of the past. Going forward, the person had to live honestly and morally. Of course, this is all "in theory" and "on paper." Integrity therapy worked as well as the therapies it was meant to replace, which is to say, not very well. It didn't work to "cure" Mowrer, but maybe cure is not the right word when it comes to a human life. Mowrer opted to commit suicide at the age of 75 when he was at the verge of another episode of major depression. This is self-disclosure made from beyond the grave.

I thought Mowrer might have been onto something by having patients self-disclose their transgressions. After all, Alcoholics Anonymous is an effective treatment for many people and confession of sins has been a sacrament of the Christian church for two millennia. But I'm no longer sure about public confession. I'm not so sure secrets are things to avoid. I'm not saying we should live immorally, but everyone is entitled to a private life. Andre Malraux, the French writer, claimed that we are what we hide from other people. Secrets aren't always burdens. Sometimes, secrets are the exuberant and thrilling parts of our identities. Sometimes, they're the parts we think about in the quiet moments. Sometimes, they're the parts we relish and cherish. Secrets don't always have to be bad and we don't have to know everything about one another. We can keep up the façade and we can let others maintain their good faces.

Let me now present a theory that has no intervening variables. This is the theory of operant conditioning associated with B. F. Skinner. As with Mowrer's, there are four components.

> *Positive reinforcement* is the situation in which the rate of a response increases when followed by favorable consequences.

> *Positive punishment* is the situation in which the rate of a response decreases when followed by unfavorable consequences.

> *Negative reinforcement* is the situation in which the rate of a response increases when the response removes undesired or aversive stimuli.

Negative punishment is the situation in which the rate of a response decreases when the response removes desired or favorable stimuli.

Note that these four statements do not involve any intervening variables. Only stimuli and responses are stated. Everything is at the surface. There is no going "inside the organism." I should say there is no going inside the organism other than the judgments of what constitutes favorable or unfavorable consequences. Certainly, there is no consideration of emotions like hope or fear or disappointment or relief.

Let's move onto a few considerations about science and theories.

There are three broad categories of science—Baconian, Newtonian, and Romantic. *Baconian science* is named for Roger Bacon, considered one of the founders or codifiers of science. I think it was named for Roger. It may have been named for Francis. I always get Roger and Francis confused. I know it's not named for Kevin. In any event, the goal of Baconian science is to build up encyclopedias of knowledge. The goal is to know everything that's knowable about particular topics. This is what the Mormon Church does with genealogy. They want to get everything that's get-able.

The goal of *Newtonian science* is to derive explicit and generalizable theories, preferably in formulaic format. For example, F = MA. Force is equal to mass times acceleration. This formula is applicable in outer space. It's applicable on highways. And it's applicable on football fields. Most learning theories are Newtonian in orientation, although not formulaic. Hull is the only theorist we cover who attempted to put concepts into formulas. Skinner, as always, is the exception. He's anti-Newtonian. He once wrote an essay, *Are Theories of Learning Necessary?*

The goal of *Romantic science* is to snuggle with our significant others while drinking champagne and listening to New Age music. Actually, it's not. The Romantic orientation focuses on solving specific problems rather than on accumulating warehouses of data. You might remember the timeworn distinction between basic science, which would be Baconian, and applied science, which would be Romantic. Using my genealogy example, we might say that in Romantic science we strive to learn who our great-grandparents were. We don't want everybody's great-grandparents. Just our own.

If science has a goal, it is to describe and explain the world and the people in it. To say the same thing differently without the egomaniacal "explain the world," *the goal of science is to describe and explain relationships among classes of events.* That is, science attempts to describe and explain *empirical regularities.*

Some of these regularities will be *correlational*—what is associated with what; what goes with what. For example, a dislike of germs is associated with an avoidance of banisters in public places. And social shyness is associated with an inability to make decisions.

Some of these regularities will be *causal*—what leads to what; what makes what happen. For example, overly severe toilet training leads to a dislike of germs and to an avoidance of banisters in public places. And excessive punishment in childhood leads to social shyness and to an inability to make decisions.

In theories of learning we want to describe and explain how organisms, lower and higher on the evolutionary scale, acquire responses. We want to describe and explain changes in behavior. And we want to describe and explain the processes responsible for changing behavior.

Theories are complex sets of assumptions about empirical regularities from which testable statements—hypotheses—are drawn (deduced). In personality theory the collected works of Sigmund Freud are twenty odd volumes long. The collected works of Carl Daddy-o Jung are even longer. We can't test every statement in these volumes. (Not that anyone has tried.) But we can deduce specific hypotheses from these books and put these hypotheses to the test. (Not that this has been overly successful.)

Theories include statements about relationships—these statements are the hearts and souls of theories. Theories also include a lot of tangential items—particular vocabularies, particular statistical techniques, particular methodologies, and general philosophical and intellectual notions about what we're looking for in our research and how we're going to find it.

There is a brief list of six honorable characteristics that we would like theories to possess. As we go through the course, I invite you to assess how each theory fulfills or fails to fulfill these characteristics. I invite you to do the same with theories you cover in other courses.

We want our theories to move beyond description and to have *explanatory power* involving new research and new hypotheses. We want to explain the future, not the past. It's too easy to explain the past after it occurs. And we need to be aware that altered descriptions frequently masquerade as explanations. This is a case of "in other words." The other words may provide better metaphors and similes, but they may not add anything to the explanation. I recall a child asking me why the peach on our kitchen table was so big. I answered, "Because it's large," which was true, but which doesn't explain why the peach was big. A neighbor once asked why the hot water tap in our kitchen sink wasn't working. I answered, "Because it's broken," which was true, but which doesn't explain why my neighbor couldn't wash the dish.

We want our theories to be *testable and to be testable independently* of the source of the original research. If a particular result is found in Union, we want it to be found in Monroe and in Seaside Heights and in the rest of our wonderful state. Not to mention in the other 49 states. Some years ago, physicists in Texas announced that they had created fusion in drinking water. If that were the case, they solved our energy woes till the end of time. I believe anything is possible in a glass of water in Texas, but laboratories in other states could not reproduce their results, so it was dismissed as some kind of procedural artifact.

We want our theories to be *productive of research and ideas.* We want our theories to leave the laboratories and go out and do some good in the world, like Tom Joad in *The Grapes of Wrath.* In the psychology of learning we have the example of operant conditioning that left the laboratories for the world of classrooms and boardrooms and consulting rooms.

We want our theories to be *parsimonious.* That is, we want our theories to explain empirical relationships with the least number of concepts required. Science is inherently conservative. We want to get as much mileage out of existing concepts before we introduce additional concepts. I think it was Harry Harlow (1905 – 1981) who said that the entire weight of psychology rests on the bars in operant conditioning chambers. If it wasn't Harry Harlow who said this, then it was the old fellow who looked like him and who hung out in the Wagon Wheel Tavern on Carr Ave. in Keansburg.

Sometimes complex processes are studied in the light of simpler processes. This is referred to as the use of *models*. In medicine human diseases and treatments are routinely studied using animals like mice and pigs. In our advanced era these animals are genetically tampered with. In psychology Eric Kandel won a Nobel Prize for studying neural processes in sea snails. Eminently Baconian, his conclusions were forthrightly applied to human memory and conditioning.

We want our theories to be *adequately communicated*. There is something desirable and esthetically pleasing in reading an interesting and well-written paper. Freud won a Nobel Prize not in science but in literature. B. F. Skinner was considered an excellent writer. He started out wanting to be a novelist. Later in his career, he wrote a novel, *Waldon Two*. He stated that he periodically reviewed the elements of grammar in order to present his concepts more effectively. Readers may not agree with him, but his writing is crystal clear and he's never boring.

The sixth and final desirable characteristic in theories is that they be *criticize-able and refutable*. That is, *they can be shown to be wrong*.

The traditional view was that scientific knowledge was certain, final and free from error. This view is no longer tenable in any field. The philosophical orientation I'll like to advance is *fallibilism*, which is the doctrine that *all knowledge is incomplete and in need of correction*. "In need of correction" is a polite way of saying that some aspect of our knowledge is wrong.

Every field in science demonstrates the incompleteness of knowledge. This is true of physics, of medicine, of biology, of paleontology, and so on through the campus directory. This is true of the hard physical sciences and of the so-called "soft" social sciences. Our concepts are always limited and *based on the knowledge available at a particular point in time*. Sometimes our theories need tweaking. Sometimes our theories need changes, minor or major. And sometimes our theories are flat-out wrong.

In the 1940s a theoretical claim arose in the psychodynamic camp that cold, emotionless parenting leads to autism. (The claim, which probably always lurked in psychology, explicitly appeared in a 1948 paper by Freida Fromm-Reichmann.) The claim soon extended into other pathologies. Bad parenting leads to schizophrenia. Bad parenting leads to anxiety disorders.

Bad parenting leads to mood disorders. The claim lasted for the rest of the century and was held by virtually every clinician with the possible exceptions of Adlerians and behaviorists. Unfortunately, the idea is still floating in the intellectual ether. In 2014 a student asked me if she did something as a parent that resulted in autism in her child.

The claim that bad parenting causes psychological disorders was mainstream in those years. It was a claim that "went viral," in modern parlance. And it was a claim that was wrong. It led to great harm, dumping horrendous guilt trips on parents and hindering successful treatments for the offspring.

People like Fromm-Reichmann were kind and gentle souls who sincerely wanted to help people. They were fine clinicians—and they were bad scientists. They made no attempt to ascertain whether their claim was correct.

Let's overlook the fact that the claim originated in case studies written by highly opinionated people full of their own importance and certain of their own insights. Before we can decisively claim that bad parenting results in psychological disorders, we need to examine three other situations. We need to explore the possibility that bad parenting results in children who have no psychological disorders. We need to explore the possibility that warm, emotionally-appropriate parenting results in children who have psychological disorders. And we need to explore the possibility that warm, emotionally-appropriate parenting results in children who have no psychological disorders.

None of these three situations were considered by generations of clinicians. Clinicians fixated on one situation to the exclusion of situations that could prove them wrong—if not wrong in total, then only partially correct.

A few additional comments before we move on. Note that an entire field can hold mistaken viewpoints—there must be a better term than "mistaken viewpoints," considering the damage this particular viewpoint resulted in. This should give us pause when we consider relying on the consensus of experts. The claim about bad parenting and psychological disorders didn't belong to a fringe subgroup of clinicians. It belonged to nearly every practicing clinician. It was a "paradigm" and "normal science" to use Thomas Kuhn's famous terms. Finally, these clinicians never fully addressed the ever-thorny issue of operational definitions. Just what is bad parenting? What is good parenting? How is bad parenting different from good parenting? And they never addressed the possibility that they had things in reverse—psychological disorders in children result in cold and emotionless parents.

The fallibilist orientation I'll advance derives from the philosopher Karl Popper (1902 - 1994). Popper is generally known as a "philosopher of science," but he made important contributions in a number of fields, including the social sciences and political philosophy. His most famous book is *The Open Society and Its Enemies* (1945).

In Popper's view the search for knowledge starts with problems. (Popper lies in the Romantic tradition.) We want to solve a problem. We want to find something out. We want to resolve a discrepancy. To solve problems, we give answers—tentative answers. Most researchers call these answers "theories" and "hypotheses." Popper called these answers *conjectures*. (I used the term "viewpoint" in the comments about bad parenting.) As a civilian (non-scientist), I can stop once I state my conjectures, sit back, and congratulate myself on my perspicuity. As a scientist, I have the additional obligation—burden, as it often turns out—to test my conjectures against reality. Have I solved the problem? Are my conjectures correct? Are my conjectures incorrect?

Conjectures occur in the context of our current knowledge. A conjecture stated in 2019 is going to conceptualize things differently than a conjecture stated in 1989. Conjectures are complex and carry a lot of background knowledge. In psychology background knowledge involves statistics and various ways of collecting data. Conjectures are creative acts akin to art and fiction. *They are the stories we tell ourselves about the world and the people in it.* However, unlike art or fiction, conjectures in science must be matched against reality. They need to *correspond* to the way the world really works.

Popper's approach is deductive and decidedly anti-inductive. We can never go from a particular instance found in New Jersey to a general law applicable everywhere. Nor can we go from a particular successful test of a conjecture to a general law. In the former, we do not observe every instance—famously, we haven't seen that every swan is white. In the latter, we do not repeat the test. Or we rarely repeat tests. The failure in psychology to repeat experiments has recently come under scrutiny. This is related to the rather nasty can of worms in which failed repetitions are never reported. We never know whether the successful outcome was one of one attempt or one of five attempts or one of twenty attempts.

Every conjecture involves a *horizon of expectations* in which we expect certain events to occur. We expect certain outcomes. For example, we expect that psychologically disordered individuals experienced bad parenting. And we expect other events and outcomes not to occur. We do not expect to find that psychologically disordered individuals experienced good parenting. If the events that we expect to occur actually occur, then the conjecture is proven (or confirmed). No! If the events that we do not expect to occur actually occur, then the conjecture is disproven (or not confirmed). Yes! We can put the conjecture in an o-pine box and bury it.

The search for truth is lopsided. We cannot go from the truth of evidence to the truth of theories. We can go from the falsehood of evidence to the falsehood of theories—that is, our theories *do not correspond* to the way the world really works.

The first situation—going from the truth of evidence to the truth of theories—is called *affirming the consequence*. It is an invalid way to proceed, according to the rules of deductive logic. So I find a white swan and I conjecture that all swans are white. We're back to the weakness of induction—there are other swans in the world than the one I observed and they may not all be white. (The Cape May zoo has black swans on exhibit.) I find an extravert who uses projection as a defense mechanism and I conjecture that all extraverts use projection as a defense mechanism. I'm back at the same inductive starting gate. There are many extraverts in the world and not all of them use projection.

The second situation—going from the falsehood of evidence to the falsehood of theories—is called the *modus tollens*. It is a valid way to proceed, according to the rules of deductive logic. I claim that all swans are white. I just saw a black swan in Cape May. My conjecture has been refuted and we're in trouble. I claim that all extraverts use projection as their defense mechanism. I just found an extravert who uses introjection. My conjecture has been refuted and we're back in trouble.

The argument is made against Popper that a particular refutation does not ordinarily knock a conjecture out of the ballpark and into the swamp. This is true. However, a refutation indicates that something is amiss. Maybe the surveys I used to assess extraversion and style of defense mechanism were not sensitive enough—this is an issue of operational definitions. Maybe there was something wrong with my sample. Maybe I should have sampled people from Bergen County rather than from Ocean County. Maybe extraverts use projection in specific situations, but not in all situations. Maybe these situations were not addressed in my research. But maybe my conjecture is wrong. Maybe extraverts do not use projection. Maybe we just don't know enough about extraversion and projection.

Popper believed that he discovered something fundamental about the scientific process. Scientific conjectures, contrasted with nonscientific conjectures, can be refuted. He believed this fact served as the *demarcation* between scientific knowledge and knowledge that is not scientific. He believed that the foremost requirement in developing scientific theories is that we state theories in ways that allow them to be criticized and refuted.

I'm not sure that refutability is the demarcation between science and nonscience, given the many nutty ideas that have appeared in the history of science, but I think it is essential that we consider refutability in assessing theories. It is a moral imperative. And it is realistic. Nature says "Wrong" to our ideas far more frequently than she says "Right." Contrary to popular opinion, science progresses not from being less right to being more right, but from being *more wrong to being less wrong*. At any given point in time our knowledge is incomplete and our understanding is limited. This is especially true at the outset of research. We often advance simple conjectures to explain complex situations. These simple conjectures are often stated as all-encompassing truths, such as cold and emotionless parenting results in psychological disorders. It's all too easy to prove ourselves right. If we're good with words and have command of the facts, we can prove anything. (If you're of a certain age, you may remember how Lou Costello was able to prove that 2 + 2 = 5 on the wall of Sidney Fields's rooming house.) For good measure, we can pump our theories full of high-level statistics—if we do, no one will challenge us.

I'll close by returning to what we teach undergraduates on day one of Introduction to Psychology. Whatever our level of sophistication, we need

LECTURE THREE

Habituation and Sensitization

Habituation and sensitization are two phenomena that, while they may not qualify as principles of conditioning, produce changes in behavior. They are certainly ubiquitous in our daily experiences. And they are phenomena that must be controlled in conditioning experiments.

Habituation is the process that results in decreased responding to a repeating (benign) stimulus.

Sensitization is the process that results in increased responding to a novel stimulus in an aroused organism. The arousal is due to a painful or emotionally-arousing stimulus. The exaggerated response or overreaction is to a second stimulus that follows the painful or emotionally-arousing stimulus.

Habituation is a common experience in our daily lives. I once worked with a gentleman named Keith. I'm not going to say his family name because you may know him—it's a small world and I don't know who you know. Keith was a fine man, but he had one flaw—he bathed in Stetson cologne. I could smell him, sight unseen, a block away. The issue regarding habituation is that after a few minutes I no longer smelled Stetson cologne. The odor had habituated. I became, as is said, "nose blind."

I once had an uncle named Albert. I'm not going to say his family name—if you're curious, it wasn't Ford. He wouldn't mind, but it's not proper to talk about departed relatives. Uncle Albert was, like Keith, a fine man. Like Keith, he had a flaw. It was a more serious flaw than Keith's. Uncle Albert smoked Cuban cigars. The cigars must have cost the little income he got from Social Security and they smelled to the place we like to think he's occupying. They were stinkers in short, positively stinkers of the sinus-grabbing kind. The issue regarding habituation is that after a few minutes I no longer smelled Uncle Albert's cigar. The odor had habituated. Once again, I became "nose blind."

Here are additional examples of habituation provided by students in previous semesters:

- ticking clocks,
- the odor of a gym,
- the odor of chlorine in an indoor pool,
- the odor of spices in a pizzeria,
- the scent of air freshener in a car,
- the scent of kitty litter,
- the scent of house candles,
- the sounds of conveyors in a warehouse,
- the sounds of fans in a room,
- the sounds of escalators in a building,
- background music in a department store.

I'll end this list of examples with my personal favorite. It actually happened. There are no Latino people in the town where I live. The self-service checkout at the supermarket allows for instructions in English or in Spanish. The young lady clerk who is supposed to watch for shoplifting has heard the English instructions hundreds of times on her shift. She no longer pays attention. She has habituated to the English instructions. I decided one day to shake things up and use the Spanish instructions. Once she heard Spanish, she instantly woke up and sprang into action. She rushed over and switched the instructions to English. "*Por favor,*" I said, "I prefer to bag the groceries in *El Español.*" It didn't do any good. She went back to her station and re-habituated and I had to bag in English.

The process of habituation is used in the study of infant perception— habituation is also used in the study of animal perception. A particular image or sound or smell is presented and the orientations of the infants are noted. After a few repetitions, the infants habituate. The infants no longer pay attention—infants habituate as rapidly as I did to Keith's cologne and

Uncle Albert's stinky stogies. At this point a different stimulus is presented. If the infants perceive the new stimulus, there will be changes in their orientation and visual fixation. The infants will react and pay renewed attention. The new stimulus is within their sensory repertoire. If the infants don't react, the new stimulus is not within their sensory repertoire.

The infants and the clerk in the supermarket demonstrate *recovery from habituation* or *dishabituation*. When a new stimulus is presented after habituation occurs, there is a return to normal responding. The organisms fixate and reorient on the new stimulus. We say the organisms "pay attention." Maybe we should say the organisms pay "renewed attention." Dishabituation is a factor that needs to be controlled in conditioning experiments. In classical conditioning there's the daily presentation of meat and suddenly on a particular day a bell rings before the meat is presented. Something different has occurred. Something new has happened. We have to be sure conditioning occurs and not recovery from habituation.

Habituation makes sense, if not in an evolutionary sense, then in the sense of efficiency. If a stimulus is nonthreatening—benign—there's no point in wasting time and mental energy paying attention to it. We are free to focus on new stimuli. Stimuli that are not benign present a different story. If a professor lectured reeking of cologne, you'd habituate to the cologne. If a professor lectured while twirling a loaded handgun, it's unlikely you'd habituate to the handgun. And it's unlikely you'd get anything out of the lecture.

The process of habituation demonstrates a few characteristics that are similar to what we find in classical conditioning. Hence, the uncertainty whether habituation is a primitive kind of conditioning.

Habituation is affected by the *frequency of occurrence* of the repeating stimulus. The greater the number of repetitions, the more likely habituation will occur.

Habituation is affected by *stimulus intensity*. The more intense the repeating stimulus, the less habituation occurs. Pipsqueak sounds are noted and promptly un-noted. Booming sounds measured on the Richter scale are noted and noted. This ties in with the idea of benign stimuli. We generally reckon that loud sounds are less benign than soft sounds. I suppose the exception is the barely audible drone of a mosquito.

Habituation is also affected by *stimulus generalization of the new stimulus,* that is, of the stimulus that results in dishabituation. The more similar the new stimulus is to the repeating stimulus, the less likely dishabituation will occur. The less similar the new stimulus is to the repeating stimulus, the more likely dishabituation will occur. If we follow a series of "la, la, la, la," with a series of "pa, pa, pa, pa," we'll get little recovery. If we follow "la, la, la, la," with "di, di, di, di," we'll get greater recovery.

I experienced stimulus generalization at a recent baptism. The ladies were standing at the bassinet, fussing and cooing over the baby, who had habituated to their high-pitched feminine voices. When I arrived at the bassinet, I also fussed and cooed, but in a low-pitched masculine voice. "How is the newly baptized one?" I asked. The baby instantly recovered from habituation. In fact, the baby looked as if she was about to answer, "I'm fine, thank you. Just get all these ladies out of my face."

Finally, habituation shows a kind of *spontaneous recovery*, as is seen in classical conditioning. If there is a period of delay between repetitions of the same stimulus, there is recovery from habituation. The shorter the period of delay, the less recovery occurs. The longer the period of delay, the greater the recovery. For example, a clicking sound repeats for two minutes. It then stops for thirty seconds and starts again. A beeping sound repeats for two minutes. It then stops for sixty seconds and starts again. Greater recovery will be shown to the beeping sound than to the clicking sound. The longer interval between occurrences turned the beeping sound into more of a novel stimulus.

In a matter of speaking, habituation calms us and makes us less sensitive to stimuli. Sensitization, to the contrary, excites us and makes us more sensitive to stimuli. Habituation occurs to a single repeating stimulus. Sensitization is more complicated. Sensitization is created by one stimulus or situation and produces increased responding to a different stimulus or situation.

Sensitization is the process in which an intense or painful or emotionally-arousing stimulus produces heightened responding to the stimulus that follows. Desensitization to anxiety-arousing stimuli in a clinical setting is perhaps a better-known process, but sensitization is a more common experience.

So we're seated around the campfire and the counselor has just informed us that multiple murders of the grisly kind have occurred in the camp. Another counselor unexpectedly leaps out from behind the shrubbery shouting "Boo!" Everyone screams and jumps. We're lucky no one jumps into the nearby lake. The counselor said man-eating alligators live in the lake.

We're alone at home and we just watched a horror movie of the grisly kind. The phone suddenly rings as the credits roll. Our response in this case is quite different than if the phone rang after we watched a comedy.

We're on a long line at the supermarket checkout and we're growing aggravated. Someone has just activated the Spanish instructions in the self-service lane—this further aggravates us. The clerk makes an offhanded comment as we arrive at the register. We overreact with indignation and ask to see the manager.

We just whacked our thumb with a hammer. As it swells and turns red, a coworker asks an innocuous question. We overreact and yell at the coworker.

We feel sore and achy. We're nauseous and feverish. Maybe we've come down with the flu. A kindly uncle asks how we feel. We overreact and tell our uncle where to go and how to get there.

The big brother just got reprimanded by his father. He walks into the bedroom and the little brother playfully tosses him a foam football. The little brother is in trouble—he better be a wide receiver.

We just rode upside down on a 60-mph roller coaster. We leave the ride and walk to ground level. A gift shop awaits. So does the opportunity to buy pictures of our distorted faces as the train descended the steepest hill. We're so excited, we can't help ourselves. We empty our wallets. Probably, we laugh at the pictures on the way out. Later, we rip them up.

My last example of sensitization is personal and not to my credit. They're not here, but I want to apologize vicariously to my family. Back in the day, I had a long commute to and from my job. Traffic was always heavy at rush hour. There were always delays. The road conditions were deplorable. I made every red light in the state. I got caught in every traffic jam. By the time I arrived home in the evenings, I was aggravated, mightily. I was sensitized, completely. A family member would ask about the commute and I would overreact and lash out. Another family member would ask how my day went and I would overreact and scream that it didn't go well. Don't ask about whether the chores were done. Don't ask about whether supper was prepared to my satisfaction.

I want my family to know that I feel badly about my behavior. I want them to know that I am not a bad person. It wasn't me. It was the process of sensitization that caused me to act in so surly a manner.

Thank you.

LECTURE FOUR

Edward Thorndike

Edward Lee Thorndike (1874 – 1949) is not a household name, but he ranks among the most important American psychologists. He's the founder of educational psychology and of tests and measurements. He's the first "learning theorist," establishing many of the issues pursued across the twentieth century. He didn't call it as such, but he pioneered the study of operant conditioning. (B. F. Skinner once wrote Thorndike that in developing operant conditioning he "… was merely carrying on your puzzle box experiments.") He was an active researcher his entire career, starting with the most important doctoral dissertation ever written and concluding with studies of the quality of life in cities. And he was a prolific author, maybe the most prolific author in the history of psychology, which is saying something. He wrote textbooks, since none existed in the fields he originated. He even wrote a dictionary, the *Thorndike Lorge Wordbook*, that listed the frequencies particular words were used.

Thorndike was born in Williamsburg, Massachusetts, the son of a Methodist minister. (I have no data to support this, but I suspect that many psychologists began life as the children of ministers.) He was drawn to psychology after reading William James's *Principles of Psychology* (1890). He subsequently studied with James at Harvard.

Thorndike did his doctoral work with James McKeen Cattell at Columbia University. His 1898 dissertation, *Animal Intelligence: An Experimental Study of the Associative Processes in Animals*, is the seminal research paper in what became theories of learning. Thorndike taught at

Columbia his entire career. His son Robert Ladd Thorndike followed him at Columbia. Robert died, aged 79, in September 1990.

In his 1936 autobiography in *History of Psychology in Autobiography* Thorndike called his career a "conglomerate of varied opportunities and demands." He wrote that "young psychologists … may take comfort in the fact that … I have done useful experiments without mechanical ability or training and have investigated quantitative relations with very meager knowledge of mathematics." And he wrote that "excellent work can surely be done by men with widely different notions of what psychology is or should be." As we'll see with Clark Hull, not all psychologists shared Thorndike's optimism about allowing "widely different notions of what psychology is or should be."

Thorndike called his research on measuring attitudes and intelligence his best work, but he is mostly remembered today as a pioneer in the field of learning. In 1938 Tolman wrote "the psychology of animal learning … not to mention that of child learning … has been and still is primarily a matter of agreeing or disagreeing with Thorndike or trying in minor ways to improve upon him." In 1962 Leo Postman, a prominent verbal learning psychologist, wrote that "the picture of the learning process which Thorndike sketched more than 50 years ago is still very much in the books." We can add an additional 50 years to Postman's comment.

Thorndike's referent experiment is the *puzzle box* or *confining box*. A cat is placed inside a box. There is a screen on one wall of the box. A bowl of milk is on the counter outside the screen. If the cat performs a particular behavior—clawing a string, for example, or scratching a wall of the box—the screen drops open. The cat is free to leave the box, which in modern parlance involves negative reinforcement (escape conditioning), and drink the milk, which in modern parlance involves positive reinforcement.

The dependent variable is *time to solution*. How long does it take the cats to escape from the box? Thorndike believed there was a *slow—and variable—decrease in time to solution*. There's no sudden "Aha!" moment in which the cats "figure out" or "get" the solution to exiting the box. Rather, the cats slowly got better at escaping the box, unpredictably and not all-at-once.

Thorndike asserted that the cats showed *trial-and-error learning*. (When I was in grammar school, the term was more appropriately called

36

"trial-and-terror learning.") If one response does not work to produce escape from the box, the cats will try another response. If the new response works, the cats will stick with it. The cats will gradually retain successful responses and gradually discard unsuccessful responses. What works, gets repeated. What doesn't work, gets rejected. It's all so pragmatic, so functional, so Darwinian, so American.

Thorndike called trial-and-error learning *selecting and connecting*. (This sounds surprisingly Skinnerian.) The environment selects the responses that are retained. As the responses are successful, connections are made between the responses and sense impressions (stimuli). The organism learns what to do in particular environments.

So we have for the first time in this course what has been a motif for a century—*associationism* in the sense of stimuli (S) and responses (R).

Thorndike conjectured (1903) that the "connection is with the *total state of affairs felt*." This allows for a broader and sophisticated analysis of particular situations. It may be that the origin of those obscure quirks and oddities in behavior that were once called "neurotic" lie somewhere in the "total state of affairs." However, in practice we usually focus on one stimulus and one response.

Thorndike advanced a contradictory idea to the one suggested above with the concept of *piecemeal activity*. In the total state of affairs there may be an especially relevant stimulus. So we're at bat in the Yankee Stadium. Our focus is not on the rabid fans in the bleachers, but on the pitcher's right arm. We're in the parking lot and encounter a rabid dog. Our focus is not on the cars in the lot, but on the dog's teeth and tail. We're driving in wintry conditions. Our focus is not on the trees dressed in shiny wraps of snow, but on the treacherous surface of the road.

Thorndike was not a behaviorist of the ilk of Pavlov, Hull or Skinner, but he suggested that *the stimulus - response connections were sensorimotor and peripheral*. The connections were not cognitive. In his dissertation Thorndike famously wrote that:

> "... the cat does not look over the situation, much less
> think it over and then decide what to do. It bursts out all
> at once into the activities in which instinct and experience

have settled on as suitable reactions to the situation
'confinement when hungry with food outside.'"

Initially, the cat responds to novel situations according to heredity
and to instincts. With practice and experience, the cat comes to respond
in more advanced and efficient ways.

The cat also responds to novel situations *by analogy*. It responds to novel
situations in the way it responded to similar situations in the past. This
is a kind of stimulus generalization—what worked in the past will work
again because the current situation is similar to situations encountered in
the past.

Perhaps following from his peripheral view of learning, Thorndike
suggested that the learning principles identified in animal research applied
to humans as well. And I should add vice versa. "No matter how subtle,
complicated and advanced a form of learning one has to explain, these
simple facts [obtained in research with animals] will still be the main, and
perhaps the only facts, needed to explain it [learning]." These views on the
unity of human and animal behavior reflected Thorndike's functionalist
perspective and his adherence to the principle of parsimony. The same
principles apply across species. As we move up the evolutionary scale, we
needn't add additional and more complicated principles if behavior can be
explained by principles established lower on the scale. Of course, we have
to be careful not to endow humans with instincts or animals with human
capabilities. The latter advice is consistently ignored by many of the dog
walkers I overhear.

Initially, Thorndike established three "laws" to explain how the
connections between stimuli and responses come to be. (Some people
prefer to use the term "lore.") They are the law of effect, the law of
readiness, and the law of practice.

The *law of effect*, which first appeared in print in 1907, has a positive
side and a negative side. The positive side states that "*if a response is followed
by a satisfying state of affairs, the strength of the connection increases.*" The
connection is "stamped in." The negative side of the law of effect states
that "*if a response is followed by an unsatisfying (annoying) state of affairs,
the strength of the connection decreases.*" The connection is "stamped out."

Thorndike added "effect"—what we now call "reinforcement" and "punishment"—to the ancient philosophical principles of *contiguity* and *repetition*. The two latter principles—without the concept of effect—are stressed by theorists who favor the stimulus side of the stimulus – response connection. These theorists include Pavlov, Watson, Guthrie and Tolman. As they posit effect (reinforcement) as the critical variable in learning, theorists such as Thorndike, Hull and Skinner favor the response side of the connection.

Unlike Skinner, Thorndike tried to define satisfying and unsatisfying states of affairs. He tried to tie them into physiological processes, but without success, mostly because many human behaviors cannot be tied to simple or specific physiological processes. He settled for a kind of practical or functional definition. Satisfying states of affairs result from environmental stimuli the organism *does nothing to avoid*. Unsatisfying states of affairs result from environmental stimuli the organism *strives to avoid*.

Like Skinner, Thorndike believed that the effect of effect, so to say, was automatic and did not have to involve awareness or consciousness. Animals may or may not have awareness of the situation and they certainly can't verbalize details. The cat can't think, "Humm, if I scratch this side of the box, the screen opens." Having awareness and the capability to verbalize details are helpful in the case of humans, but they are not necessary for connections to get stamped in or stamped out.

The law of effect operates through the *law of readiness*, which involves the *context* in which satisfying and unsatisfying effects work their magic. The law of effect operates depending on what the organism has been doing.

The law of readiness states:

- when someone is ready to perform an act, to do is satisfying;

- when someone is ready to perform an act, not to do so is unsatisfying;

~ when someone is not ready to perform an act and is forced to act, to do so is unsatisfying.

Thorndike didn't add a fourth component—when someone is not ready to perform an act and is not forced to perform, to not do so is satisfying.

The first two components in the law of readiness remind me what happens in conversations. I'm ready to make a clever response—I make the response and feel mighty pleased. Everyone now knows how clever I am. But I feel mighty annoyed if I'm ready to make a clever response and someone speaks ahead of me. I hold the response in and await the next chance to let my cleverness shine.

The third component and the imaginary fourth component happened to me in high school. When I didn't do my homework and got called on, I felt mighty annoyed. I suppose I felt a little embarrassed, too. But I felt mighty satisfied—mighty relieved—when I didn't prepare and didn't get called on. I suppose I said to myself, "Phew, I got away with that one."

The third law was the *law of practice or exercise*. This law stated that connections between stimuli and responses are strengthened as they are repeated. Connections between stimuli and responses are weakened as they are not repeated. This law is similar to the old concept in memory research of *use and disuse*. In ordinary circumstances we retrieve frequently rehearsed memories more quickly and reliably than infrequently rehearsed memories.

The three laws operate under the guidance of *set*.

Set is what the organism brings to the learning situation—notably "instinct and experience." Set, which serves as an intervening variable, includes genetics, emotional states, previous learning, and temporary states like fatigue and deprivation. With the addition of set, we have the contributions of the organism and the environment to the learning experience—*setting, stimulus, set, response*.

Set sets up what Thorndike called *prepotency of elements*. (This is similar to the concept of piecemeal activity.) In a particular setting only a selection of relevant stimuli is connected to a response. If a cat is hungry, only the food in a particular setting will matter. If a cat is thirsty, only water in a particular situation will matter. If the cat is in heat, only particular stimuli will be prepotent—I'm not sure whether, at the level of cats, we can call such stimuli "erotic."

Prepotency of elements exists in humans. Recently, I was seated at the entrance of our local supermarket. It is a busy, crowded place. The people who passed me were not paying attention to the totality of stimuli. They were paying attention to prepotent slices of the totality. Customers were looking for cashiers. Cashiers were looking to avoid customers. Elderly people were looking for shopping carts to hold onto. Thieves were looking for pocketbooks carelessly exposed in carts. Security guards were looking for thieves. Hotties were looking for admirers. Appearance-challenged people were looking to slip inside before anyone noticed. And children were looking for the little car rides and amusements the store keeps at the entrance.

At a conference in September 1929 Thorndike announced changes to his laws. He prefaced the changes with the remark, "I was wrong." After the other conferees were lifted off the floor and revived, Thorndike described the changes. Karl Popper was in the stands and cheering.

The law of readiness sailed into oblivion. The law of exercise was renounced—repetition depends on effect. As with the idea of use and disuse in the study of memory, exercise (repetition) leads to inconsistent results. Sometimes we forget words we use frequently. And sometimes we remember words we rarely use. The major change in the laws was the elimination of the negative side of the law of effect. Unsatisfying or annoying effects do not stamp out stimulus - response connections in the same fundamental manner that satisfying effects stamp in such connections. Rather, *unsatisfying effects produce response variation.* They get the organism to do something different. To put this change in modern parlance, reinforcement produces decisive changes in behavior. Punishment does not produce decisive changes. It produces different responses that may, or may not, get reinforced.

There are two notable points about these changes in the laws. The first has to do with their sources. The original laws were based, in part, on research with cats in confining boxes. The changes in the laws were based, in part, on verbal learning experiments with college students—collegiate cats. It didn't trouble Thorndike to create laws based on one species and then refute the laws based on a different species. He held to the combustion engine concept of universal principles. It has troubled other psychologists, however, who believe that different learning principles may be required as we ascend the evolutionary ladder. Certainly, learning grows in complexity. And learning occurs in a verbal context that is altogether lacking in lower organisms. It's not that the basic principles become invalidated as we ascend the ladder. It's that complex situations overlay the basic principles with new explanatory requirements.

The second point concerns the effectiveness of punishment in changing behavior. After 1929 Thorndike took the position that what we now call "reinforcement" is the fundamental learning principle. Modern psychologists generally follow Skinner's interpretation of punishment— punishment is as effective as reinforcement in changing (decreasing) behavior, but has so many unpleasant side effects it should be used sparingly. (Unless something bad happens, we'll look at these side effects in a later lecture.) The modern consensus is that Thorndike had it right the first time. Like many the freshmen student on multiple-choice quizzes, Thorndike argued himself out of the right answer.

As an aside, I recollect from my grammar school days that the same students always seemed to be rewarded and the same students always seemed to be punished. This went on literally for eight years. So maybe punishment doesn't work. The rewarded students never fell from the teachers' good graces. The punished students never wised up and corrected their behavior. Maybe punishment worked in ways that are analogous to reward in these students. Maybe these students were confused and construed punishment as reward. Whatever the explanation, they didn't have a pleasant experience in school.

In 1933 Thorndike introduced the concept of *spread of effect*. This is the phenomenon in which the reinforcer given to one response spreads to contiguous responses. The reinforcer given to one response spreads to the responses immediately preceding and following it. Thorndike believed that the spread of effect demonstrated the "blind," noncognitive, nature of effects—they work, whether or not we notice or verbalize them.

The spread of effect, which has been supported in additional research, can be observed in verbal learning experiments. For example, we have a list of incomplete sentences. Participants have to complete these sentences. The experimenter says "Right" to some of the sentence completions. The experimenter says "Wrong" to some of the sentence completions. The idea is that saying "Right" is analogous to positive effect (reinforcement) and saying "Wrong" is analogous to punishment. The dependent variable is whether participants will change their answers to the sentence completions followed by "Wrong." Thorndike found that this did not necessarily happen in the sentences immediately preceding and following a completion followed by positive effect. Contrary to expectations, participants stayed with the wrong answers.

So in this made up list, participants hear "Wrong" to the completion of sentence #13. Participants hear "Right" to the completion of sentence #14. Participants hear "Wrong" to the completion of sentence #15. On the next presentation of the entire list, we focus on what completions are offered to sentences #13, #14 and #15. Because of positive effect, we expect the same answer to sentence #14. Based on the idea that punishment produces variations in response, we expect different completions to sentences #13 and #15. But that is not what we find. We get the same completions as previously given, despite the fact that the participants were told that they gave the wrong answers. According to Thorndike, the positive effect following sentence #14 spreads backward to sentence #13 and forward to sentence #15.

The implication of the spread of effect, especially in education, is that an undesirable response may increase because of its temporal proximity to a reinforced response. The undesirable response shares in the reinforcement given to a different and perhaps unrelated response. So, for example, a student is tapping on the desk. The teacher grows annoyed and wants the tapping to stop not by commenting on it but by putting the student on the spot. Expecting the student to give the wrong answer, the teacher snaps sarcastically, "When was the War of 1812 fought?" To the teacher's dismay, the student snaps back snugly, "1812," followed by the sound "Dud." The tapping continues because it occurred immediately before the response that led to reinforcement.

Thorndike is considered a reinforcement-oriented theorist, obviously because of the law of effect. But in the 1930s he focused on the stimulus side of the "S - R" connection and introduced an important concept called "associative shifting."

In *associative shifting* a response is connected to a new stimulus by gradually removing the old stimulus and replacing it with the new stimulus. The response is slowly disconnected from one stimulus and reconnected to a different stimulus. There is a period of time in which both the old and new stimuli are present. Our organism currently responds in the presence of a blue stimulus. We want it to respond in the presence of a red stimulus. In associative shifting we gradually fade out blue and fade in red. There is a balance of blue and red stimuli—the stimulus is maroon for a time—until the red entirely replaces the blue.

Associative shifting has been used in the sex therapy business—I'm sure what's left of Thorndike is blushing in his grave. The practice was called *orgasmic reconditioning*. This was back in the heady days when we believed sexuality was strictly a matter of conditioning. The idea was that certain people masturbate to the wrong stimuli. Gays and lesbians masturbate to images of the same sex, obviously. In orgasmic reconditioning images of the opposite sex replace images of the same sex as the person approaches orgasm. When I was in college, I had a teacher, a clinical psychologist, who was involved in this kind of therapy. He had a deck of photographic slides, each of which slowly transformed the images from the male body into the female body. Discontented gay men were supposed to pleasure themselves as the slides clicked forward. If all went well, orgasm occurred at the last slide, which was a sexually explicit image of a female. Going forward, they would be sexually attracted to the opposite sex.

That was then, this is now. We recognize this kind of "therapy" as misguided and unproductive. I heard this teacher now works as a park ranger in the Rocky Mountains.

I can't resist adding a second example of orgasmic reconditioning. I assure you I am not making this up. This example involves rekindling the fires in stale marriages. A husband—for some reason, this therapy always was directed at the husband—is no longer attracted to his wife. The man is instructed to masturbate while viewing images of glamorous naked women. As he nears orgasm, images of his wife are inserted amid the glamour. Images of his wife couldn't be inserted too early in the slide show or he might startle and lose interest in sex altogether. If all went well, orgasm occurred to images of his wife. The wife would be made—would be remade—attractive by being paired with glamorous women and her image would once again become potent by occurring precisely at orgasm. The fire would be back, or so we like to think.

Thorndike was an important figure in psychology for nearly half a century. He was a lifelong experimenter and educator. Many of his ideas about education are now commonplace. These ideas are the use of rewards rather than punishment, the importance of formulating clear objectives, and the importance of active learning. Educators need to take the set of students into account—the personal histories of students may facilitate or hinder the learning process. Famously, Thorndike emphasized the importance of *transfer of training*—since we respond to new situations to the degree they resemble old situations, we should teach what students need to master in the world outside the schoolhouse. We should not teach subjects that have no relevance in the world that students face, even if such subjects (supposedly) strengthened "mental muscles." I wish someone had told this to my Latin teacher in high school and to my calculus teacher in college.

Thorndike can be considered the first learning "theorist." As such, he set the table of discourse on which later generations of psychologists dined. Among the items on the menu were:

- the confining box as a referent experiment;

- the importance of "effect"—reinforcement, as we now call it;

- the secondary role that punishment plays;

- the idea that learning does not necessarily involve cognition;

- the universality of learning principles across species.

Thorndike's theory—and his general perspective—was one of the first experimental challenges to *mentalism*, as the cognitive viewpoint was then called. Mentalism is the belief that the mind—mental processes—is the cause of behavior. As you might suspect, most of the theorists in this course opposed this idea, Watson and Skinner most strenuously.

We meet in Thorndike a view that we will find in the theorists in this course. This is the belief that science and scientific psychology can make the world a better place. In 1940 Thorndike wrote that "Knowledge of psychology and its application to welfare should prevent or at least diminish some of the errors and calamities for which the well intentioned have been and are responsible."

We've come a long way from this naïve faith in science. Hobart Mowrer wrote in the introduction to *Leaves from Many Seasons* (1983), a collection of his papers, that "neither I nor my children now have the faith in Progress that formerly sustained and energized my generation … We thought we were making the world a better place … Today, however, progress is no longer spelled with a capital letter."

Most of Thorndike's contributions have been criticized—this is how science is supposed to work. Many psychologists challenged the emphasis on effect as the almighty principle in learning. Many psychologists challenged the idea that learning does not involve cognition. Many challenged the idea that the same principles apply across species, willy-nilly. When it comes to punishment, the current view is that Thorndike had it right before he changed his laws.

Psychologists criticized the simplicity of his approach—one stimulus attaching to one response. They point out that a cat escaping from a puzzle box operates at a different level than a collegiate cat mastering the contents of a college course. In fact, Thorndike recognized four levels of complexity in learning. The first level is *connection forming without words*, such as with cats in puzzle boxes. The second level is *connection forming with words*, such as in learning paired associates and in responding to commands. The third level is *discrimination learning*, such as differentiating colors and symbols. The fourth level involves *reasoning with words and sentences*, such as mastering the contents of a course. These levels are a demonstration of what exists "in theory" and what exists "in practice." The theory that has come down to us is pretty much limited to the first level.

I'm going to offer a final, and philosophical, criticism of Thorndike. Some people, like Thorndike and Skinner, were not troubled by this criticism. Other people are knocked off stride and into the swamp by it. The criticism has to do with the seeming defiance of one of the core principles of science—the idea that causes precede their effects. In operant conditioning the effect (reinforcement) occurs after a response. The effect increases the rate of a response that comes before it. We have stimulus, then response, then effect. The effect appears to act backward in time, which is not how causes are supposed to act. By the time the effect occurs, the response may be concluded. The cat is out of the box and drinking the milk after the response of scratching the side of the box occurred.

There is a way in learning theories to answer this criticism, but it involves classical conditioning and Clark Hull's theory. You'll have to treat this like a cliffhanger in a television series. We'll present the solution, but in a forthcoming lecture season.

Thank you.

LECTURE FIVE

A Primer on Operant Conditioning

Parents, educators and managers at every corporate level are, even as I speak, applying the principles of operant conditioning across our gun-toting land. These attempts are made with the best intentions in the most mundane situations. Psychology instructors, to the contrary, like to introduce operant conditioning not by ordinary applications but by extraordinary applications—by the conditioning of mute psychotics to use speech, for example, or by Skinner's conditioning of patriotic carrier pigeons to drop bombs on Axis targets.

I'm no different, but my examples are current. In our time dogs are conditioned to respond to the odor of tuberculosis emitted by patients, as well as to the odors of other diseases, and Giant African pouched rats are conditioned to respond to the odor of TNT in buried land mines. Sadly, land mines kill as many as 25,000 people a year in former battlefields in Third World countries.

The central idea in operant conditioning as it was developed by Skinner and many others can be succinctly stated—*the recurrence (or not) of a behavior depends on the immediate consequences of the behavior.* To restate the same in an older vocabulary—*the rate of a response depends on the immediate consequences of the response.*

Favorable consequences are called *reinforcers. Reinforcers increase the rate of responses.* The overall process of stimulus/setting, response (behavior) and reinforcer is called *reinforcement.*

Unfavorable consequences are called *punishers*. *Punishers decrease the rate of responses.* The overall process of stimulus/setting, response (behavior) and punisher is called *punishment.*

Skinner took a pragmatic approach to reinforcers and punishers. Whatever worked to change behavior worked. He never relied on physiological or, God help us, on psychological concepts to explain the action of favorable and unfavorable consequences. As everyone knows, except for the people who don't, he successfully avoided introducing intervening variables into his system throughout his long career.

There are a few guiding principles to reinforcers and punishers.

Consequences may be biological and unlearned (*primary* in the older vocabulary) or social and learned (*secondary* in the older vocabulary). An example of a primary reinforcer is a sweet substance. An example of a primary punisher is pain. Examples of secondary reinforcers are praise and money. Examples of secondary punishers are insults and fines. Secondary consequences are effective in a variety of situations not linked to biological states. To that extent, they are more effective in changing human behavior than primary consequences. Social reinforcers do not satiate—we may be overstuffed with linzer cookies, but we can never get enough praise or money. Nor do social punishers satiate—I may be in pain, but I have a reputation that forbids me to reveal the pain to someone I dislike.

Reinforcers and punishers have to be defined *from the perspective of the person experiencing them*, not from the perspective of the person giving them. Parents across the state have experienced the situation in which they believed they punished their children when, in fact, they inadvertently reinforced their children. (Teachers are often in the same predicament. So are district attorneys.) Children act up at the dinner table and are sent to their rooms. The parents congratulate themselves on timely punishments meted out, but this is what the children wanted. The children don't pout, the children gloat. Similarly, parents believe they reinforce children when they are, in actuality, punishing the children. "If you're good, we'll visit Grandma," they promise. But this is what the children loathe.

Reinforcers and punishers must be *defined in context*. This is what Thorndike was reaching for with the law of readiness. I love linzer cookies, but if I ate too many at one sitting, I may become sick. (This is the concept behind avoidance training techniques. For example, if I catch my son sneaking a cigarette, I may force him to smoke an entire pack, thereby making him ill of the behavior he once enjoyed.) The opposite is true—if I were starving, I would find a fig newton convincingly satisfying.

Robert Louis Stevenson once wrote that everyone eventually sits down to a "banquet of consequences." Our vices catch up with us—that's why we can't let ourselves slow down. In operant conditioning consequences follow behavior *immediately*. Operant conditioning is strictly present tense. If we intend to reinforce Joline, we reinforce the behavior that occurred *immediately before* the reinforcer appeared. If we intend to punish Joline, we punish the behavior that occurred *immediately before* the punisher appeared. We don't reinforce or punish past behavior. We don't reinforce or punish future behavior. It's only behavior in the here-and-now—behavior actually occurring—that gets reinforced or punished.

Some reinforcers and punishers are referred to as *positive*—positive reinforcement and positive punishment. "Positive" means "additive." These consequences add something to the situation that was not present before a response was made. Positive reinforcers add something favorable—like a linzer cookie. Positive punishers add something unfavorable—like an insult.

Some reinforcers and punishers are referred to as *negative*—negative reinforcement and negative punishment. "Negative" means "subtractive." These consequences remove something from the situation after a response was made. Negative reinforcers remove something unfavorable or aversive from the situation—like a pill melting a headache. Negative punishers remove something favorable from the situation—like the cash in my pocket when I get caught running a stop sign.

In the early days of psychology reinforcement was generally viewed as *getting something* or as *getting rid of something*. The "something" was always physical—a pellet of rat food, a linzer cookie. David Premack (1925 - 2015) perceived that *reinforcers could be behaviors*. He noted that organisms will work to engage in particular behaviors. That is, organisms will work *to perform* certain behaviors as much as they will work *to get* certain things. A preferred behavior could be used to increase the rate of a less preferred behavior. Premack called this after himself—the *Premack principle*. It was rechristened, likely to Premack's chagrin, as the *differential probability principle*.

The differential probability principle may be the most applied behavioral principle in homes. Here are a few examples. To be allowed to play video games (more preferred), children have to finish homework (less preferred). To use the family car (more preferred), teens have to mow the family lawn (less preferred). To have sex (more preferred), Romeo has to put on a condom (less preferred). I'm sorry that this example is risqué, but it's a good one and an example a student gave in a former semester. I'm sure she spoke from experience.

The differential probability principle exists on a cosmic scale. Some people work because they love their jobs, and good for them. Other people don't love their jobs. They work to make money to do something else. Maybe they have hobbies. Maybe they're creative. Maybe they like to travel. Maybe, as Oscar Wilde observed, they like to drink. Whatever the case, these people engage in a less preferred task (work) in order to perform a more preferred task.

Finally, *behavior, and not the person, is reinforced or punished.* Skinner's system was called a "skin bag psychology," and that's pretty much what it is. It refuses to deal with personalities or with anything inside the organism. We say we reinforce Sally, but what we should say is we reinforce a particular behavior Sally performs. We say we punish Sam, but what we should say is we punish a particular behavior Sam performs.

There are two ways to be reinforced—we can receive what we deem are outright rewards or something punishing can be removed from our presence. And there are two ways to be punished—we can receive what we deem are outright punishments or something rewarding can be removed from our presence. These statements summarize the four basic situations or contingencies outlined in operant conditioning.

Positive reinforcement (reward conditioning) is the contingency in which a favorable consequence immediately follows a behavior. The rate of the behavior increases. The consequence may be biological or social, it has to be defined from the perspective of the organism experiencing it, and it must be defined in context. Examples include a pellet of rat food following a bar press in the operant conditioning chamber and a child receiving praise for successfully picking out the right color in an array.

Positive punishment (punishment conditioning) is the contingency in which an unfavorable consequence immediately follows a behavior. The rate of the behavior decreases. The consequence may be biological or social, it has to be defined from the perspective of the organism experiencing it, and it must be defined in context. Examples include an electric shock following a bar press in the operant conditioning chamber and a child being yelled at for choosing the wrong color in an array.

Negative reinforcement (relief conditioning) is the contingency in which a behavior immediately eliminates unfavorable or undesirable stimuli. The rate of the behavior increases. The consequence is the removal of biologically or socially aversive stimuli. (Whatever eliminates punishment is rewarding.) The aversive stimuli must be present as the behavior occurs. The aversive stimuli and its elimination must be defined from the perspective of the organism experiencing it and it must be defined in context. Examples include a rat pressing a bar to stop electric shock and a child selecting the right color in an array to stop the parent's yelling.

Negative punishment (penalty conditioning) is the situation in which a behavior immediately eliminates favorable or desirable stimuli. The rate of the behavior decreases. The consequence is the removal of biologically or socially favorable stimuli. (Whatever eliminates reward is punishing.) The favorable stimuli must be present as the behavior occurs. The favorable stimuli and its elimination must be defined from the perspective of the organism experiencing it and it must be defined in context. Examples include a rat pressing a bar to (inadvertently) remove food from the tray and a child selecting the wrong color in an array to (inadvertently) terminate a parent's words of praise.

Extinction is the situation in which a response is no longer followed by reinforcement, although it once was.

For *newly learned behaviors* and for behaviors that have been *continuously reinforced,* the removal of a reinforcer leads to a rapid decrease in rate of behavior. The situation is trickier with respect to *well-learned and chronic behavior* and for *behaviors reinforced on a schedule (intermittent reinforcement).* In these situations the removal of reinforcement results in a *temporary increase in rate* followed by a decrease in rate. This *extinction burst* leads to what may be the most common mistake in applying behavioral principles.

Examples of extinction include the following. A parent ignores a child's pestering. "Mom, are we there yet? Mom, are we there?" The pestering worsens and then slowly stops. A teacher ignores a child's rude comments. The rude comments worsen and then slowly stop. A young woman once paid attention to the favors of a gentleman caller. Unfortunately for him, she has found a different suitor. The number of favors increase. The gentleman calls and texts repeatedly. He buys gift cards at department stores and mails them to her. He leaves presents at her front door. He hires a band and serenades her. Fortunately for everyone, such actions slowly decrease.

Care must be taken in the use of extinction. Once the process of extinction commences, parents, educators and inamorata must not *give in*. To do so is to reinforce behavior at its worst. People who implement extinction sometimes fail to understand that *behavior worsens before it gets better.* If we're not willing to withstand the onslaught, it's best not to implement extinction.

The parent gives in and responds, "No, we're not there yet!" The teacher gives in and chastises the rude child. The young lady returns a message from the gentleman caller. Giving in results in outcomes we probably don't want.

(As an aside, I would advise the young lady to place the new suitor's favors on a schedule. By not responding to every favor, she intensifies the ardor of the courtship).

With extinction, we find the occurrence of *frustration*—the usual response doesn't work and we get aggravated. We also find that extinction produces *response variability.* We try different behaviors to get the usual reinforcer—the jilted suitor never thought to hire a band before he was dumped. And we find the *reappearance of older behaviors*—the child reverts to less socialized responses like crying, yelling, and fit throwing, before they arrive at their destination.

Extinction is probably a ubiquitous practice—we've all decided at some point or other not to pay attention to our mates' undesirable behaviors. And it's an important principle in learning theories. Clark Hull viewed *resistance to extinction* as a measure of learning. We say a response is better learned as it persists in the absence of reinforcement compared to a response that disappears rapidly.

Behaviors maintained on schedules of reinforcement persist longer than behaviors maintained on a schedule of continuous reinforcement. It may be that organisms on a schedule perceive non-reinforced instances as part of the learning experience. I know that I will not always win when I play slots. I expect more losing tries than hits, but I stay in the game. If the candy machine in this building supplied candy every time I put a coin in and it suddenly stopped supplying candy, I would probably not insert additional coins. If the candy machine supplied candy every so often and not every time, I would probably insert a second coin if the first one failed.

There's an important strategy in utilizing the disparity between intermittent reinforcement and continuous reinforcement. To achieve rapid decreases in rate, it's recommended to convert intermittent reinforcement into continuous reinforcement before the process of extinction commences.

Mark Bouton introduced an important principle called *renewal* (1988). Unlike acquisition of behavior, extinction that occurs in one situation does not generalize to different situations. Extinction is specific—limited—to the place where it occurs. For example, learning occurs in an environment with bright light and loud noise. Extinction takes place in an environment with dim light and no noise. When the organism returns to the site of the original learning, extinction fails and behavior reverts to its original state. The fact that extinction may not generalize has important implications for psychotherapy and for drug and alcohol rehabilitation. Undesirable behaviors are often extinguished in a different place from the setting in which they were acquired. When the person returns to the site where the behaviors were learned, extinction fails and the problem behaviors commence anew.

The term "operant" refers to a group or class of behaviors that *operate* on the environment to achieve particular outcomes. These outcomes involve both a changed environment and a changed organism. To satisfy hunger, I may walk to a French restaurant, call a Chinese take-out, or drop eggs and bacon on the griddle. Although they are disparate, these behaviors result in the same outcome—each satisfies hunger. To that extent, they are comparable or equivalent. To get a box of cereal off the topmost shelf in a supermarket, I may climb in the carriage, use a broomstick to knock the box down, or ask a clerk to get a stepladder. Again, the behaviors are disparate, but the effect is the same—I will have raisin bran for breakfast. In an operant conditioning chamber I want the rat to press the bar—that is the objective. It doesn't matter to me if the rat uses its right paw or its left paw or its snout or its entire body. The effect of these behaviors is the same—a nugget of rat food and a satisfied experimenter.

The concept of *differential reinforcement* offers a refinement to the idea of an operant class of disparate behaviors. In applying differential reinforcement, *a reinforcer follows a specific behavior in a group of behaviors.* Reinforcers do not follow any other behaviors in the group. *The non-reinforced behaviors are not punished.* We reinforce a rat for bar pressing only with its right paw. If the rat bar presses with the left paw, or with its snout, or with its body, it receives no reinforcement.

From the perspective of the organism, we find *induction* or *response generalization* at the outset of the procedure. Reinforcing bar pressing with the right paw commonly results in bar pressing with the left paw. For the rat, bar pressing is tantamount. For experimenters, bar pressing only with the right paw is tantamount. As the procedure continues, we find *response differentiation.* Responses are limited to the specific behavior that results in reinforcement and only to that behavior. Responses that are not followed by reinforcement eventually drop out.

We'll meet with the same phenomenon on the stimulus side when we examine classical conditioning. This is an important principle of learning—at the outset of learning, organisms show generalization, but with practice and experience learning becomes refined and demonstrates differentiation.

Differential reinforcement is commonly applied in ordinary life. A parent reinforces a child's correct grammar with attention and ignores incorrect grammar. A teacher reinforces good penmanship with praise and ignores sloppy penmanship. A coach reinforces a player's correct batting stance and ignores an incorrect batting stance. A therapist responds to a client's consensual speech and ignores the client's delusional speech.

Differential reinforcement can be used to reinforce the *omission of behavior.* For example, praise is given within a particular time frame for the absence of smoking or for the absence of the use of profanity. The occurrences of such behaviors are not punished. They are ignored—of course, the absence of attention can be conceived as a kind of punishment.

Differential reinforcement can also be applied to establish a *low rate of response*. We extend praise and attention to a student if he or she talks in class at a lower rate than a pre-set criterion. We ignore the student's talking if it exceeds the criterion. We don't want the student to become mute, nor do we want the student to hog up class time at the expense of other students. The opposite can also be achieved—differential reinforcement for a *high rate of response*. In this case we reinforce behavior only if it exceeds a pre-set criterion. For example, we might want students to speak up in class more than they do or to express a greater number of creative ideas in group discussions.

Shaping is the process by which we learn a complex behavior. The final, target, behavior is broken down into a *series of simpler component behaviors that are learned in a sequential manner*. Differential reinforcement is applied to each component. As each component is mastered, differential reinforcement is applied to the next component.

Initially, reinforcement is given to *any behavior that approximates the target*. Standards are lax at first. The requirement for receiving reinforcement becomes more stringent as practice continues. This is called the *method of successive approximations*. As practice proceeds, the behavior of each component and, ultimately, the target behavior must progressively match the desired criteria.

Pitching is the perfect example of the process of shaping. Pitching involves a series of steps, each of which must occur correctly for the pitcher to hurl a strike. Pitchers must learn how to grip the ball, how to throw the ball at three-quarters arm motion, and how to raise and lower the leg in the delivery. Each skill must be mastered in turn before the next component is introduced. Coaches are lenient at first, praising any attempt and ignoring mistakes, but the pitchers must eventually match the target of winding up and delivering the ball accurately over home plate. Probably, coaches start the pitchers close to home plate and gradually move them back toward the pitching mound.

Shaping is not a gradual increase in a particular behavior, such as jogging slightly more distance or lifting slightly greater weights. Rather, shaping involves a series of different behaviors, *all of which are retained* in the final performance.

Operant conditioning is decidedly partial to the response side of the S - R acronym, but it does not altogether neglect the stimulus side. *Stimulus control* is the situation in which *reinforcement occurs only when specific stimuli are present*. These stimuli are referred to as *discriminative stimuli*. They are abbreviated *S+*. Discriminative stimuli do not cause the reinforcement. They signal that reinforcement is possible. The stimuli are not reinforcers, but they can become associated with the occurrence of reinforcement. Through this association they may take on some reinforcing properties.

Similarly, there are situations in which stimuli signal that reinforcement is not possible. These stimuli do not prevent the reinforcement. They happen to be present when behavior will not result in reinforcement. These stimuli are referred to as *non-discriminative stimuli*. They are abbreviated *S-*. I suppose they result in disappointment.

For example, bar presses result in reinforcement only if the chamber is brightly lit (S+). Bar pressing does not result in reinforcement if the chamber is dimly lit (S-). Ralph asks Alice if he can go to the Raccoon convention only if she has a happy face (S+). He does not ask if she has an angry face (S-). Grandpa gives the children money only when Grandma is present (S+). Grandpa does not give the children money when Grandma is absent (S-). A house in New Orleans lights a green candle in the window (S+) to indicate the ladies are available, or so I've been told. The house does not light the candle (S-) when the ladies are unavailable.

Stimulus control also occurs with punishment. Discriminative stimuli (S+) signal that punishment is forthcoming. The stimuli do not cause the punishment. However, through association, they may come to share in the punishment. The organism sees them and thinks, "Oh boy, I'm in for it now." Non-discriminative stimuli (S-) signal that punishment will not follow a response. The organism is on safe ground and thinks, "Whew!"

For example, a child is brought to the principal's office. If the vice principal in charge of discipline is present (S+), the child knows he or she will be punished. If a child is brought to the principal's office and the vice principal in charge of unconditional good will is present (S-), the child knows he or she will not be punished.

There's an interesting example of stimulus control in ethology. A particular type of South African monkey will descend from the trees and risk walking on the jungle floor only when humans are present. Humans serve as a type of non-discriminative stimulus that the monkeys will not be attacked by leopards. When humans are present, leopards are absent. When humans are absent, monkeys walking on the jungle floor risk getting devoured, which is pretty severe punishment in any species.

I'll like to add two wrinkles to the concepts of reinforcement and punishment.

It may be that some people prefer reinforcements at the risk of receiving punishment. And it may be that some people prefer to avoid punishment at the risk of losing reinforcements. I'm reminded of a line from a distinctly unmemorable movie called *Tenderness*— "Some people chase pleasure, other people run away from pain." Sometimes bad movies have insightful lines.

The British psychologist Jeffrey Alan Grey (1934 – 2004) developed what he called *reinforcement sensitivity.* He conjectured that we possess a *behavioral activation system* that responds to rewards and regulates approach behavior and a *behavioral inhibition system* that responds to punishment and regulates avoidant behavior. People vary in which system dominates. Some people are sensitized to the activation system. They want reinforcement even at the risk of earning punishment. As this sensitivity increases, they become impulsive. Other people are sensitized to the inhibition system. They want to avoid punishment even if it means missing out on reinforcers. As this sensitivity increases, they become anxious.

Think about approaching a yellow light at the end of the road. Some people want to make the light no matter what. They speed up and risk a ticket or a collision. Other people want to make the light, but not at the risk of a ticket or a collision. These people slow down.

The second wrinkle is whether the motivation to perform a behavior is based on extrinsic or intrinsic reinforcement. *Extrinsic reinforcers are external to the person.* They involve performing a behavior for praise and for money. *Intrinsic reinforcers are internal to the person.* They involve performing a behavior for the sheer pleasure and delight in performing it.

Some people write for pay and for the chance to become famous, such as having their books on the best-seller list. Other people write just for the fun of writing. They don't care about writing best sellers. (In fact, some of the most popular items in bookstores are blank journals.) Some people prepare culinary delights for the chance to have a show on the food network. Other people prepare culinary delights just for the fun of cooking. They don't care about being on the food network.

This is all pretty obvious, but what is interesting is when intrinsic reinforcers convert to extrinsic reinforcers and vice versa.

On the surface it would appear that replacing intrinsic reinforcers with extrinsic reinforcers is an ideal situation. We are now being paid for what we once did for free. We are now famous. We are now on television. But this is not necessarily an ideal situation. Previously, we wrote for enjoyment and for nothing else. Now writing comes with editors and critics and a demanding public. Now we have agents and are told what to write. Previously, we cooked alone in the kitchen. (Maybe Dinah was there, but we didn't have a studio audience.) Now we have servers to deal with and food critics and finicky customers who send the dishes back with complaints.

Replacing extrinsic reinforcers with intrinsic reinforcers is equally dicey. Once we wrote for money and fame, but now no one is buying our books. Are we going to buy blank journals and write for free? Maybe, maybe not. Once we had a program on the food network, but our ratings tanked and we're off the air. Are we going to cook culinary delights out of the goodness of our colanders? Maybe, maybe not.

There's an idea current in educational circles that schools should pay students for attending class. The logic is school is work, so students may as well get paid. The danger is reliance on extrinsic reinforcement. Paying students to attend class works only as long as we have money to dispense. If we stop paying students, they may react like our writer and chef—they may not want to continue without the paycheck. I suppose the assumption is that money will lead to intrinsic reinforcement. Because they love money, students will eventually come to love learning. This may be the case or it may not be the case.

Paying students to attend school may kill whatever intrinsic reinforcement existed before we put everyone on the payroll. Some students—teachers like to think a lot of students—love to learn. Now they are paid to learn. Now they have to learn. They may come to dislike learning.

Another danger of converting intrinsic to extrinsic reinforcement is that paying students signals the behavior is unpleasant. "Something's fishy if you have to pay me to attend school," students think. "School mustn't be a place I want to be." The attempt backfires. The classic example of this concept is getting children to eat vegetables. "You can have an extra lump of ice cream if you eat the spinach," parents promise. Children think, "The spinach must taste awful if I'm getting an extra lump of ice cream to eat it." The attempt backfires.

The attempt backfires because of another—immensely overlooked— concept in behavioral science called *reactance*. People, including the variety of people called "children," do not like to feel that they are being manipulated. People do not like to feel that they are being forced to do something (go to school, eat spinach). They proceed in the opposite direction and reject the attempt, even if it involves the loss of reinforcers. The crassest and most dangerous example of reactance involves tailgating. Someone is riding our fender, wanting us to speed up or get out of the way. Ordinarily, we like to speed, but not when someone is forcing us to speed. What'd we do? It's happening everywhere on the Parkway even at this moment—we slow down. We think, "No one is going to make me drive fast." We stay in the lane and repeat the advice Clarence Bickett, an old-time long-haul truck driver from Secaucus, once gave us—"If they want to get ahead of me, they can pass me or they can fly over me."

Thank you.

LECTURE SIX

Ivan Pavlov and Classical Conditioning

In the same way that the name of B. F. Skinner is synonymous with operant conditioning, the name of Ivan Petrovich Pavlov (1849 - 1936) is synonymous with classical conditioning. As was Skinner, Pavlov was an intrepid experimenter for decades. We might say he was a dogged experimenter. As with operant conditioning, many other people made contributions in the development of classical conditioning.

Let me say at the outset that in all the years I've taught this course no student has asked where the term "classical" came from. It's a good thing no one asked, because I don't know the answer. I don't believe anyone does. Well, there was a man in Point Pleasant who claimed to know, but he went swimming one afternoon and never returned to the shore, so we're rather in the lurch. The likeliest origin for the term "classical" is that Pavlov's experiments provided a behavioral rendition of the hoary philosophical concepts of the frequency, similarity and contiguity of ideas.

Classical conditioning commenced with a serendipitous observation. Pavlov, a famous scientist who had won a Nobel Prize for his research on the physiology of the digestive system, was studying salivation, which is the first step in digestion. A dog was attached to a harness so it couldn't move. Surgery had been done to the dog's snout so saliva could be collected in test tubes rather than in puddles on the floor. Pavlov could assess how much saliva the dog was spewing from moment-to-moment—this is messy, wet research, but it's the kind of research that wins Nobel Prizes. Pavlov noticed that the dog *started to salivate before it was given any meat*—this was the serendipitous observation that led to classical conditioning. Pavlov wondered, "What was that all about?" I doubt he entertained the conjecture that the dog wanted to take a bite out of him. He spent the rest of his long and productive life answering that question. It's sad to think that if Prof. Ford was in that lab, he would have noted the saliva and carried on with the day's program.

Pavlov was interested in conditioning as a way to study the "physiology of the higher nervous system." He viewed the cerebral cortex as a mosaic of constantly changing points of excitation and inhibition. A "dynamic stereotype" is created with the pairing of stimuli. Cortical activity occurs more readily or easily with such pairings. This view was, of course, based mostly on guesswork. It was early in the twentieth century, very early. Knowledge of the brain was, as is said, "in its infancy."

American psychologists tended to be more practical in their views of classical conditioning. They were interested in using classical conditioning as a way to change behavior in homes, classrooms and institutions. Like our other theorists, Pavlov wasn't averse to using classical conditioning as a way to improve the world. In 1928 he wrote that "Only science, exact science about human nature itself, and the most sincere approach to it by the aid of the omnipotent scientific method will deliver man from his present gloom."

Thorndike's law of effect pretty much faded from experimental psychology soon after he published it. Effect (reinforcement) didn't return into prominence until the 1930s. The first behaviorist movement of Watson and others was based on classical conditioning. Since 1903 there have been something like 10,000 published classical conditioning studies involving organisms from protozoa to people, including psychotic people. Toward the end of his life Pavlov performed experiments on dogs that he believed mimicked the development of psychological disorders. He paired circles with food and ellipses with pain and then presented a stimulus that was, like the Nephilim of Hebrew lore, half a circle and half an ellipse. Discrimination became impossible. Dogs became agitated and reacted according to temperament. Aggressive breeds became more aggressive and timid breeds became more timid.

Interestingly, there have been a few Russian experiments assessing the state of conditioning after "clinical death." The dogs were trained, then flatlined, then revived and retested. I hate to keep you hanging, but I don't read Russian, so I don't know whether the reanimated dogs responded correctly or returned as canine zombies.

It's not easy to define classical conditioning. I'll try two approaches and then outline the "structure" of classical conditioning. I'll go on to suggest that everything I said needs to be qualified. As Robert Rescorla, a prominent experimenter, wrote, "Pavlovian conditioning—it's not what you think it is."

We might say, not altogether correctly, that classical conditioning is a kind of *stimulus substitution*. One stimulus comes to substitute for a second stimulus. To say this another way, the organism comes to respond to one stimulus the way it does to another stimulus.

Classical conditioning can also be considered the process by which *neutral stimuli acquire meaning*. They do this by being paired with stimuli that possess meaning. This pairing depends on the twin processes of *repetition* (frequency) and *contiguity*. Contiguity refers to stimuli that occur together in space and time.

The structure or arrangement of classical conditioning begins with a *reflex*—an *unlearned stimulus elicits or produces an unlearned response*. In the case of Pavlov's dog, meat elicited saliva. We might note that meat is not a neutral stimulus. It means something to a dog, something the dog does not need to learn. Pure breeds know what to do with meat. So do mutts.

In order to avoid cognitive connotations to the word "unlearned" and to indicate that the process of conditioning is tied to specific experimental procedures, the word was changed to *unconditioned*—the *unconditioned stimulus* of meat elicits the *unconditioned response* of saliva. In fact, the original term "unconditional" was wrongly translated as "unconditioned." Another translation error involved Pavlov's name. It should have been translated as "Pawlow." They should have gone with a better translator.

Pavlov selected a stimulus that had no meaning to the dog. He initially selected a metronome. The majority of people in Union County erroneously believe he used a bell, so let's go with the bell. The question is, "What does a bell mean to a dog that has never heard it before?" The answer, of course, is "Nothing." If we pair the bell with the meat and do this often enough, the bell comes to mean something—meat is on the way. If we paired the bell with electric shock, the bell would have quite a different meaning.

The once neutral bell has become learned—*conditioned,* as we say. Because of repetition and contiguity, it now elicits saliva. The *conditioned stimulus* of a bell elicits the *conditioned response* of saliva. The dog responds to the bell more or less as it responded to the meat—by generating saliva. Its mouth waters, just as our mouths water when we walk into a pizzeria thick with the odors of oregano and garlic. In many, but not all instances of classical conditioning, the conditioned response is a weaker or reduced version of the unconditioned response. Our mouths water when we walk in, but it's not like we just bit into a pepperoni Sicilian.

There are "hard versions" and "soft versions" of classical conditioning. (Guthrie distinguished studies involving *conditioned reflexes* from studies involving *conditioning* without reflexes.) The hard versions require a reflex. The soft versions do not. The soft versions amount to associationism, which is the pairing of stimuli that may or may not possess biological significance. The underlying principles in all the versions are repetition and contiguity.

The *key or controlling element* in classical conditioning is the unconditioned stimulus. If we have one, learning or acquisition occurs. Sometimes, the acquisition involves favorable or desirable stimuli, stimuli the organism does nothing to avoid. These are instances of *appetitive conditioning.* Sometimes, the acquisition involves unfavorable or undesirable stimuli that the organism strives to avoid. These are instances of *aversive conditioning.* And sometimes conditioning of the appetitive and aversive kinds involves time. This is referred to as *temporal conditioning.* The conditioned stimulus is the passage of time. Regular occurrences of stimuli at specific times produce expectations that an unconditioned stimulus will appear. With respect to aversive temporal conditioning, consider what would happen if an allergy attack occurred at the same time every day. With respect to appetitive temporal conditioning, I recollect a kindly neighbor who lived a few doors down from us. This neighbor arrived home from work at 5:00 PM. He always placed open cans of cat food on the sidewalk—over the years this must have cost a fortune. It never failed that stray cats arrived at his house around 4:30 PM. I don't know what they did the rest of the day. Probably, bad things. But at 4:30 PM they were waiting patiently on the sidewalk.

If we do not have an unconditioned stimulus, no acquisition occurs. Or, rather, the dog learns that the bell leads to nothing. If the bell keeps ringing and nothing happens, the dog will habituate to it. If we have an unconditioned stimulus and then remove it from the situation—the bell once did, but no longer leads to meat—we have *inhibition*. The new pairing of "bell—nothing" replaces and inhibits the old pairing of "bell—meat." Conditioning disintegrates. It's senseless to waste saliva on bells that are never followed by meat.

The association of "bell—meat" never disappears entirely. It is suppressed by the new combination "bell—nothing." If the dog is kept from the lab for a period of time after the process of inhibition occurred and then returned to the lab and a bell suddenly rings, we're going to get a spurt of saliva. This is the phenomenon of *spontaneous recovery*. *Reconditioning* occurs rapidly if the bell continues to be paired with the meat.

Disinhibition is an interesting phenomenon. In disinhibition a novel stimulus is introduced in the inhibition process. A buzzer suddenly sounds as the dog experiences "bell—nothing." What follows the buzzer is the sudden reappearance of the conditioned response. "Bell and buzzer—saliva." I suppose the moral is we have to be careful not to introduce a new stimulus as inhibition is occurring.

An example of disinhibition in human behavior is the following. A young man was once afraid of making small talk with young ladies. He has since lost that fear. As he chats with a young lady in the club something expected occurs. Maybe a bottle shatters. Maybe someone falls off a stool. Formerly inhibited, the fear suddenly returns, quite as if it never went away.

In the hard versions of classical conditioning the conditioned stimulus must come before or overlap (*delayed conditioning*) the unconditioned stimulus. If the conditioned stimulus concludes before the unconditioned stimulus turns on (*trace conditioning*), there must be minimal delay between the two. In order not to violate the principle of contiguity, this delay is a matter of seconds. The interval between the two stimuli is referred to as the *inter-stimulus interval*. Trace conditioning played an important role in Clark Hull's theory, as we'll see, unless something untoward occurs.

Situations in which both the conditioned and unconditioned stimuli turn on and off at the same time *(simultaneous conditioning)* do not produce much evidence of conditioning. Similarly, *backward conditioning*, in which the unconditioned stimulus precedes the conditioned stimulus, does not produce acquisition. There are some exotic examples of backward conditioning in the laboratory, but it's not found in "the real world." Those of you who own dogs can try this experiment. Stand over your dog the next time it eats and ring a bell. Watch what happens.

The *unconditioned stimulus is the controlling element* in classical conditioning—I think I said that. The *conditioned stimulus serves as a signal* that the unconditioned stimulus is about to occur. The *conditioned response serves as the test of learning or as the dependent variable.* If it occurs, we have conditioning. If it does not occur, we do not have conditioning. *With repetition and contiguity, the conditioned response starts to move forward in the process.* It serves to prepare the organism to experience the unconditioned stimulus. In conditioning with aversive stimuli such as shock, this serves as a defensive maneuver. Pavlov called this the "paradox of inhibition." In a later lecture we'll examine avoidance learning. The moving forward of the conditioned response is what Pavlov originally observed with the dog in the harness—the dog started to salivate before the meat was presented.

I'm going to return to this process shortly, but first I'll like to relate some examples of classical conditioning provided by students in former semesters.

The beeping sound of the microwave oven serves as a conditioned stimulus. The warm food serves as the unconditioned stimulus. Saliva serves as the conditioned response.

The yellow arch outside McDonald's serves as a conditioned stimulus. A Big Mac serves as the unconditioned stimulus. Saliva serves as the conditioned response.

A bag of peanuts serves as a conditioned stimulus. A chemical in the peanuts serves as the unconditioned stimulus that elicits the unconditioned response of an allergic reaction. The next time the bag of peanuts appears it elicits the conditioned response of fear.

The jingle of the ice cream truck "Mr. Softee" serves as a conditioned stimulus. The ice cream serves as the unconditioned stimulus. Saliva and the good feeling of hearing the jingle serve as the conditioned responses.

The buzzing sound of an electric can opener serves as a conditioned stimulus. The smell of Nine Lives cat food that permeates the apartment serves as the unconditioned stimulus. Saliva serves as the conditioned response.

The sound of a bell in a high school serves as a conditioned stimulus. Lunch in the cafeteria serves as the unconditioned stimulus. Increased saliva and the rush to the cafeteria serve as the conditioned responses. Of course, it's hard to believe students' mouths water in anticipation of cafeteria chow.

The noises of gurgling and sprayed water heard in the waiting room of a dental office serve as conditioned stimuli. Drilling of teeth serve as the unconditioned stimulus. Pain serves as the unconditioned response. Fear and nausea felt in the waiting room serve as conditioned responses.

The last example has been related to the class every semester for decades. It has taken on the aura of an urban legend. A student is taking a shower. The water is lukewarm. Suddenly, there's the sound of the toilet flushing in the upstairs apartment. The water in the shower becomes boiling hot. The next time the student is showering and hears the toilet flushing over his head, he averts the nozzle, thereby preventing a scalding. In this example the flush of the toilet serves as the conditioned stimulus. The hot water serves as the unconditioned stimulus. The scalding serves as the unconditioned response. Panic and fear serve as the conditioned response. Averting the nozzle is an avoidant response.

I'll like to return to the concept that the conditioned response moves forward in the conditioning process. As noted, this was the feature of conditioning that grabbed Pavlov's attention. I'll like to demonstrate the concept by reference to an early and noteworthy 1938 intervention by Hobart Mowrer and his wife Willie May Mowrer, who was also a psychologist, on the problem of bedwetting.

Bedwetting (enuresis) is a serious problem in a fair number of children, mostly boy children. About one-in-four children aged five and under chronically wet their beds. About one-in-twenty children aged six and older wet their beds. This can lead to personal and social issues. These children can't sleep at their friends' houses. They can't go to summer camps—some camps have cabins for bedwetters. Parents try all sorts of techniques to stop the bedwetting. They wake the children up periodically throughout the night. They stop the children from drinking fluids after a certain hour. Probably, they shame the children into showing urological will power. Such techniques inevitably fail. Friction can occur if parents believe the children are defiant or wetting their beds on purpose. Nothing can be further from the truth. As everyone knows except for the parents, the bladder works reflexively and releases urine when full.

Any number of explanations for bedwetting have been offered throughout the years. The psychoanalysts, as we might expect, had a field day. Mowrer viewed bedwetting in terms of classical conditioning. Children who wet their beds have failed to learn to wake up when the bladder is full.

Mowrer's task was to wake the children up in the act of urinating. (He and his wife ran a group home for boys.) His initial attempt was to design a collapsible bed. When a circuit in the bed got wet from urine, the bed would tip and the boy would drop to the floor. The second and less dangerous attempt was the famous bell and moisture-sensitive pad. (Sears Roebuck sold the pad for many years.) When the pad got wet, a circuit caused a bell to ring, waking the boy up in the act of urinating.

In this case the bell serves as the unconditioned stimulus and waking up serves as the unconditioned response. The full bladder and beginning urination serve as the conditioned stimuli. A full bladder and beginning urination lead to a bell ringing and to waking up. Waking up—the result of urinating—serves as the conditioned response. If this happens a sufficient number of times, *a full bladder leads to waking up before urination occurs.* Waking up—the conditioned response—moves forward in the process.

There's an unadvertised catch to the procedure. Many boys will blithely sleep through the ringing of a bell. For the procedure to be maximally effective, parents are advised to sit beside the bed. They have to be awake—maybe they can do their theories of learning homework. Once the bell rings, they have to grab the boy and jostle him, making sure he wakes up as he urinates. This may necessitate wearing raincoats or wetsuits.

The procedure sounds esoteric, but it corresponds with what Pavlov experienced with the dog and with what we experience when we start to use an alarm clock. The first few days after we set the alarm, we wake up only as it rings. We may even sleep through the ringing. With further practice and experience we wake up and shut the alarm off before it rings.

We note in the bedwetting procedure that a biological reflex served the role of a conditioned stimulus – conditioned response. It is obviously not a neutral stimulus, but it doesn't much matter. It is the *order of pairing of stimuli* that is crucial in classical conditioning. The stimulus that is presented first, whether neutral or biological/reflexive, comes through repetition and contiguity to elicit the response associated with the stimulus that is presented second. In the case of the Mowrers' intervention, emptying the bladder elicited the response to a bell, which was waking up. A bell, decidedly not biological or reflexive in nature, served in the place ordinarily reserved for an unconditioned stimulus.

In his 1954 presidential address to the American Psychological Association Mowrer followed up on Pavlov's suggestion that language is unique to humans. Pavlov entitled language the *second signal system* and compared it to the *first signal system*, which is universal among mammals and which involves classical conditioning pure and simple.

Mowrer suggested that syntactic *predication*—combining nouns and verbs—*is analogous to conditioning*. The example involves Tom. Maybe you know Tom. He's tall, tan and mustachioed. Most of the year he resides in a beach house in Oahu. You perform obsequious behavior in his presence. You rush to shake his hand. You want to stand at his side. You want to sit next to him.

Consider the word "thief." We have many associations to this word— criminals have a different set of associations than law-abiding folk. When we hear the word "thief," as in "There's a thief in the room," we engage in particular behaviors. We check for our wallets and purses. We move our belongings closer.

Now I inform you that "Tom is a thief." If you believe me, your behavior may change. You may no longer want to shake Tom's hand or stand next to him or sit beside him. You may check for your wallet when he enters the room and move your possessions closer. You never did such things before, but you do them now, simply because I told you that Tom is a thief. I've changed your behavior by joining the words "Tom" and "thief."

Even the people in Tuckerton can see where this is going. Propaganda depends on the pairing of words (associations). "Tom is a liberal." "Tom is a progressive." "Tom is a far-right winger." "Tom is a skinhead." If I keep repeating these slogans, you may consider Tom differently and you may act differently toward him. You may act toward Tom in accordance with the associations these terms elicit. Some of these terms carry so much associative baggage, it may take only one pairing to change your behavior.

The nature and arrangement of stimuli are important in classical conditioning. Let's look at a few issues involving stimuli.

Organisms will spontaneously respond to a range of similar conditioned stimuli. This is the phenomenon of *stimulus generalization*. Pavlov referred to this as *brain irradiation*. The likelihood of occurrence of the conditioned response increases as the similarity of the stimuli increases. This is the beauty of using bells and lights. Their properties can be precisely defined.

Because of practice and experience the organism may come to respond, not to a range of similar stimuli, but to a single, specific conditioned stimulus. This is the phenomenon of *stimulus discrimination*. Pavlov referred to this as *brain concentration*. Discrimination results from prolonged training and from the selective use of the unconditioned stimulus. So we have three bells—loud, medium, soft—each defined in volume and pitch. We present the unconditioned stimulus of meat only after the loud bell. Initially, the dog salivates to all three—they're bells, after all. But with continued training the dog ceases to respond to the medium and soft bells. Why waste saliva on bells that are never followed by meat? Inhibition occurs to the medium and soft bells.

We have with generalization and discrimination an exceedingly important learning principle. *Learning commences as generalization and with practice and experience becomes discriminated.* Initially, organisms respond to all similar stimuli. Gradually, organisms come to respond selectively.

So we're languishing in a jail somewhere in Turkey. There are three jailors. Initially, we cringe and curl up defensively whenever one enters our cell. This demonstrates generalization. But we learn that only one of the three—the short smelly one—mistreats us. We cringe and curl up only when he enters the cell. This demonstrates discrimination. And it's lucky for us that only one of the three mistreats us.

The *stronger and more salient*—more obvious—the conditioned stimulus and unconditioned stimulus are, the more expeditious the conditioning. *Unfamiliar (novel) stimuli are easier to condition than familiar stimuli.* Familiar stimuli carry their associative histories and are more difficult to disconnect from old stimuli or attach to new stimuli.

Repeated presentations of a neutral stimulus without an unconditioned stimulus impede the learning process. This situation is called *preexposure* or *latent inhibition*. If a bell rings repeatedly and nothing follows the bell, the organism learns "bell—nothing." If the bell is now paired with meat, the organism doesn't respond as quickly as if it never heard the bell. It has to replace (inhibit) "bell—nothing" with "bell—meat."

Pseudoconditioning is the situation in which the unconditioned stimulus is presented by itself for a number of trials. A neutral stimulus is then presented, leading to a strong and temporary response. Probably, the strong response is due to sensitization. The organism reacts strongly to a novel stimulus.

Sensitization and habituation are processes that always need to be controlled in conditioning experiments. We have to be careful that repeated presentations of stimuli do not result in habituation. And we have to be sure that responses are due to association (learning) and not to recovery from habituation or to sensitization. There have been a number of procedures that try to control for the nuisances of habituation and sensitization. Currently, the procedure used is called *discriminative control*. The conditioned stimulus—the neutral stimulus that eventually becomes conditioned—is paired with the unconditioned stimulus for half the trials. A second neutral stimulus is presented without the unconditioned stimulus for the other half. If it occurs, sensitization should follow the presentation of both stimuli. Association should occur only to the stimulus followed by the unconditioned stimulus. The test, of course, is the occurrence of the conditioned response.

External inhibition is the situation in which, after reliable conditioning has been established, a novel stimulus occurs at the same time as the conditioned stimulus. We've been pairing "bell—meat" for a while and suddenly we pair the bell with a light. The organism hasn't been expecting that. The novel stimulus serves as a distractor or intrusion and it impedes the performance of the conditioned response.

There have been revisions over the years to how the fundamental facts of classical conditioning are interpreted. As practicing fallibilists, we expect no less. Gone are the days when classical conditioning was perceived as a sensorimotor and mindless process. In our time classical conditioning is perceived in nearly cognitive terms. The formerly sacrosanct concepts of contiguity and the inter-stimulus interval have been challenged. I'll describe three challenges—the procedures of overshadowing and blocking and the concept of preparedness.

In *overshadowing* (Pavlov, 1927) a salient stimulus prevents the association of a less salient stimulus. We start with a compound stimulus—bell and light, presented simultaneously, are paired with shock. (Compound stimuli hardly capture the complexity of the sensory world, but they are better than single stimuli.) We make one of the stimuli more salient than the other, say a loud shrill bell and a brief flash of dim light. After reliable conditioning has been established, we test each of the components of the compound stimulus separately. The notion of contiguity predicts that each stimulus will elicit the conditioned response. But that is not what we find. The salient bell leads to the conditioned response. The less salient light does not, despite being paired with the unconditioned stimulus the same number of times. It's as if the organism ignored the less salient stimulus.

Rescorla and Wagner (1972) suggested that there is only so much association possible in the pairing of stimuli. In overshadowing the salient stimulus carries all of the associative value. The less salient stimulus contributes little or nothing to the association.

In *blocking* (Kamin, 1969) a single stimulus is converted into a compound stimulus. Originally, we had a bell. Now we have bell and light. Pairing with the unconditioned stimulus occurs the same number of times for the compound stimulus as it did for the original single stimulus. As in overshadowing, the two stimuli are separated and tested individually. The notion of contiguity predicts that each stimulus will elicit the conditioned response. But that is not what we find. The bell elicits the conditioned response. The light does not. The original stimulus interfered with learning the second stimulus. Kamin suggested that the second stimulus doesn't work because it doesn't add anything new or different to the situation.

Kamin had an intriguing view of learning. He suggested that learning involves *being surprised*. Something new is added to the situation, something different. We already know what leads to what. If the second stimulus fails to add anything new or different to the learning situation, it is redundant and superfluous. In a different context I'm reminded how the late New York *Times* reporter and columnist John Hess once defined "the news." The news, Hess observed, is not what we read in the papers. The news is what we don't read.

Leon Kamin (1927 - 2017) was an interesting psychologist. He exchanged the tranquil laboratories of learning for the thermal politics of intelligence testing and authored an important book, *The Science and Politics of IQ* (1974). Kamin pointed out that since the 1920s intelligence tests have served political and ideological purposes, most famously in curtailing immigration. He opposed the notion that a score on an intelligence test reflects biological or racial factors. In his estimation a score on an intelligence test reflects political and educational decisions to create a set of questions that result in an average score of 100. Alternate universes may define intelligence using a test whose average score is 80 or 120. The topics on the test reflect categories educators define as comprising "intelligence." Educators put math and vocabulary on the test. They did not put art or music or gymnastics on the test.

Kamin challenged the category of "identical twins reared apart" frequently used in intelligence testing research. He pointed out that with selective placement in adoption identical twins were rarely raised in environments that differed widely in terms of cultural background or educational opportunities. Twins born in upper socioeconomic classes were both placed in upper socioeconomic foster homes. Twins born in lower socioeconomic classes were both placed in lower socioeconomic foster homes.

Many years ago, Kamin delivered a lecture here at Kean in Hutchinson Hall. I never forgot his answer to the observation a faculty member brought up. This teacher asked whether the correlation—approximately .60— between SAT scores and college grade point averages demonstrates that intelligence is mostly biological (with the implication that it is inherited).

Kamin replied that the correlation demonstrated that colleges were failing to educate students. The knowledgeable students who entered college, as defined by their scores on the SAT, stayed knowledgeable. The less knowledgeable students, sadly, stayed less knowledgeable as they plodded through the curricula.

The third challenge to traditional Pavlovian conditioning involves *preparedness* (*selective association*). The challenge also involves the concepts of *taste aversion* or the *Garcia effect*, named after James Garcia (1917 - 2012), who performed some of the crucial experiments.

Preparedness challenges contiguity, specifically the inter-stimulus interval. And it challenges the notion of "inter-changeable stimuli." I have to say that probably no psychologist ever entertained the improbable notion that any stimulus could be paired with any other stimulus, whatever they were and willy-nilly. I can say there was little regard in theories for any biological constraints on the pairing of stimuli. The work of Garcia and others demonstrated that there were biological constraints on the pairing of stimuli. These constraints could make it difficult to pair certain stimuli. And to the contrary, biological factors could facilitate the pairing of stimuli.

Perhaps the most famous experiment in this regard was that of Garcia and Koelling in 1966. There were four groups of rats.

Group One drank sweet (saccharine) water. While drinking, a paw was shocked.

Group Two drank ordinary water from a bright (backlit) and noisy dispenser. (The noise was a clicking sound.) While drinking, a paw was shocked.

Group Three drank sweet (saccharine) water. While drinking, they were irradiated with X-rays. They became sick half an hour later.

Group Four drank ordinary water from a bright and noisy dispenser. While drinking, they were irradiated with X-rays. They became sick half an hour later.

The dependent variable was what dispenser the rats avoided after conditioning. (The procedure involved conditioned avoidance.) Group One did not avoid drinking from dispensers that provided sweet water. Group Two avoided bright and noisy dispensers. Group Three avoided dispensers that provided sweet water. Group Four did not avoid drinking from bright and noisy dispensers.

Garcia and Koelling concluded that there is a biological preparedness to associate pain with visual and auditory stimuli (Group Two). And there is a biological preparedness to associate sickness with gustation (Group Three). No association was formed between taste and pain (Group One). No association was formed between visual and auditory stimuli and the effect of irradiation (Group Four). The temporal delay between drinking sweet water and getting sick in Group Three challenged the principle of contiguity. Despite an interval of half an hour between experiencing the conditioned stimulus and the unconditioned response, avoidance conditioning occurred.

What happened to the rats is analogous to what might happen to us if we suffered food poisoning. (There are approximately 200,000 cases of food poisoning yearly in the United States.) We ate chicken marsala on a red-and-black checkerboard tablecloth. Afterward, we got sick and nauseous. Going forward, we're leery about ordering chicken marsala. But we would not be leery about dining on a red-and-black checkerboard tablecloth. The situation would be different if we cut our hands on a piece of glass lying on a red-and-black checkerboard tablecloth. We might prefer to sit at a differently colored tablecloth on our next visit.

The association between taste and subsequent sickness depends on the *novelty of the stimulus that makes us sick*. The subsequent aversion to the food is greater if the food is new and different. If we regularly ate chicken marsala and got sick one time, we might not be deterred from ordering it again. If we ate chicken marsala for the first time and got sick, we might be permanently deterred from reordering it. The effect of novelty is utilized with people undergoing chemotherapy. The medications can induce nausea. Rather than pair the nausea with foods that are regularly consumed, patients are encouraged to eat foods they never tried before. The novel substances would be paired with the medication and with the subsequent nausea. Foods ordinarily consumed would be left unaffected.

Taste aversion has been applied to humans and animals, but with incomplete success.

In former years there was a "treatment," often court-mandated, for alcohol abuse. In this treatment the person consumed a drug called

"Antabuse." By itself, the drug is harmless, but in combination with alcohol it results in nausea and sickness. The idea was to recondition alcohol from something that led to pleasure, presumably, to something that led to misery. The belief was that no one would drink a substance that made them sick. Like so many beliefs, this one was in need of correction. Sadly, there are people who will continue to drink despite being nauseous and sick.

Taste aversion was applied in efforts to control predation. Coyotes prey on sheep and chickens in the American West. Traps were set and rifles taken off the mantels to send coyotes into the canine afterlife. Gentler ranchers applied the Garcia effect—maybe these ranchers took a theories of learning course. Carcasses of sheep and chickens contaminated with chemicals that made coyotes sick were deposited in fields. The belief was that coyotes would avoid attacking the creatures that made them sick. As with the treatment of alcoholism, this method—called *bait shyness*—has not proven to be a panacea. Coyote predation continues unabated. Sheep and chickens continue to live in fear.

The Garcia effect does not appear to work in humans. We still frequent buffet counters despite the occasional food poisoning. We still go bar-hopping despite the recurrent hangovers. People still use narcotics despite the cycle of getting sick from not getting high.

There are a number of factors that may counteract the Garcia effect in humans. Animals eat to survive. So do humans, but we also eat for social reasons and to comfort ourselves from the woes of this world. When it comes to alcohol and drugs, there is peer pressure to get drunk and to shoot up. And when we are addicted there is the necessity to drink or shoot up to avoid the unpleasant consequences of not drinking or shooting up. With addiction, there are changes in the brain and in cognition that impair judgement. We know we should avoid these substances, but we can't help ourselves. These substances may be so ingrained in our daily routines that we overlook the sicknesses their consumption creates.

Thank you.

LECTURE SEVEN

John Watson and Behaviorism

Sigmund Koch suggested that there have been three versions of behaviorism in the history of psychology in America. The first version is associated with John Watson. This version occurred in the 1910s and was based on classical conditioning. The second version, which Koch called "the Age of Theory," is associated with Tolman and Hull. This version occurred in the 1930s - 1950s and was based on a gumbo of classical and operant conditioning salted with the spices of intervening variables. The third and most influential version is associated with B. F. Skinner. This version started in the 1950s and was based on operant conditioning. This version, which is still present in some quarters, revolutionized psychology and education. Although it was based on a far richer experimental foundation, the third version held to Watson's original perception of what psychology should focus on.

I consider behaviorism in all its versions to be a misguided approach to the study of human beings. It led to the neglect of the topics that make us human—creativity, consciousness, forethought, personality, to name a few. (This negligence caused the study of such topics to fall into the inept hands of clinicians.) Given its insistence on prediction and control, behaviorism was based on a truncated slice of the human experience. It was certainly based on a stultifying methodology that conflated experimental tactics with a worldview.

That said, we have to understand behaviorism—certainly, Watson's version—in the context of the history of psychology. Watson's behaviorism was a reaction to what was going on in psychology at the time. In the long run Watson's behaviorism set psychology back. In the short run Watson's behaviorism was an advance.

The psychology of the period was amazingly non-observational and non-experimental. Psychologists in the period came by their theories the old-fashioned way—they sat in lounge chairs, drank brandy, smoked imported cigars, and pontificated. For example, Freud's conjectures about children were based on memories of disturbed men and women and on his case study of raising his children. This is hardly a broad base to erect a theoretical cathedral. To his credit, Watson actually observed babies. He sat for hours writing down everything particular babies did in what were called "baby biographies." If he did that today, he would use a camcorder.

The psychology of the period was excessively theoretical. The period was full of big theories, vast theories, heavy theories, theories that encompassed everything and explained everything, the kitchen sink included. Freud's psychoanalysis and Jung's analytical psychology are typical. Every educated person knows about those two. Here's a theory that was influential at the time, but is pretty much forgotten today—hormic psychology. This was the brain dumpling of William McDougall (1871 - 1938), a British psychologist who immigrated to America. McDougall was quite famous in his time. He's not so famous in our time. If he's remembered for anything, it's for founding the parapsychology laboratory at Duke University later made notorious by J.R. Rhine. Here's the opening sentence of McDougall's masterpiece, *Social Psychology* (1908):

> "The human mind has certain innate or inherited tendencies which are the essential springs or motive powers of all thought and action, whether individual or collective, and are the bases from which the character and will of individuals and of nations are gradually developed under the guidance of the intellectual faculties."

This leaden level of theorizing continues for several hundred pages.

Watson's behaviorism was a reaction against the non-observational and non-experimental psychology of his time. His behaviorism was also a reaction against the prevalent instinct theories of the period. These theories evolved out of—what else?—the theory of evolution. Everything that organisms did, humans included, was based on instinct. If I acted friendly, this showed the instinct for friendliness. If I acted unfriendly, this showed the instinct for, I don't know, unfriendliness. If I helped you, this showed the instinct for altruism. If I failed to help you, this showed the instinct for selfishness. If I told the truth, this showed the instinct of truthfulness. If I told a lie, this showed the instinct for mendacity.

The notion of instinct really added nothing to the description of behavior. It was circular reasoning at its finest. I help you because of the instinct of altruism. I demonstrate the instinct of altruism by helping you. None of this was based on anything genetic or biological. It was strictly a word stew that sounded scientific.

Instinct theories created a false dichotomy between learned and unlearned behavior. There's a vast difference between the instinctual behavior of insects and whatever instinctual behavior exists in mammals. Never mind humans. Consider that the instinctual behavior of many organisms involves the practice and refinement of inherited capabilities ("instincts," if you will). For example, the nest building and song making of birds involve considerable practice and fine-tuning, beyond whatever instinctual base exists.

Years ago, the comparative psychologist Frank Beach suggested that we need to see the origin of a behavior before we conclude that it is learned or instinctual. On an island somewhere in the Pacific there's a group of monkeys that washes their fruit before consuming it. If we were on a cruise and took an excursion to this island, we might conclude that this behavior was instinctual. But we would be wrong. Uniquely, an observer was present to note the first occurrence of this behavior. A young monkey, raised perhaps by an anally retentive mother, happened to wash a piece of fruit before eating it. Other monkeys saw this and did what monkeys do best. Only a few monkeys of mature age resisted.

Watson, like Skinner after him, preferred an environmental orientation. The environment makes us who we are. Watson's most famous statement (1930) occurs in his rejection of instinctual explanations in favor of environmental explanations:

"Give me a dozen healthy infants, well-formed, and my own specified world to bring them up in and I'll guarantee to take any one at random and train him to become any type of specialist I might select—doctor, lawyer, artist, merchant and, yes, even beggar man and thief, regardless of his talents, penchants, tendencies, abilities, vocations and race of his ancestors."

Watson believed psychology was a natural science. It should be experimental in methodology. It should strive for the prediction and control of behavior. Its subject matter was behavior, pure and simple. It should eschew cognition and avoid intervening variables. And it should be modest in formulating theories. These views were exactly those we later find in B. F. Skinner.

Watson was born in Greenville, South Carolina, in 1878. We shouldn't hold this against him. He died in 1958. He received a doctorate from the University of Chicago in 1903. He taught at Johns Hopkins from 1908 – 1920. His scandalous affair with Rosalie Rayner forced him to leave Johns Hopkins and to withdraw from psychology. He left the ivy-draped halls of academe for the glass-and-steel boxes of Madison Avenue where he applied classical conditioning to great effect and to great wealth. Watson's insight was that consumers would transfer favorable associations from one stimulus to another. I well remember advertisements in magazines in my youth. A shapely lady in a bathing suit stood next to a car in one ad. Another shapely lady in a bathing suit stood next to a refrigerator in another ad. There doesn't appear to be any logical connection between the shapely ladies and the products, but the idea was that men would transfer their liking for shapely ladies to the products. In no time, men would be opening their wallets and buying cars and refrigerators.

We're all sophisticates in this class, or so we keep telling ourselves. We chuckle at the idea that a shapely lady in a bathing suit could make us buy anything, but the concept made Watson a rich man and I don't doubt a lot of cars and refrigerators were sold. And maybe times haven't changed as much as we like to think. A commercial in a recent Super Bowl featured a shapely actress named Kate Upton wearing a skimpy outfit and standing next to a Mercedes-Benz. Women's groups reacted to the ad by accusing the car company of using "sex appeal" to sell their product and of portraying degrading images of women. I'm sure Watson was rolling over in his coffin and I'm not sure the ad was ineffective. I had all to do to keep from rushing to the local Mercedes-Benz dealer.

The focus on observable behavior led to a relentless attack on mentalism—today, we would say "cognition." Wilhelm Wundt, another forgotten giant of the formative years of psychology, believed psychology was the study of the conscious minds of normal adults using introspection as the primary method. Sigmund Freud believed psychology was the study of the unconscious minds of disordered people using dream interpretation and free association as the primary methods. Watson rejected both definitions of psychology. And he rejected introspection, dream interpretation and free association as methodologies.

I suppose Watson's main objection was that we cannot see the mind. We can only ask, "What's on your mind?" Respondents may or may not know what's on their minds. Respondents may or may not tell us. We never know for sure that we get the right answers. Watson's point is well taken. It's shaky business to proceed on the basis of not knowing if we hear a truthful answer. But an exclusive focus on observable behavior lops off sizeable chunks of human experiences. And the exclusive focus on observable behavior does not guarantee the accuracy or truthfulness of behavior. We've all had experiences in which a person said or did one thing while thinking something else entirely. It's not to my credit, but I've done this. One time, I lied to dear Aunt Ethel. I hated her lemon pie, but I said I loved it. I even asked that she bake another.

It's one thing to say we should avoid studying cognition because of its invisibility. It's another thing to say that cognition doesn't exist. In 1919 Watson wrote that he "finds no evidence for mental existences" or for "mental processes of any kind." In an essay entitled *The Unconscious of the Behaviorist* Watson wrote that "the behaviorist finds no mind in his laboratory." He further wrote that, contrary to what Freud claimed, "there can be no festering spot in the substratum of the mind … because there is no mind."

This is very strange—sometimes I think Watson was pulling our collective axons with these statements. He just blew off all the introverts in the world who are preoccupied with what he claimed doesn't exist. And he just blew off all the people who engage in meditation to explore what he claimed doesn't exist. And he just blew himself off—he was the man, after all, who came up with the *idea* to place shapely ladies in bathing suits next to cars and refrigerators.

For Watson, consciousness amounted to *verbalized responses*. I am conscious if I can put something—an idea?—into words. I am unconscious to the extent I cannot put something—another idea?—into words. This is pretty much Skinner's position and it is pretty much an inadequate position. There are people who know full well what they want to say but who cannot put it into words. There are people who incessantly verbalize without any consciousness of what they are saying—I know a number of such mindless chatterboxes. And there is a difference between the complete absence of behavior and behavior that is unverbalized because it is automatic or because a particular thought is not easy to express. I suppose what I'm saying is that there may be different types of "unconsciousness" with different relationships to behavior.

Whatever we may think of Watson's behaviorist program, we have to acknowledge his importance. Watson *changed the role of the observer* in psychology. Data was no longer to be obtained from private experience observed through introspection and reported as self-disclosure. Data was now to be obtained from observation of another person's (or animal's) public behavior. In a broad sense Watson shifted psychology from an introverted to an extraverted format. Watson said as much—he said he wasn't interested in his dreams as in what his neighbors were doing.

Watson launched the behaviorist assault on mentalism in 1913 with the article entitled *Psychology as the Behaviorist Views It*. His major book, *Psychology from the Standpoint of a Behaviorist*, was published in 1919. Watson was a prolific writer in professional psychology. He also wrote for popular magazines and he published books on parenting and childcare. His most influential book on children, *Psychological Care of Infant and Child* (1928), was written with his wife Rosalie Rayner. In the book they suggested that parents should not develop overly emotional bonds with their children—"mother love is a dangerous instrument" is a typical quote. They appear to have practiced what they preached with their two sons, who they raised in a kind of experiment applying behavioral principles in their upbringing.

Watson made a load of money in advertising and in publishing. We shouldn't be envious of him in this regard. It's a different matter when it comes to parenting and childcare. I don't doubt that his advice wrecked any number of families. I don't want to judge them, but the Watsons don't seem to be successful parents. One son committed suicide, another son attempted suicide. James, the surviving son, wrote that he regretted the way his parents raised him.

We've seen how we can understand Watson's program as a reaction against the practice of the psychology of his time. Watson's theory, as such, was quite modest. For Watson, learning was a kind of *general adjustment to the environment*. This adjustment involved the *whole body*, with the mind included in the "whole body."

Watson never attempted to establish formal "laws" of learning, as Thorndike and the experimenters in the "Age of Theory" attempted. His principles included frequency, recency and stimulus change. *Frequency* involves repetition of stimulus - response associations. *Recency* is the concept that organisms will do next in a situation what they last did in the situation. *Stimulus change* is the concept that the performance of a response changes the overall situation. The latter two concepts were further developed by Edwin Guthrie.

There were three classes of stimulus - response habits—*manual habits, laryngeal habits* and *emotional habits*.

Laryngeal habits involve speech and thinking. Thinking involves *talking to oneself* and, following the movement forward of conditioned responses, *preparatory action*. Think, for example, how you act when you leave this classroom. If you're like me, you have the keys out before you reach the car. Except for avoiding getting struck by a car as students race off campus, the walk to my Hyundai is a silent and mostly mindless trek. Notice how verbal I would become if I arrived at the spot where I parked my car and it wasn't there. I would say "What!" rather loudly and start talking to myself, "Just where did I park?" I suppose I would be thinking out loud—very out loud.

We should note that this is a limited view of the thinking process. Thinking occurs for many reasons besides preparing ourselves for further actions. Thinking occurs rather aimlessly in dreams and rather aimfully in intellectual and creative pursuits. Watson must have engaged in serious thinking in writing his books and developing the concepts of behaviorism.

With respect to emotional habits, Watson suggested that there were three basic emotions—*fear, love,* and *anger.* These emotions serve as unconditioned responses. He incorporated these emotions in his dubious advice to parents. Parents should avoid eliciting too much fear in their children, else they create timid offspring. Parents should avoid eliciting too much anger in their children, else they create aggressive offspring. And parents should avoid eliciting too much love in their children, else they create pampered offspring. The first two suggestions aren't controversial, but the third suggestion about avoiding too much love goes against modern sensibilities.

Fear is a basic emotion instilled in us by God and Watson. We do not have to learn to fear. We have to learn who and what to fear. Similarly, we have to learn who and what to love and we have to learn who and what makes us angry.

The idea that fear is an unconditioned response that can be attached to different conditioned stimuli is the concept behind Watson's most famous experiment—the experiment with *Little Albert.* The experiment is one of the most famous, if not infamous, in psychology. The conclusions drawn from it are often secondary to the scandal behind the experiment and to the search for the identity of Little Albert. And the conclusions are by no means as clear cut as Watson indicated.

Watson's partner in the experiment was a graduate student named Rosalie Rayner. Rosalie was 22 years younger than Watson. She was also his mistress. He was, as these affairs go, a married man. When I first taught this course, I joked that Watson was the John F. Kennedy of psychologists. I have since updated the joke to "Watson was the Bill Clinton of psychologists." Only he wasn't as lucky as our lecherous presidents. Rosalie's brother got wind of the affair and tried to blackmail Watson. When that didn't work, he informed the administration of Johns Hopkins about the affair. That worked. Watson was promptly fired. As I indicated, he went into advertising and made a fortune. He also divorced the first Mrs. Watson and married Rosalie. Unfortunately, Rosalie died in 1935 at the age of 37.

Over the years psychologists have tried to uncover the identity of Little Albert. Little was known about him other than his age—nine months—and the fact that the experimental sessions took place only on weekends. In January 2010 an article by Hall et al. in the *Monitor* identified Little Albert as Douglas Merritte, the son of Arvilla Merritte, a wet nurse at Johns Hopkins. Sadly, Douglas died at the age of six.

Onto the experiment. The purpose of the experiment was to demonstrate that fear becomes attached to particular stimuli through the process of classical conditioning. Little Albert was not frightened of white lab rats. (In fact, the rats were in greater danger from Little Albert than Little Albert was in danger from the rats.) Little Albert was frightened of an unexpected loud noise. Watson and Rayner paired a white rat (conditioned stimulus) with an unexpected loud noise (unconditioned stimulus). The conditioned response of fear was operationalized as crying and withdrawal in the presence of the white rat.

There were two pairings at the first session. A week later there were five additional pairings. A week later Watson and Rayner used a variety of items to assess whether the fear generalized. The items included a rabbit, a dog, a Santa Claus mask, and Watson's white hair. Little Albert showed fear to some, but not to all, of the items. (We assume the fear generalized to small white items and not to the site of the experiment.)

A week later they paired the rat with noise an additional time. They tried at this session to pair a tiny white dog with the noise, but the dog failed to cooperate and started to bark. A month later they reassessed generalization. As before, Little Albert showed fear to some, but not to all, items.

Watson and Rayner demonstrated that a child can become conditioned to develop a specific fear. Little Albert was not afraid of the rat before it was paired with the loud noise. After it was paired with the noise, he showed fear when he saw the rat. The issue of generalization is trickier to assess. Little Albert showed fear to some small white items, but not to all small white items. The time period of testing was brief—a little more than a month. I use to joke that there's a hundred-year-old man with a fear of white rats wandering the streets of Baltimore, but that's surely not the case.

As parents know, the fears of children inexplicably come and go. Pets, toys, dolls, water, the babysitter, Uncle Dennis—children are frightened of these items for a while and then the fears dissipate, mysteriously as they originated.

As many psychologists do, even famous psychologists, Watson exaggerated the results of the experiment, in this case the generalization of Little Albert's fear. He and Rayner (by then the second Mrs. Watson) wrote in 1921, "When you condition a child to show fear of an animal, this fear transfers or spreads in such a way that without separate conditioning he becomes afraid of many animals." This may or may not be the case. Recollect that we are dealing with one child in a brief window of observation. Further recollect that all learning starts as generalization. It would have been useful to learn how Little Albert behaved in the presence of small white items six months or a year after the final conditioning session.

It's doubtful that Watson and Rayner ruined Little Albert for life, but they came under severe criticism for their apparently cavalier treatment of a nine-month-old. Watson commissioned another graduate student, who he didn't have an affair with, to demonstrate how classical conditioning can be used to eliminate the fears of children.

In a seminal 1924 paper, *A Laboratory Study of Fear: The Case of Peter*, Watson's student, Mary Cover Jones (1897 - 1987), applied conditioning techniques to eliminate fear in a two-year-old child. The techniques have since become standard in behavior therapy. Peter—no one ever called him "Little Peter" or cared to learn his surname or his subsequent fate—was deadly afraid of a white rat and a white rabbit. As Jones describes it, "At the sight of the rat ... Peter screamed and fell flat on his back in a paroxysm of fear."

Jones, who was called "the mother of behavior therapy," outlined a desensitization strategy that would become associated with Joseph Wolpe a quarter century later. In Peter's case the desensitization was *in vivo* as she used real stimuli and not imaginary stimuli. Her strategy resembled what Guthrie later called the "incompatible response method" and the "threshold method" of inducing behavior change.

Jones reasoned that Peter could not experience disparate emotions simultaneously. He could not experience fear and comfort at the same moment. One strategy to replace fear with comfort involved play. She brought a rabbit into the room while Peter played with other children and gradually moved the rabbit closer to him. Another strategy to replace fear with comfort involved food. The rabbit was brought into the room while Peter was in a high chair eating. The rabbit was always kept far enough away so as not to cause agitation. Jones developed a twelve-step program that brought the rabbit gradually closer to Peter. For example, in step two Peter tolerated the rabbit if it was kept at a distance of twelve feet from the high chair. In step four Peter tolerated the rabbit if it was kept at a distance of three feet. In step five Peter touched the rabbit while Mary held it. In step ten Peter held the rabbit on his lap. In step twelve Peter played with the rabbit in a friendly manner. The entire procedure took 45 sessions. (The sessions were interrupted when Peter came down with scarlet fever.)

Like Little Albert, Peter showed inconsistent generalization. In Little Albert's case it was the generalization of fear. In Peter's case it was the *generalization of the absence of fear*, which is a more subtle outcome. More carefully than her mentor, Jones concluded, "By 'unconditioning' Peter to the rabbit, he has apparently been helped to overcome many superfluous fears, some completely, some to a lesser degree." At the conclusion of the sessions Peter showed no fear to a fur coat or to feathers. He showed reduced fear to a fur rug and to a white rat. He may not have been happy doing so, but he touched the rug and picked up a box containing the rat. These behaviors may be small gains, but they are better than no gains.

Thank you.

LECTURE EIGHT

Operant Schedules of Reinforcement

So far, we've examined individual units of discrete stimuli melded to discrete responses by daubs of reinforcement. We've also worked with the assumption that every response is successfully followed by reinforcement. Looking at *schedules of reinforcement*—synonyms are *partial reinforcement* and *intermittent reinforcement*—opens up the sequential or temporal nature of stimuli, responses and reinforcers. (Punishment can also be placed on schedules.) Schedules of reinforcement ask us to examine longer slices of behavior. And schedules provide a more realistic view of events. Crocodiles do not always grab wildebeests. Customers do not always buy their first choices. Obviously, gamblers do not always win. And the Lotharios of Morris Avenue more often sleep alone than with their conquests.

A notable element with schedules is that they result in *greater persistence in responding after extinction has commenced*. In Clark Hull's terminology, schedules show *greater resistance to extinction*. When reinforcement is no longer available, we might expect an organism to persist in performing a behavior that has been continuously reinforced compared to an organism that has been sporadically reinforced, but that is not the case.

When it comes to reinforcement, less is more.

The schedules are organized on the basis of *predictability of obtaining reinforcement*. The occurrence of reinforcement is either predictable (*fixed schedules*) or unpredictable (*variable schedules*). *Ratio schedules* are based on rates of response. *Interval schedules* are based on intervals of time.

The basic schedules dependent on rate of response are fixed ratio (FR) schedules and variable ratio (VR) schedules. The basic schedules dependent on intervals of time are fixed interval (FI) schedules and variable interval (VI) schedules.

Let's take a look at each.

In fixed ratio schedules reinforcement follows a fixed and predictable number of responses. In a FR-4 schedule reinforcement follows every fourth response. In a FR-8 schedule reinforcement follows every eighth response. Not just any response will do. The responses have to be correct—they have to be designated as reinforceable by the administrator of the schedule.

We find stepwise increases in rates of response in fixed ratio schedules. There's a pause after the reception of the reinforcer. The pause is followed by a rush of renewed responses. This rush is referred to as a *ratio run*. The extent of the pause depends on the extent of the schedule. The higher the schedule, the longer the pause. A FR-10 schedule produces a longer pause than a FR-5 schedule. A FR-20 schedule produces a longer pause than a FR-10 schedule.

It's not difficult to find examples of fixed ratio schedules in "real life." Commissions in sales follow fixed ratio schedules. Years ago, the ladies who sold cologne on the ground floor in Macy's at Herald Square were on a FR-3 schedule. They had to sell three bottles of Stetson to earn their commission. Distribution centers sometimes put their employees on a fixed ratio schedule. Employees have to fill a set number of orders before they earn a bonus. The intention is to maximize worker production, but I've heard of cases where such programs backfired. To get their bonuses employees worked at a rate that was bankrupting the company.

Incentive cards in retail demonstrate fixed ratio schedules. In my town there's an ice cream stand that hands out a free ice cream cone for every ten purchased. I don't know what this does to my health or to my weight and I'm not sure this is much of a bargain, but every summer I systematically lick my way through nine strawberry cones to earn the tenth one free.

You may not tell it from looking at me now, but I was quite a party animal in my college days. I frequented a tavern that handed out free drinks on the basis of a fixed ratio schedule—the free drinks were called "knockers," as Kevin, the Irish barkeep, knocked on the bar as he refilled the glass. The schedule was FR-4. Every fourth drink was on the house. In the same way that I ate my way through nine strawberry cones, I systematically drank my way through three snifters of California brandy to get the fourth one free.

It is possible to produce extraordinarily high rates of response—FR-200, FR-300, and so on, numbers that reflect my success with the ladies in my college days. However, the schedule has to start at a low rate and slowly build up. Initially, it may have to start with FR-1, which is *continuous reinforcement*. FR-1 becomes FR-2 and FR-2 becomes FR-3 all the way up to the Himalayas of response rates.

The second category of schedules based on rate are variable ratio schedules. *In variable ratio schedules reinforcement follows a varying and unpredictable number of responses.* In a VR-3 schedule reinforcement follows *an average* of every third response. On its next occurrence the reinforcer may follow the third response. Or it may follow the sixth response. Or it may follow every response. In a VR-5 schedule reinforcement follows an average of every fifth response. On its next occurrence the reinforcer may follow the fifth response. Or it may follow the tenth response. Or it may follow every response. The organism never knows. As with the fixed ratio schedules, the responses have to be correct. Not just any response qualifies in obtaining reinforcement.

Variable ratio schedules result in a steady and high rate of response. There are no pauses between reinforcers, as we find in fixed ratio schedules. In a fixed ratio schedule the organism knows exactly how many responses are necessary to obtain reinforcement. In a variable ratio schedule the organism doesn't know how many responses are necessary. If the organism is lucky, the next response may result in reinforcement. If the organism is like me, it may have to work like the devil.

Variable ratio schedules result in higher rates of response than fixed ratio schedules. This is also true of interval schedules. Variable interval schedules result in higher rates of response than fixed interval schedules.

The premier example of a variable ratio schedule is gambling. If the gambler knows exactly how many pulls on the one-arm bandit result in a payoff, it wouldn't be gambling and casinos would be out of business. The gambler could simply drop in the necessary number of coins. Better still, the gambler could watch Grandma drop in the coins and push her out of the way when the moment came to earn the reinforcement.

I'm sure it's the unpredictability that fuels the high rate of response. We're on a winning streak. We want to keep the hits coming. We're on a losing streak. We want to work faster to reverse course and start a winning streak. We just never know when the next hit comes. We hate the thought that stinginess results in going home broke.

Telemarketing is another example of a variable ratio schedule. Telemarketers don't succeed on every cold call. Probably, they fail after most calls. But like gamblers, they keep dialing—they never know when the next call succeeds. If they live wholesome lives and religiously say their prayers, they may get two sales in a row. They can go home early if they do.

I suppose I retained my good health due to the fact that Kevin, the Irish barkeep, never took a theories of learning course in college. He kept us carousing on a fixed ratio schedule. We would have turned into irredeemable lushes if he used a variable ratio schedule. I knew exactly how many snifters of California brandy I had to inhale before I heard the cherished tap on the bar. If I never knew how many snifters were required, I'd knock back the drinks doubly quick. If the wine god Dionysus was my friend, the very next pour might have been on the house.

There are two basic schedules that involve time. They are the fixed interval schedule and the variable interval schedule.

In the fixed interval schedule reinforcement follows the first correct response after a fixed or predictable period of time has elapsed. After making the correct response, the organism has to wait till the fixed interval is over. Making the correct response during the fixed interval will not result in reinforcement. As soon as the interval ends, the next correct response will result in reinforcement.

The organism does not have to make the response precisely as the interval ends. It can wait for as long as it wants. But it has to wait the entire fixed interval. Note that reinforcement is not automatically given at the conclusion of the interval. The organism has to perform the correct response to receive reinforcement.

The organism responds at a high rate of response early in the learning process involving a fixed interval schedule. But with practice and experience the organism learns that responding in the interval does not produce reinforcement. (Responding in the interval is a waste of time.) In a sense, the organism learns time—it learns to wait. Responding slows down and stops at the start of the interval and picks up in rate as the conclusion of the interval nears.

So we have a FI-60" schedule—a fixed interval of sixty seconds. Inexperienced organisms respond at a high rate throughout the interval. Reinforcement does not occur. Experienced organisms stop responding after receiving reinforcement. They start responding again around fifty seconds into the interval.

As with ratio schedules, we can build up lengthy intervals of time between reinforcements. But we have to start with very brief intervals and we have to slowly lengthen the intervals. We start with FI-5", then FI-10", then FI-20" and so on to intervals that are so long organisms can get a shave and haircut between reinforcements.

There are human behaviors that operate under fixed interval schedules. Every Thursday the manager hands employees green slips of paper—it beats handing employees pink slips of paper. New hires continue to work at a steady pace on Friday. Old hires goof off on Friday. They shape up on Wednesday in anticipation of receiving their paychecks on Thursday.

Stores have special timed events in which sales occur. Macy's at Herald Square use to hold a One Day Sale once a month on Wednesdays. Pandemonium broke out on these sales days as customers jostled for deals. The rest of the month the store was so empty sales associates had to shanghai tourists off Seventh Avenue to make their commissions.

We have regularly scheduled tests in college. The syllabus prints the dates so the students know what's coming. Many students "coast" until the scheduled test approaches—this makes the students "coasters." The students diligently study in the week before the test and at no other time. They start coasting again immediately after the test. And so on throughout the semester. Of course, the situation is more complicated taking tests than bar pressing in an operant conditioning chamber. A passing grade is not guaranteed. It may be a student's diligence results in punishment—a low grade or failure—rather than in reinforcement. Teachers hate to think the reverse is true.

In variable interval schedules reinforcement follows the first correct response after a varying or unpredictable period of time has elapsed. After making the correct response, the organism must wait till the interval is over. Making the correct response during the interval will not result in reinforcement. As soon as the interval is over, the next correct response will result in reinforcement.

As with fixed interval schedules, the organism does not have to make the correct response precisely as the interval ends. It can wait for as long as it wants. But it has to wait the entire interval, whatever the length. Reinforcement is not automatically given at the conclusion of the interval. The organism has to perform the correct response to receive reinforcement.

There is a different pattern of response with a variable interval schedule than with a fixed interval schedule. In the fixed interval schedule the organism comes to learn when the next reinforcement is available. In the variable interval schedule the organism does not know and cannot predict when the next reinforcer becomes available. A VI-30" schedule is one in which reinforcement is available an average of thirty seconds from trial to trial. After making the correct response, the organism may have to wait thirty seconds or longer for the next reinforcer. But it may have to wait only five seconds or ten seconds. As with the variable ratio schedule, the organism responds at a high rate. Reinforcement may be delayed. Or reinforcement may follow immediately. The organism doesn't know, so it responds rapidly, as if it hoped that the luck was with them and the wait was brief.

Human examples of variable interval schedules are not easy to come by. Managers can't hand out paychecks whenever they feel like. Stores don't usually hold haphazard sales events. In past semesters students have suggested that fishing and working as servers in restaurants qualify as demonstrations of variable interval schedules. Fishers never know how long they have to wait till the next bass takes the bait. Servers never know how long they have to wait till the next high-roller orders a full-course meal.

One event that demonstrates a variable interval schedule is the occurrence of "sneak" or "pop" quizzes. (This practice is uncommon at the college level.) Students took a test today. In a variable interval schedule the next quiz occurs unpredictably. It may occur tomorrow. It may occur next week. It may occur next month. Students never know. Diligent students in the class study and stay prepared after today's quiz. Slouches in the class do not study or stay prepared. If the world is a just place, they perform poorly on the next unannounced quiz.

In interval schedules the organism does not need to respond immediately at the conclusion of the interval. It can wait, conceivably for as long as it wants. This can lead to exasperation on the experimenter's part. *Limited hold schedules* are applied to avoid situations in which organisms do not respond quickly. This is the situation in which the organism must respond within a set period of time after the interval has elapsed. If it doesn't, it loses the chance for reinforcement. For example, in a FR-30" schedule with a limited hold of 60" the organism has sixty seconds to respond after the interval has elapsed.

I noted an interesting application of a limited hold schedule with a colleague in the department. He conducted courses in which students were required to hand in assignments on specific days. This is a fixed interval schedule that was printed on the syllabus. He gave students a one-day grace period in which to hand in the assignments. If they didn't submit the assignment during this grace period, they failed. The one-day extension corresponds to a limited hold.

Some organisms exhibit odd patterns of behavior in the intervals. On occasion organisms become aggressive or increase their activity level in erratic ways. Sometimes there is an increase in consummatory behavior, such as excessive food or water intake. These patterns are referred to as *adjunctive behaviors* or *schedule-induced behaviors*.

We might view adjunctive behavior in the sense that the awake organism must do something in the intervals between reinforcements, especially if the intervals are lengthy. In a sense the organism needs to fill time. There may also be an element of frustration and impatience, both of which can lead to aggression. Think, for example, how a preschooler acts if forced to wait. And think how a young dog behaves in training sessions if forced to wait for reinforcement.

Response rates are greater for variable schedules than for fixed schedules. The variable ratio schedule produces the highest rate of response. The fixed interval schedule produces the lowest rate of response. Ratio schedules produce greater numbers of responses than interval schedules because organisms are not constrained by time. Interval schedules place limits on how many reinforcers can be received in a given period. Organisms do not have to wait in ratio schedules. The faster organisms respond, the more reinforcers they receive. Of course, this can backfire when it comes to such behaviors as gambling.

I'll like to mention two additional schedules. They are the conjunctive schedule and the chained schedule.

In *conjunctive schedules* two or more schedules must be learned before reinforcement is given. For example, a FI-30" and VR-5 schedule. Or a VI-25" and FR-10 schedule.

Conjunctive schedules are not uncommon in our lives. There are college courses in which there are assigned test dates (fixed interval) and assignments that can be turned in at the student's leisure throughout the semester (variable ratio). And there are occupations in which employees must work an assigned number of hours per week (fixed interval) and produce a set number of piece goods or make a set number of sales (fixed ratio).

Conjunctive schedules can be completed in any order. When a conjunctive schedule *must be completed in a particular order, it becomes a chained schedule.* As with conjunctive schedules, reinforcement occurs after both schedules are completed.

Chained schedules are often implemented in combination with discriminative stimuli, which are stimuli that are present when the reinforcer can be obtained. The discriminative stimuli inform the organism which contingency is operative. For example, we have a chained schedule FR-10 followed by a FI-30". The discriminative stimulus for the ratio schedule is a green light. The discriminative stimulus for the interval schedule is a blue light. When the organism completes responding under the ratio schedule the green light changes to a blue light and the interval contingency goes into effect. An example in human terms may be a job in which employees have to produce a fixed number of piece goods followed by an interval in which they have to perform clerical behavior, say data entry into a computer. The former behavior is performed in a warehouse. The latter behavior is performed in an office.

Generally, *chained schedules are learned backwards*. The second contingency is mastered before the first. In addition, the second contingency produces more reliable and predictable responses than the first. This occurs for the obvious reason that the second contingency is closer in time to the reinforcer.

Fred Keller (1899 - 1996), a colleague of B. F. Skinner, wrote a famous paper in 1968 with the clever and appropriate title, *"Good-Bye, Teacher ..."*. The article contained an original premise that became hugely influential.

Keller noted that most college courses operate on fixed interval schedules—assigned test dates, assigned project and term paper dates. As we noted, this often leads to periods of slacking off between evaluations. Keller suggested that it might be more productive to use ratio schedules as the grading system. In addition, he suggested scraping the entire lecture-based classroom for a system of individualized instruction in which students work through the course material at their own pace. Overall, the concept was entitled *self-paced instruction*.

When I first started at Kean University—it was Kean College then—we conducted a number of introductory courses using a program of self-paced instruction called *Personalized System of Instruction* (*PSI*). The textbook was divided into a number of units. It's been a lot of years, so I can't swear to it, but I think each unit was ten - twenty pages. Students studied each unit on their own. When they felt ready, they came to class and took a multiple-choice quiz on the unit. If they achieved a particular score on the quiz—I remember it as eighteen correct of twenty questions—they could proceed to the next unit. If they didn't achieve a passing score, they could review the material privately and retake the quiz at a later date or they could meet with a proctor and review the material in a one-on-one tutoring session. The proctors were junior and senior psychology students who performed this task for credit.

Students could proceed at their own pace and stop at whatever grade level they desired. The achievement-oriented students hurriedly proceeded to the "A" level. The party animals and procrastinators stopped at the "C" and "D" levels. Students could proceed at a breakneck pace and complete the course early or stretch the units out across the entire semester.

The major problems we encountered were cheating and inadequate facilities. We tried to reduce the former by instituting a time table in which a set number of units had to be completed by particular dates. We also introduced a mid-term and final exam that accounted for percentages of the final grade. We had no control over the facilities—classrooms aren't built for ten or more separate conversations going on at the same time and it was difficult to hold class in the auditorium in Hutchinson Hall, which was what the administration gave us.

Introductory students and the proctors liked PSI, but the program ended a few semesters after it began. The last thing the college administration wanted was innovation, so PSI quietly went away and slacking off between assigned evaluations promptly recommenced.

Thank you.

LECTURE NINE

Edwin Guthrie

Edwin Ray Guthrie was born in Lincoln, Nebraska, in 1886. We shouldn't hold this against him. He died in Seattle, Washington, in 1959.

Guthrie started in academia with a degree in philosophy from the University of Pennsylvania. He slowly gravitated toward psychology. He taught at the University of Washington his entire career. His major work is *Psychology of Learning* (1935; revised in 1952). If he had a referent experiment, it was Thorndike's puzzle (confining) box. He and Donald Horton filmed cats escaping from the box. They published their results in *Cats in a Puzzle Box* in 1946. To anticipate, their conclusion was that the cats exhibited a great deal of *stereotypy* in making their escapes.

Guthrie's theory is a version of associationism, with contiguity as the leading principle. He does not present a classical conditioning view of learning, but he is closer to Pavlov and Tolman in favoring the stimulus side of the stimulus - response mantra than he is to Thorndike and Skinner.

In our course Guthrie is the preeminent example of a theorist who favors the methodological concept of *parsimony*, as we'll see in his views on reinforcement. He tended to write in a folksy manner with lots of homespun examples. Think in this regard how Sheriff Andy Taylor of Mayberry would write, if he were a learning theorist. He wasn't much interested in building elaborate theories, such as Tolman and Hull were. It was left for his students to convert his statements into axioms and present them in a formal scientific style. The best known of these efforts was by Virginia Voeks in 1950.

If there is a fundamental principle in Guthrie's system, it is this—"*a combination of stimuli which has accompanied a movement will on its recurrence tend to be followed by that movement* (1950)." This concept is called the *recency principle*. It's also called the *postremity principle.* The idea is straightforward—whatever the organism last did in a given situation, it will tend to do the next time it is in the situation.

It follows that the more alike the situations are, the more alike the behavior will be. Identical situations call out identical behaviors.

We are all creatures of habit. Cats in puzzle boxes. Children in playgrounds. Customers in stores. Students in the East Campus. I notice that students sit in the same places every class. I also notice that students tend to arrive in class at the same time. The same students come early. The same students come late. If I may self-disclose—no, I'm not going to disclose what happened in Las Vegas—like everyone else, I'm a creature of habit. I get up at the same time every day. I eat the same breakfast. I drive the same roads. I change lanes at the same mile markers. I listen to the same radio stations. I park in the same spot on campus. I park in that spot even if closer spots are available. I do that in the event I go senile during the lecture. If nothing else, I'll find my way back to my car.

Contrary to the emphasis on frequency and repetition, Guthrie suggested that learning occurs in a single trial. This is one of the slogans associated with his theory—*one-trial learning.* "A stimulus pattern gets its full associative strength on the occasion of its first pairing with a response (1942)."

This concept sounds at variance with the education system. "Practice makes perfect"—"better," anyway, teachers keep telling students. This concept sounds at variance with training in sports in which players are advised to drill relentlessly and to overlearn the plays. And it sounds at variance with the world of theories of learning. Thorndike and Pavlov, among others, inform us that learning is incremental, occurring in baby steps toward some optimum level.

One-trial learning may sound odd, but there is a catch to what it means. Perhaps "response" was not the right word in Guthrie's statement.

Guthrie distinguished three levels of behavior—movements, acts and skills. *Movements* are the muscular contractions that accompany behavior.

For example, the muscular activity in holding a hardball or in pressing a letter on a keyboard.

Acts consist of innumerable movements. "Act" is Guthrie's term for the level of behavior understood in the ordinary sense of an "operant response." Like operants, acts have effects on the environment. Examples are throwing a curve ball toward home plate and typing an essay.

Skills are higher levels of performance than acts. Skills involve greater levels of complexity. Examples are pitching a ball game and creative writing. Pitching involves considerable cognitive activity as the pitcher tries to outthink the batters. Creative writing involves considerable thought as the writer proofreads at the same time as he or she drums the keyboard.

Consider driving a car. This consists of innumerable movements of the muscles of the hands and the feet. I suppose it also involves movements of the thighs and the fanny. The act of driving involves more than muscle movements. It involves hand-eye coordination, judgment and anticipation. The skill of driving involves what happens on a NASCAR track—or on the Garden State Parkway any hour of the day or night.

One-trial learning occurs at the *level of movements*, not at the levels of acts or skills. Guthrie (1930) viewed conditioning at the level of movements as "an all-or-nothing affair, analogous to the setting of a switch, and not analogous to the wearing of a path." I suppose there's only one way to grip a curve ball. And I suppose there's only one way to use the index finger to tap the letter "h" in the word "the."

Practice and repetition are important not because they increase associative strength, but because they allow for *slightly different pairings of stimuli and responses* (or movements). *Habits are complex bundles of stimulus - response associations*—slightly different stimuli paired with slightly different responses. So a pitcher learns to hurl curve balls on sunny days and on cloudy days and on humid days and on rainy days. The movements are similar, but the external stimuli in which the act of pitching occurs are slightly different. The ball may feel slightly different depending on conditions. The mound may feel slightly different.

I've learned to drive on fair-weather days. This being New Jersey, I've also learned to drive on wet roads and on icy roads and on snow-covered roads. The movements are similar, but the external stimuli in which the act of driving occurs are slightly different. I have relatives in Florida who have never driven on snow. If they drive in New Jersey in winter, they're going to be in trouble.

In sports there's something called "the home field advantage." This seems to be a real phenomenon—it's a reason why the Super Bowl is played at a neutral site. Home teams learn to play on their home fields in a variety of situations. The home field pitcher knows how the mound feels in many weather conditions. The visiting pitcher needs to learn this in a hurry.

We mustn't get too carried away by the concept of home field advantage. I recollect watching a playoff game some years ago between the Green Bay Packers and the New York Giants. The game was played in Green Bay under Arctic conditions. Presumably, the Packers had played and practiced under these conditions. They had more experience with snow and wind than the Giants. The game was tied after four quarters. The Giants' kicker had missed something like nineteen field goals—clearly, he wasn't experienced kicking field goals in the Arctic Circle. The Packers won the coin toss in overtime. They were led on the field by Brett Favre, one of the greatest quarterbacks in the history of football. I was sure the Packers were going to win. Despite having played and practiced in snow and ice, Favre proceeded to throw the weakest pass imaginable. The Giants intercepted and, against climactic odds, proceeded to win the game. So much for the home field advantage. The Packers could have saved a lot of money by suiting me up and putting me on the field. I never practiced in snow and ice, but I could have thrown the same lame pass that Brett Favre threw.

Guthrie suggested that the role of practice was not to add movements and acts in performing a particular behavior, but to eliminate movements and acts that are not needed. "Improvement demands more *detachment* of stimuli *from* responses than *attachment* of stimuli *to* responses (1930)." We learn through practice and experience what responses can be eliminated. We learn what we *don't need* to do in order to perform our daily tasks. Whether in sports, business or academia, we generally become more efficient with experience. With experience, behavior becomes simplified and refined. Superfluous responses no longer get in the way.

Guthrie introduced two classes of stimuli that affect organisms beyond the external stimuli that are immediately present to the senses. These classes are maintaining stimuli and movement-produced stimuli.

Maintaining stimuli originate in biological needs. Think, for example, of an organism stimulated by hunger or by thirst or by temperature control or by the need to eliminate pain. And think of an organism stimulated by sexual impulses—maybe we don't want to think about this example. The organism persists in specific kinds of behavior until the needs that maintain the behavior are satisfied. The organism searches for a meal or for water or for a blanket or schedules a visit with a vet or dials an escort service. If organisms are interrupted in pursuing their goals, the maintaining stimuli will redirect behavior once the interruption is over. For example, if a hungry organism is interrupted by the need to avoid a predator, the hunger will resume once the threat is over.

Movement-produced stimuli are kinesthetic stimuli that accompany acts. Presumably they become conditioned to external stimuli and to maintaining stimuli. They serve as guidance and as feedback to keep ongoing behavior on course. They may come to serve as preparatory movements that precede behavior. We toss a ball to a child—the child's body tenses, the hands extend, the knees bend, before we release the ball. We're climbing stairs in the dark and we've miscounted—our feet rise in preparation before we take the final step, but we've already reached the upper level. Our feet land awkwardly. We believe a glass of water is going to topple off the counter and wet our homework—we lunge for the glass before it falls.

Movement-produced stimuli became an important, if subtle, concept in Guthrie's theory. He believed that movement-produced stimuli were fundamental components of associations. We associate overt responses with overt stimuli. We also associate the kinesthetic feedback that accompany overt responses with the same overt stimuli. Guthrie offered the example of a boy sharpening a pencil. The association of pencil, sharpener and what to do with both involve connections between sensations and movements—and between sensations and movement-produced stimuli as the pencil revolves in the boy's hand. The boy doesn't see it, but he knows by touch alone when the point is sharp.

I described Guthrie as an adherent of the principle of parsimony. This adherence is best observed in his treatment of the concept of reinforcement.

We've seen reinforcement construed as *getting something*, such as a pellet of food or a word of praise. We've seen reinforcement construed as *getting something taken away*, as in removing pain or poverty. And we've seen reinforcement construed as *getting the opportunity to perform a behavior*, as in playing computer games after completing household chores. Guthrie disagreed with these conceptions of reinforcement.

Guthrie viewed reinforcement as a strictly procedural event. *Reinforcement works because it changes the situation and preserves associations.* Whatever we did last in a situation we will do the next time we're in the situation. Reinforcement is not the cause of stimulus - response associations and it is not responsible for increasing behavior. Reinforcement works because it changes the situation and prevents another response from occurring.

So there's a cat in a puzzle box. It claws a wire and nothing happens. The situation is unchanged. It nudges the left wall of the box and nothing happens. The situation is unchanged. It nudges the right wall of the box and the lid drops open. The situation has changed. No additional behavior can be performed with the lid closed because, obviously, the lid is now open. The next time the cat is inside the box it will do what it did last— nudge the right wall. We might add that reinforcement also changes the organism. The cat escapes the puzzle box and laps the milk. It was hungry a moment ago. It is no longer hungry.

In Guthrie's view adding any other detail to what reinforcement is—a satisfying state of affairs, as Thorndike did, or the concept of drive reduction, as we'll see Hull did—is an unnecessary step. The simplest, most parsimonious, explanation of reinforcement involves only the procedural, very nearly mechanical, level of preserving stimulus - response connections. The situation changes and no additional associations are possible.

Guthrie was assuredly not a psychotherapist or a behavior therapist. In the time period in which he worked there was precious little psychotherapy and precious few methods to change behavior. Many students think the subfield of clinical psychology is very old, but it is quite recent. Clinical psychology, as we know it, commenced only after World War Two when it became necessary to help veterans who were maimed in the mind.

Guthrie's practical advice and the concepts advanced in his views on learning are compatible with later developments in the clinical field.

Reinforcement preserves stimulus - response connections, making new learning impossible. Odd as this sounds, we may not want reinforcement to occur. (We'll see this in the lecture on avoidance learning—the organism gets better and better at avoiding anxiety-arousing situations.) We don't want maladaptive associations to form. When they do form, we must *disconnect the associations*. We must get the organism to perform the same responses to new stimuli. Or we must get the organism to perform new responses in the presence of old stimuli. We must get the organism *to do or to feel something different* in the situation.

Guthrie offered three useful techniques to change behavior. These techniques are the incompatible response method, the threshold method, and the fatigue method.

In the *incompatible response method* a new (different) stimulus is introduced into the situation. The new stimulus is more potent than whatever stimuli are present and results in a response that is incompatible with the response that formerly occurred to the old stimuli. The idea is that the organism can't do two things at the same time. Or feel two incompatible emotions at the same time. If this reminds you of systematic desensitization, you are reminded correctly. And if this reminds you of Mary Cover Jones and Peter, you are also reminded correctly.

So a child is frightened of water in a swimming pool. The parent, who is more potent than the water, goes in the pool with the child. A child is frightened of the babysitter. The child sees a parent laughing and talking in a friendly manner with the babysitter. A child is frightened of the dark. The parent sits on the bed in the dark and commiserates with the child.

The idea is that the child can't experience incompatible behaviors— crying and laughing—at the same time. (However, I once saw simultaneous crying and laughing at a bridal shower.) The child can't experience incompatible emotions—fear and contentment—at the same time. And the idea is that new and more powerful stimuli produce reactions that are more potent than the reactions the old stimuli produced. The new stimuli result in behaviors and feelings that overwhelm—disconnect—whatever behaviors and feelings were previously present.

In the *threshold method* a new stimulus is introduced into the situation at weak levels that are gradually increased. In some instances the level of the new stimulus is gradually reduced. The new stimulus is always kept below the level at which it will be rejected. (The threshold and incompatible response methods are often applied in tandem.) In *Pudd'nhead Wilson's Calendar* Mark Twain observed that, "Habit is habit and not to be flung out of the window by any man, but coaxed downstairs a step at a time." Keep in mind that Guthrie is a stimulus-side theorist. The threshold method is conceptualized not as doing more of a behavior, but as the gradual change in a novel stimulus.

In Robert Parker's mystery novel *Valediction,* the stalwart detective Spenser lowers his caffeine intake by adding slightly higher levels of milk into the mug. Similarly, alcoholics may try to reduce their alcohol intake by adding slightly more seltzer to their drinks. Parents throughout our homeland have long tried to implement the threshold method by slowly adding nourishing food to their children's diets, but never in sufficient quantity (or obviousness) that the food will be rejected.

A child is frightened of the water. Wearing arm floats, the child is introduced to the water at the shallow end of the pool. The air in the child's arm floats is slowly reduced, but never at a rate in which the child goes under. (The air is reduced so the child has to work harder at staying afloat.) A child is frightened of the babysitter. The child is allowed to hold favorite toys when in the presence of the babysitter. The toys are slowly reduced in number. A child is frightened of the dark. The lights are gradually dimmed, but never at a rate that produces fear. Alternately, a night light is introduced into the room. The level of the night light, bright at first, is gradually dimmed.

In the *fatigue method* organisms are exposed to a stimulus at high intensities for a prolonged period. The exposure results, initially, in disagreeable states. The long-term effects are changed feelings and behaviors. A child is frightened of the water. If we use the fatigue method, we throw the child in and let him swim or sink. (Of course, we do this at the shallow end.) A child is frightened of the babysitter. We let her stay with the babysitter by her lonesome for longer periods of time. A child is frightened of the dark. We turn the lights off and keep them off. The child initially cries and panics, but eventually learns that no monster is lurking in the dark.

The fatigue method is clearly related to punishment and to aversive techniques. Years ago, there was a "psychotherapeutic" technique to eliminate smoking. Presumably, there is some pleasure in smoking—some of the pleasure may lie in the anxiety-reducing effects when we light up to avoid the un-pleasure of not lighting up. The therapy worked by disconnecting smoking from pleasure. The technique involved subjecting smokers to intense levels of tobacco fumes. People were forced to chain smoke while spending hours in smoke-filled rooms decorated with overflowing ash trays and powdery rugs. The goal of the therapy was to make smokers sick of what previously provided pleasure.

The technique sounds altogether disagreeable—and it was. The technique was actually the plot lines in horror vignettes on television shows.

The fatigue method doesn't seem to have permanent effects. We could repopulate ghost towns in the Pine Barrens with people who have sworn off smoking after such a disagreeable experience. These people say they "are sick of smoking," but we soon find them buying packs of cigarettes at the local pharmacies. And we could repopulate these ghost towns with people who have sworn off drinking alcohol after a weekend binge. These people say they "are sick of drinking," but next weekend we find them hugging the bar at the local tavern.

To change behavior we must engage with new stimuli or we must perform new (different) behaviors in the presence of old stimuli. The operative term is "engage"—the operative term may also be "disengage." Guthrie advised that we cannot *sidetrack* a habit by avoiding the stimuli associated with the habit. Some people who want to stop smoking avoid the local pharmacies. Some people who want to stop drinking alcohol avoid taverns.

Sidetracking a habit by avoiding stimuli associated with the habit won't work because no new (different) responses are performed in the situation. Nothing is disconnected. Nothing is given the opportunity to change. If we want to stop smoking, we must visit pharmacies and not buy packs of cigarettes. If we want to stop drinking, we must go into taverns and not drink alcohol.

Let's conclude with an example. A particular five-year-old niece was terribly afraid of her uncle, kindly man though he was. Fortunately for the family, her mother had taken the theories of learning course and was familiar with Guthrie's techniques for behavior change. She applied the incompatible response method by having the child eat ice cream while the uncle stood in the doorway. The mother applied the threshold method by having the uncle take baby steps into the room while the child was eating the ice cream. (The uncle always carried candy with him as he approached—he had also taken the theories of learning course.) The mother avoided the fatigue method. The uncle never intruded on his niece's personal space without her permission. And the mother avoided sidetracking the habit. The uncle was always welcome in their home. I'm glad to say the mother's strategy paid off. The little girl came to love her uncle. She grew up and became his favorite niece and inherited all his money when he strolled through the turnstile at the Pearly Gates. Or so we like to think.

Thank you.

LECTURE TEN

Edward Tolman

Edward Chace Tolman was born in Newton, Massachusetts, in 1886. He died in California a few months after Guthrie in 1959. He taught at the University of California at Berkeley. His major work was *Purposive Behavior in Animals and Men*, published in 1932 (revised 1949). Tolman's referent experiment was the *maze*. He must have been a cartographer in a previous life. In understanding Tolman's approach we have to think geographically, literally geographically.

Tolman is one of the most admired and important experimental psychologists. He's admired because he stood up to "The Man" and triumphed. During the McCarthy years in the 1950s the university required faculty members to sign a "loyalty oath" declaring that they were not communists. Tolman was not a communist, but he refused to sign. He sued when the university moved to fire him. He won the lawsuit in 1955 when the California Supreme Court overturned the use of a loyalty oath in academia. The psychology building at Berkeley is named for Tolman and, yes, they have an entire building devoted to psychology.

Tolman's importance in experimental psychology derives from a number of reasons.

Tolman was instrumental in introducing intervening variables into psychology. This turned out to be fortunate for him. Like other theorists in what Sigmund Koch called the "second behaviorism," Watson's being the first behaviorism and Skinner's being the third, Tolman relied on a number of intervening variables to describe and explain the learning process. Some critics said he relied on an excessive number of intervening variables.

Contrary to the learning psychology of the 1920s and 1930s, Tolman emphasized *molar behavior*. He derided the focus on "twitch-ism"—discrete muscle movements made in response to discrete stimuli—in favor of a focus on global and holistic behavior.

Contrary to the learning psychologists of the 1920s and 1930s, Tolman focused on *motivation*—on *goal-oriented behavior*—as an important factor in learning. And he differentiated learning from motivation.

Tolman created a specific theory of learning—we can call it *sign theory* for want of an accurate term. The theory is so expansive it comfortably contains classical and operant conditioning.

Finally, Tolman preferred an *eclectic approach* to psychology. A student once expressed the view that Pavlov and Skinner were "purebreds" in comparison to Tolman, who was a "mutt." He was a "dust bowl" behaviorist who ran experiments with rats. He included cognitive elements in his theory—famously, the *cognitive map*. He can be considered a precursor of cognitive psychology. He was philosophically inclined, a characteristic lacking in his peers. He was interested in perception and friendly toward Gestalt psychology. Finally, he applied psychoanalytical concepts in the attempt to study what he called the "drives toward war."

Tolman believed that all behavior was inherently *purposive*. Organisms demonstrate *persistence of behavior* despite changed conditions. If the men's room is closed on the second floor, I'll proceed to the men's room on the first floor. If a student interrupts me on the way to the first floor, I'll continue after the interruption. At a minimum, organisms move to or away from stimuli—from *signs* in Tolman's vocabulary. At a maximum, humans demonstrate complex and long-term motives as we plan for marriages, careers and creative productions.

Maybe I'm selling lower organisms short. Jane Goodall reported that chimps will walk miles to their favorite termite mounds. I don't think it's a stretch to conjecture that the chimps are thinking of termites along the way. Otto Tinklepaugh reported in 1928 that organisms become upset if their preferred food is switched surreptitiously to a less preferred food. Tinklepaugh was studying memory. He was interested in how long animals remember where they last saw food. Midway in the research, he got the idea to switch foods and study how the organisms responded. Not well, apparently.

Tinklepaugh has, in my view, the second funniest name among psychologists. In decades of teaching theories of learning no student has asked what is the first funniest name among psychologists. I'll tell it to you, anyway—Edwin Twitmyer. In an early psychology convention—this is around the same time as Pavlov's discovery—Twitmyer independently described what we now call classical conditioning. His version went unnoticed, which is a bad thing for the progress of American psychology, but a good thing for naming purposes. If things went differently, we might be speaking of Twitmyerian conditioning rather than of Pavlovian conditioning.

We can see the concept of *expectation* in the examples I provided. *With previous experience with the environment, organisms expect certain signs to occur*—men's rooms, termite mounds, favored foods. Signs that are not present to the senses serve to guide behavior toward (or away from) specific places. *As organism foresee signs, the signs are psychologically real.* I think this view of expectation destroys the possibility that we can have a theory of learning without intervening variables. This view destroys the kinds of theories Watson and Skinner strove to develop. And this view led Hull to strive to develop a theory that could, odd as this sounds, account for expectation without cognition.

Learning for Tolman involves *learning the causal texture of the environment.*

Organisms learn "what goes with what" and "what leads to what." These statements refer in a way to classical conditioning. And organisms learn "what do I have to do to make what happen?" This type of learning was referred to as *means-end readiness* and it can be conceptualized along the lines of operant conditioning. In Tolman's vocabulary the first "what" in these statements was called a *sign-gestalt*, but we'll discard the "gestalt" and limit ourselves to the word "sign." The second "what" in these statements was called a *significate*, but we'll stay with the word "sign."

Tolman had a dynamic view of signs. They carry information and they are changeable and tentative. He coined terms to try to capture the dynamic nature of signs. *Discriminanda* are the properties of signs that result in sensation and perception. What in the rose results in its color?

What in the trash results in its odor? What in the filament results in its light? What in the bell results in its sound?

Manipulanda are the properties in signs that make behavior possible. This table allows for my notes to be scattered on top of it. A toaster would not allow this scattering. This chair allows me to sit on it. A fog bank would not allow sitting. This piece of chalk allows me to grasp it. Water does not allow grasping.

James Gibson (1966) later developed an influential view of perception similar to Tolman's. This was the theory of *affordances*. Gibson believed that there were properties inherent in stimuli that afforded perception and behavior. A table affords the scattering of notes, toasters do not. A chair affords sitting, a fog bank does not. A piece of chalk affords grasping, water does not.

Tolman suggested that *perception involves making propositions about signs.* He distinguished between *hypotheses*, which are tentative, and *expectations*, which are better established and reliable. We note the propositional nature of perception in driving. Is that object in the distance an abandoned car or a police cruiser? Is that smear on the pavement a piece of trash or a pothole? Is that black streak ice or a skid mark? We can note that lower organisms also make propositions when it comes to signs. A bird misjudges a pane of glass for vacant air. A lion misjudges the speed of a zebra. A deer misjudges the speed of a car on a county road.

Tolman believed propositions can be rank ordered from more likely to less likely.

When I drive on Route 22, I generally propose that the patterns of shadows on the road are reflections of trees and telephone poles. The possibility that the shadows are pedestrians is lower in rank. If I were tired or sick or, God forbid, driving under the influence, the rank order of possibilities can become jumbled. The possibility that the shadows are pedestrians may move upward or forward in rank. I might misinterpret the shadow of a tree as a pedestrian and, to the misfortune of the car behind me, slam on the brakes.

Tolman believed that *signs carry information* and that there are categories of signs. These ideas were novel in learning psychology at the time. Remember this is the 1930s and we're breathing arid air in the "dust bowl" of behaviorism.

Good signs lead to appetites. We want to perceive good signs. We want them to come to us. We want to go to them. We do nothing to avoid them. ("Appetites" denote physiological events, but the word can be used in a general motivational sense.) Good signs include the following. A dog wags its tail with its ears raised. A server unfolds the food tray beside our table. A child hands a parent a report card with superior grades. A manager smiles as he calls an employee inside the corner office. A friend strolls into the schoolyard. A warning light on the dashboard turns off.

Bad signs lead to aversions. We do not want to perceive bad signs. We want them to go away and leave us alone. We do not want to go to them. We strive to avoid them. Bad signs include the following. A dog lowers its tail beneath its legs and draws its ears back. A server places a billfold on the tablecloth. A child hands a parent a report card with failing grades. A manager frowns as he calls an employee inside the corner office. The neighborhood bully strolls into the schoolyard. A warning light turns on the dashboard.

Ambiguous signs lead unpredictably to either a desired goal or to an undesired goal. We're not sure what will follow when we perceive an ambiguous sign. Examples include a message from the lab left on the answering machine, "Contact the doctor." It may be good news or it may be bad news. Another message is left on the answering machine, "Call the principal." It may be good news or it may be bad news. The department runs a secret grab bag exchange during the Christmas party. Our bag may contain a valuable prize or it may contain a worthless tchotchke. We go on a blind date. A heartthrob may drive up in a limo or a hobo may shuffle up behind a shopping cart loaded with empty soda cans. We're on a game show. A sportscar may be behind door number one or a bag of buttered popcorn may be behind door number one.

Ambivalent signs lead to both desired and undesired goals. Examples include spending a wonderful afternoon at the beach and a not so wonderful evening rubbing ointment on a sunburn. We spend a thrilling night at the casino and we leave our paycheck behind. We attend graduate school where we talk shop with the scholars and we stay at the poverty level in income. We go to the local pub and we get tipsy. Getting high is fun and it results in a hangover. We find the fugu first-rate at a buffet and we spend the rest of the night getting our stomachs pumped. We have sex—well, that's temporarily exciting and now we have a baby.

Misleading signs lead to the opposite of the desired goal. I suppose this is the learning theories version of "the joke is on us." Examples include taking a free vacation sponsored by a time-sharing development. Somehow, the vacation evaporates our paycheck. We finally meet the person we corresponded with on the on-line dating site. To our dismay, the word "glamorous" doesn't apply. A car ahead of us on Morris Ave. has the left blinker on and, to our surprise, turns right. We're in the mob and the crime boss is unusually nice to us. After a big meal at the steakhouse we don wings and take up harpsicord lessons. A suitor takes his paramour to dinner. He hands her a small box. She opens the box. It's not the engagement ring she anticipated, but a pair of cheap earrings. Two young ladies go to the club. A heartthrob is seated at the bar across from them. He's looking at them. He catches her eye. Her friend goes to the ladies' room. He walks over. Her heart races as he arrives at her side. Alas, it's not what she expected. He asks if she will introduce him to her friend.

The five categories of signs can be *reliable* or *unreliable* as they recur.

I'll like to mention with respect to ambivalent signs an important, but complicated, study by Mowrer and Ullman in 1945. They presented both rewarding and punishing consequences following behavior. They found that *the order in which the consequences occur is crucial.* When two consequences follow behavior, it is *the first consequence that takes precedence.* If favorable consequences come first in the sequence, the organism will persist in the behavior, even if punishment follows. If unfavorable consequences come first, the organism will not persist in the behavior, even if reinforcement follows. The study was small in scope, involving only 21 rats, but it may help explain why we never seem to break bad habits.

Learning for Tolman involves acquiring the causal texture of the environment. Learning involves developing *accurate expectations* about the environment. This is to say, learning amounts to developing a *cognitive map* of the environment.

The cognitive map is the major concept in Tolman's theory. It is the phrase he is best known for, analogous to "one-trial learning" for Guthrie or to "drive reduction" for Hull. I would like to stress that we should understand cognitive maps in a literally geographical manner. We learn where things are in the environment. We learn where to go to get what we need. We learn orientation with respect to the environment. We learn to conduct commerce with the environment, for example, how easy or how difficult it is to get around. In a literal sense, *we learn the layout of the physical environment.*

Think, for example, of driving to the East Campus. We know the route "by heart"—I should say "by mind." We know where all the choke points are. We know alternate routes to the East Campus. We know where things are along the different routes. We know where the gas stations are and where the convenience stores are. We know the routes so well, we can replay the trips strictly in our mind, as if we were running a tape. We can do this sitting in this classroom.

Think what would happen if the lights suddenly went out in this building. It would be a chore, but we would find our way out. Probably, we'd hug the walls. We would have an easier chore if the lights went out in our apartments. We know the rooms. We know where things are. We just have to hope the kids didn't leave roller skates at the head of the stairs.

Tolman's referent experiment is the *maze*, as we might expect from a theorist so geographically fixated. Mazes were introduced into psychology by Willard Small in 1901 and have been used by many psychologists over the years. It was Tolman and his Berkeley team that most developed the methodology. They developed it to such a point that it became a worldview or philosophical orientation.

The simplest maze is a *T-maze.* This is a long straight runway that concludes at what Tolman referred to as a *choice point.* At the choice point the rat can turn right or left and proceed to its reward. Tolman believed events at the choice point are critical in the learning process. In his 1948 paper *The Determiners of Behavior at a Choice Point* Tolman wrote, "I believe that everything important in psychology ... can be investigated in essence through the continued experimental and theoretical analysis of the determinants of rat behavior at a choice point in a maze." This may be stretching it a tad, but this is what he said and we have to run with it.

Let's take a rat that's never been in a T-maze. It walks ahead and arrives at the choice point. (We place blocks behind it so it can't backtrack.) The rat turns left and finds nothing. It reverses course and proceeds to the right and finds a pellet of food. Tomorrow, the rat is back in the maze and at the choice point. Tolman conjectured that at this point in the learning process the rat engages in *vicarious trial-and-error.* This is a kind of surrogate behavior made before and in place of the final behavior. The rat is testing options by replaying or reviewing its cognitive map. Of course, the rat doesn't use words, but it's as if the rat is thinking, "Should I turn left? Should I turn right?" Maybe it hasn't learned the maze and turns left again. We can be sure that the next time the rat runs the maze it will turn right.

Through practice and experience with the maze, the rat develops hypotheses about the maze. These hypotheses further develop into expectations. The rat becomes efficient and avoids mistakes (dead ends or blind alleys). If we leave aside the verbal aspects (and the fact that we can review multiples of cognitive maps while sitting in the comfort of this classroom), the rat has acted—has solved the maze—much like a human.

Tolman frankly equated animal and human maze learning. He once admitted he imagined what he would do at a choice point if he were a rat—he would act like a human. It may not be farfetched to equate the development of cognitive maps in rats and humans. I behaved much like a lab rat in learning the route from Jersey City to Kean College. I was hired by Prof. Hank Kaplowitz—I like to think it was one of his better hires. I had no idea where Kean was. I had never been in the vicinity. Hank supplied directions. Take One-Nine South. Stay in the local lanes. Turn right past the brewery onto North Ave. Stay straight till the intersection at Morris Ave. Turn right on Morris.

I found Kean without incident. On the second trip I definitely exhibited vicarious trial-and-error, and plenty of it. I had a rough idea of distance, but I wasn't sure of the turn. I came to Madison Ave. and looked right. Without making it, I tried to figure out if that was the turn. I came to Newark Ave. and looked right. Without making it, I tried to figure out if that was the turn. I came to North Broad St. Without making it, I tried to figure out if that was the turn. I was looking ahead, looking down the road and trying to foresee where the right turn was. I was matching geography with what I remembered of my first visit. At some point I made the correct discrimination—this was the right turn at Morris Ave. That was the moment of *insight*—I now knew the route. I had no difficulty on the third trip or on any trip thereafter.

Humans and rats share a number of characteristics when it comes to mazes. Both learn *distance* and both prefer the *shortest route*. In complex mazes rats come to prefer *diagonal routes*. Humans do, too. Consider a vacant lot at a corner. We don't take the longer route by walking to the corner and making a sharp turn. We cut across the lot on the diagonal. This happens so frequently, visible paths get cut in the grass.

Humans and rats prefer the route that gets us to the goal in the *least amount of time*. Web sites that provide maps and directions inquire whether we want the quickest route to our destination or the longer scenic route. Tolman and Sams demonstrated this with rats in 1925 in a simple experiment. If the rats turned left in a maze, they had to wait longer than if they turned right before continuing. Distance was the same on both sides of the maze. Rats started turning right. I presume they weren't sightseers.

Both humans and rats learn *alternate routes* to a destination. If a path is blocked, humans and rats will blithely take a different route. Of course, this depends on whether or not we have experience with the environment and with alternate routes. I know five routes to this building. If all five were blocked in a monumental traffic jam, I like to think I could figure out a sixth route. To the contrary, I have frequently sat in traffic because I did not know an alternate route. We've all had the experience of wanting to, but daring not, leave the traffic jam because we didn't know whether the exit ramp led to our destination or to a place described in tales of horror.

Tolman believed that humans and rats learned *specific places* (and the routes to get there). Other psychologists believed that humans and rats learned *specific responses*. A robust controversy erupted over this issue—do we learn places or responses?

In this research a *cross maze* was used.

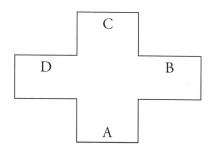

The rat starts at point A and learns to make a right turn. The rat is then placed at starting point C. The maze is now reversed from the rat's perspective. If the rat learned a specific place, it will turn left to B. If the rat learned a specific response, it will turn right to D. In fact, the rat turns left to B.

Humans learn the general layouts and orientations of the places we inhabit. We can reverse course and find our way back. I did the first day I drove to Kean. We learn that Bergen County is north of Hudson County. We learn that Atlantic City is south of Seaside Heights and north of Wildwood. New Yorkers know that "the Bronx is up and Staten Island is down." I drive a lot in West Jersey. I know that, going north, Route 1 is to the west of Route 130 and that Route 130 is to the west of the Turnpike.

The concept of the cognitive map was Tolman's greatest contribution to psychology. It is a concept that has been embraced by science in general. I once saw an article about the cognitive maps of insects. As recently as January 2016 an article in *Scientific American* referred to cognitive maps. John O'Keefe, Edvard Moser and May Britt Moser shared the 2014 Nobel Prize for their research on cognitive maps and the brain.

O'Keefe and others demonstrated that specific neurons in the hippocampus called *place cells* monitor the location of the organism in the environment, as well as the organism's direction and speed. Single-cell recordings of neurons in the rat's brain indicated that different place cells fire as the rat moves through a maze. It's as if each cell corresponds to a different place in the maze.

Subsequent research by the Mosers and others identified a different type of neuron, called *grid cells*, in the entorhinal cortex adjacent to the hippocampus. Grid cells connect to a number of different places organized in hexagonal patterns in the physical layout of the environment. Grid cells fire as the organism crosses the different points (vertices) of the hexagons. Place cells are connected to specific places or steps. Grid cells are connected to six places or steps.

The entorhinal cortex can be arranged from the dorsal to the ventral direction. The hexagons are more closely spaced at the dorsal end. At the topmost level of the cortex rats have to traverse thirty centimeters between vertices for grid cells to fire. At the lowest ventral level rats have to traverse several meters between vertices for the cells to fire. This is a truly astonishing discovery—the architecture of the brain relates in a geometrical pattern to the physical layout of the environment.

Other neurons in the entorhinal cortex relate to cognitive maps. In the 1980s Ranck and Taube described cells that exclusively fire when the rat faces a particular direction. Another type of cell fires only when the rat approaches a border or barrier. And there are "speed neurons" that fire faster or slower depending on the rat's actual locomotion.

The majority of research has been done with rats, but there is an obvious application to humans. People afflicted with Alzheimer's and other types of dementia often exhibit geographical confusion. They don't know where they are and they can't follow geographical directions. The hippocampus and surrounding cortex are among the first areas affected in Alzheimer's and it's now clear that these brain sites are instrumental in utilizing cognitive maps.

The concept of the cognitive map has drifted into common parlance. I suppose the term is so widely embraced because we encounter or demonstrate cognitive maps daily. There's a roadblock on the way to campus. We have to find an alternate route. We have to ask for directions. We have to follow directions. We have to give directions. We have to get someplace and don't know how. The last thing we want is to be lost.

We think of cognitive maps in a geographical sense involving getting from one location to another, as in getting from Jersey City to Union. But cognitive maps include the layout of our homes and neighborhoods. Cognitive maps also include the layouts of offices and stores. I know the layout of my local supermarket and could continue to shop if the lights went out. I'm in trouble if they change the layout. I'll have to relearn where things are and I just may take my business elsewhere.

Cognitive maps involve the acquisition, storage and utilization of information about the location of places and objects in the everyday spatial (geographical) environment. Cognitive maps include distance, direction, alternate routes and the general orientation of the layout of the environment. They may be verbal, as in following directions. They may be visual, as in reading a map. They may involve other senses. We know where we are when we smell the garbage dump. We know where we are when we hear the river.

Cognitive maps are *incomplete and not identical with the environment*. We do not learn a verbatim representation of the environment. Details are left out. Details are inserted. Often, distance is distorted. We think a place is closer than it really is. Or we think it will take longer to get to a place than it really does.

Cognitive maps are *functional*. On the drive to campus I may need to remember if there's a gas station on the way. I may need to remember if there's a convenience store on the way or if there's a pharmacy.

Cognitive maps include *stereotypes*. We know where "the strip" is and where "the slums" are and where the "business district" is.

Cognitive maps include *landmarks*, which are physical objects along routes used for reference. I can tell you to turn right at Jerome Avenue or I can tell you to turn right at the big oak tree with the yellow ribbon tied around it. I can tell you to turn left at Beekman and Broad Streets or I can tell you to turn left when you see the cemetery with the rusted green gates. The use of landmarks facilitates movement through the environmental mazes we inhabit. Kevin Lynch described the usefulness of landmarks in *The Image of the City* (1960). One of the cities Lynch studied was Jersey City, which, happily, is full of usable landmarks.

Tolman distinguished *learning* from *performance*. *Learning involves acquiring cognitive maps*. We do so routinely and automatically through the obvious fact that we live in a physical world. *Performance involves utilizing and demonstrating our cognitive maps*.

Learning is a function of contiguity. Performance is a function of motivation, which, in turn, is a function of reinforcement. Learning occurs whether or not we receive reinforcement. It is a function of daily commerce with the world. Reinforcement provides the motivation to perform what we have learned.

Tolman utilized experiments involving *latent learning*, a term coined by H.C. Blodgett. This is learning that is not immediately performed. There are a number of experiments that demonstrate latent learning. The one I'll like to cover was published by Blodgett in 1929.

Blodgett ran three groups of rats in a maze. Dependent variables were *time to solution* and *number of errors (entering a blind alley)*. Each rat ran the maze once a day. As is common in maze research, blocks were inserted so rats couldn't backtrack.

The first group found food at the end of the maze on every trial. The group's performance consistently improved. On day one this group averaged 2.97 errors and took about a minute to complete the maze. On day seven this group averaged less than one error and ran the maze in less than ten seconds.

The second group found food at the end of the maze starting on the third trial. On day three this group averaged 2.72 errors and a speed of 42.60 seconds. On the fourth day—the day following first receipt of the reinforcer—average errors dropped to 1.20 and the average speed dropped to 25.44 seconds.

The third group ran the maze for seven days before receiving reinforcement. Their performance did not improve. On day seven they averaged 2.28 errors and a speed of 46.70 seconds. On the eighth day—the day following first receipt of the reinforcer—average errors dropped to less than one and the average speed dropped to 12.46 seconds. With one trial of receiving reinforcement, this group performed comparable to the first and second groups, both of which received considerably more reinforcement over the course of the experiment.

Blodgett argued that the second and third groups were learning the maze every time they ran it. The sudden occurrence of reinforcement served as a *motivator* to bring out the learning they already acquired. The rats didn't show what they had learned until they found reinforcement. Their attitude was, if I can use this phrase in reference to a murine species, "What's in running the maze for me?"

There were a number of experiments, most coming out of Clark Hull's research program, called *shift in reward*. These experiments supported the notion that reinforcement affects performance rather than learning. Perhaps the most noted of these experiments was reported by Crespi in 1944. (To my knowledge, no one ever called him "the Amazing Crespi.") Crespi ran two groups of rats. One group found bran mash, a preferred food, at the conclusion of the maze. For rats, bran mash is like filet mignon to experimenters. This group learned the maze more quickly and made fewer errors than a second group that found sunflower seeds, a less preferred food, at the conclusion of the maze. For rats, sunflower seeds are like baloney sandwiches to experimenters. The point is the nature of the reinforcer—preferred or less preferred—affected performance.

After both groups learned to run the maze, Crespi switched reinforcers. The group that found bran mash suddenly found sunflower seeds at the conclusion of the maze. The group that found sunflower seeds suddenly found bran mash at the conclusion of the maze. The performances of the groups shifted depending on the change in the reinforcer. The performance of the group that found sunflower seeds rather than bran mash deteriorated. They ran the maze slowly and they started to make errors. The performance of the group that found bran mash rather than sunflower seeds perked up and improved. They ran the maze more quickly and made fewer errors.

I think we can extrapolate rather easily from the performances of the rats to human behavior. Think how we would respond on the job if our pay was cut or some valuable benefit taken away. Beyond the resentment we'd feel, our performance would deteriorate and we wouldn't much care about avoiding mistakes. And think how we would respond on the job if our pay was increased substantially or some valuable benefit added. Beyond the elation we'd feel, our performance would improve and we would be very careful to avoid mistakes, else these boons be rescinded.

Behavioral contrast is a similar notion to shift in reward. This was introduced by Reynolds in 1961. In the first part of the procedure pigeons were trained to peck at keys lit either red or green. The schedule was the same and pigeons received equivalent reinforcement at both lights. In the second part of the procedure pecking at one of the keys no longer provided reinforcement. This is to say, extinction commenced. Let's say pecking the red key no longer provided reinforcement. Reynolds found that pecking at the remaining key—in this case at the green light—increased dramatically. It was as if the pigeons were trying to recoup the lost reinforcers by increased pecking at the light that still worked.

I think behavioral contrast applies, if only by analogy, to human behavior. Let's say we work two jobs and lose one of the jobs. I think we would be very careful and very productive in the remaining job. Previously, two jobs provided us with income. Now all the eggs are in one paycheck. Given the economic situation of the nation, we'd be most careful not to crack the remaining egg.

Tolman worked at a time in the history of psychology when it was fashionable to posit any number of intervening variables into theories. And he worked at a time when large and comprehensive theories were in vogue. Tolman, Hull and many others believed they needed to develop theories that *included all relevant variables* in describing and explaining behavior. Tolman wanted to account for all relevant variables in the goal-directed behavior of learning mazes. From the get-go, cognitive factors were a part of the account. Hull opposed Tolman's cognitive orientation and attempted to explain maze learning without reference to cognitive concepts. Doing so, he outlined a different set of intervening variables.

Tolman's first statement in 1936 of a formal system was rather modest. There were two broad categories of independent variables. They were *governing variables* that included genetics, physical maturation and previous training in mazes, and *releasing variables* that included whatever stimuli and physiological drives were present. Governing variables and releasing variables blended in some unspecified manner to form *readiness*. Presumably, readiness meant to perform a particular behavior and to receive a particular reinforcer. Think in this regard of a trained rat waiting at the start of a maze and of a trained runner waiting at the start of a race. The dependent variable in the system was *goal-directed molar behavior*.

Two years later Tolman threw caution overboard in *The Determiners of Behavior at a Choice Point* and sailed full steam ahead at listing intervening variables. There were six intervening variables, each linked to a specific independent variable. The intervening variables somehow blended into *vicarious trial-and-error*. Like readiness in the 1936 paper, vicarious trial-and-error led to the dependent variable of *goal-directed molar behavior*.

The independent variable of the *layout of the physical environment* (think discriminanda) led to the intervening variable of *discrimination*.

The independent variable of *response requirements* (think manipulanda) involved in running the maze led to the intervening variable of *motor skills*.

The independent variable of *previous experiences with mazes in general* led to the intervening variable of *beliefs*.

The independent variable of *previous experiences in the specific maze being learned* led to the intervening variable of *hypotheses*.

The independent variable of *maintenance schedules* led to *demands* for particular substances or to avoid particular substances.

Finally, the independent variable of *goal objects* (*incentives*) led to the intervening variable of *appetites*. (Incentives are qualities of reinforcers that make them preferred and valuable.)

Tolman further suggested that there were *background variables* that influenced the transformations of independent variables into intervening variables and vicarious trial-and-error into the dependent variable of goal-directed behavior. Perhaps as an ironic nod to his Quaker heritage, perhaps as a mnemonic, he called these variables by the acronym HATE—*heredity*, *age* (and physical maturation), *training* in the broadest sense, and *endocrine* and momentary body states.

Tolman was a central figure in the history of theories of learning. He was a key figure in the introduction of intervening variables and of operationism into psychology. Both concepts have been criticized across the years, the former by B. F. Skinner, the latter by Sigmund Koch. Like the other mid-century theorists, Tolman developed a large and comprehensive system. Unlike the other theorists, his system straddled both behaviorist and cognitive horses. Probably, this expansiveness expressed Tolman's eclectic orientation. Whatever we may think of the breadth of the theory—comprehensive theories have fallen out of favor in psychology—his system generated a large body of data, which is a criterion of the value of a theory.

The cognitive straddle got Tolman into the most difficulty. Guthrie derided him for leaving his rats "buried in thought." Critics rightly pointed out that there was no specification of how independent variables became intervening variables or how intervening variables blossomed into goal-directed molar behavior. The system looked good on paper, but a lot of things look good on paper. And critics pointed out that Tolman was unable to specify the physiological or psychological underpinning of cognitive maps. It wasn't until the 1970s that place cells and grid cells provided the physiological underpinning. The psychological underpinning remains unknown in the case of rodents, but the concept of a cognitive map is intuitive—"immanent," in Tolman's terminology—in the case of humans.

Anyone who has ever been in a blackout has experienced a cognitive map and anyone who has ever been lost on a back-country road has consulted a cognitive map.

His arch-rival Hull developed a mindless approach to maze learning that was, for a time, successful. Unless something bad happens, we'll look at Hull's attempt in the next lecture. Hull won the intellectual battles in their lifetimes, but given the subsequent history of American psychology, Tolman clearly won the war.

Before we conclude, I'll like to examine cognitive maps in an international context.

In a 1942 book entitled *Drives Toward War* Tolman conjectured that cognitive maps relate to issues of war and peace. Certain regions of our maps are perceived as *home territory*. Other regions are perceived as *enemy territory*. We behave differently when we are in our home territory than when we are in enemy territory. Different rules—different moralities—apply depending on where we perceive we are.

The borders of these territories are changeable, sometimes quickly. In the early 1940s the United States perceived Germany as enemy territory and bombed it day and night. We may not have seen the Soviet Union as home territory, but it was certainty not enemy territory. By the late 1940s the situation had changed. We were willing to go to war, even to nuclear war, to defend our half of Germany and we perceived the Soviet Union as our greatest enemy.

Tolman conjectured that another aspect of cognitive maps relates to war and peace. This was whether the home territories in our maps were *broad* or *narrow*. Broad home territories include more of the world than narrow home territories. Do we see the world as home? Or North America and Europe as home? Or North America? Or the slice of North America called New Jersey? Or the slice of New Jersey called Union County? And so on down to the neighborhood where we live.

Narrow home territories were formed owing to *limited experience* with different places (and peoples) in the world. Narrow home territories kept people from seeking out wider and corrective experiences. Narrow home territories also formed owing to *excessively strong and unsatisfied motivations*. Tolman's conjectures took on a psychoanalytic nuance at this point. "Id wants," such as sexual frustration, predispose people toward narrow maps. So do "ego wants," such as unsatisfied drives for personal power and prestige. I'm not sure history has borne Tolman out, but the conclusion is that unhappy, sexually frustrated and interpersonally insecure people develop narrow home territories and are, subsequently, prone to conflict and violence. Happy, sexually satisfied and interpersonally secure people develop broad home territories and are less prone to conflict and violence.

The idea that happiness makes people less violent is an old one in Western philosophy, going back to Epicurus. Certainly, happiness is incompatible with frustration, anger and rage. In *Cognitive Maps in Rats and Men* (1948) Tolman famously wrote that "We must ... subject our children and ourselves (as the kindly experimenter would his rats) to the optimal conditions of moderate motivation and of an absence of unnecessary frustrations, whenever we put them and ourselves before that great God-given maze which is our human world."

Thank you.

LECTURE ELEVEN

Clark Hull

The name of Clark Leonard Hull doesn't ring a bell among the general public, unlike the names of Pavlov or Skinner. In the twenty first century the name of Clark Leonard Hull may not even ring a bell in psychology departments across the land. But in the middle of the twentieth century Hull was the most influential psychologist in America. His orientation toward psychology and science dominated experimental psychology. His vocabulary became standard in many psychological subfields. In 1940 four percent of the papers published in the *Journal of Experimental Psychology* referenced Hull. In 1950 39% of the papers in that journal referenced Hull. In 1960 24% of the papers referenced Hull. In 1970 the number had returned to four percent. The number of papers in the journal was small in comparison to what the number of papers is today, but we can see the enormous influence Hull had.

Hull's influence derived from a number of sources. He was an active experimenter and he introduced a number of concepts, some of which remain in the textbooks. His orientation was strikingly behavioristic—in this, he was Tolman's nemesis. He developed a network of important colleagues and students, some of whom were major intellectual figures in their own rights. They included Kenneth Spence (1907 - 1967), Hobart Mowrer (1907 - 1982) and Neal Miller (1909 - 2002), to name three heavyweights.

Hull's influence declined for a number of reasons. The behavioristic program he espoused was simply too stultifying for the students of the 1970s. He tended to write in a technical scientific style—all right, he was dull to read. And he tended to write in a quasi-mathematical style that many students disliked. Of course, this says more about the students than it does about Hull. On the surface, the theory looks intimidating—it looks difficult because of the quasi-mathematical aura, but don't be deterred. Plow on. Plod on. With a few translations, we'll see that Hull's theory is similar to the theories we've reviewed to this point.

And Hull's influence declined because his theory was shown to be inadequate and erroneous. This shouldn't trouble us as fallibilists. That's what happens to most theories in psychology. Hull's theory is likely the most examined and tested theory in the history of psychology. (Sigmund Koch wrote a massive critique of Hull's approach.) No theory in the social sciences could survive such scrutiny. The fact that it was shown to be in need of correction doesn't make it a bad theory or unworthy of study. Theories that are wrong can teach us many things and they address fundamental issues. In showing us the blind alleys, wrong theories reveal more productive paths in the weedy garden of science.

Hull was born in Akron, New York, in May 1884. He died in New Haven, Connecticut, in May 1952. He received a doctorate in psychology from the University of Wisconsin in 1918. He taught at Wisconsin from 1918 - 1929. Subsequently, he taught at Yale University for the remainder of his life. Before he studied conditioning in the early 1930s, he did extensive experimental work on rote learning, aptitude testing and, surprisingly, hypnosis. His autobiographical statement was published in *Volume Six* of the *History of Psychology in Autobiography*. His major book is *Principles of Behavior*, published in 1943. Abram Amsel and Michael Rashotte reprinted a number of Hull's 1930s journal articles in *Mechanisms of Adaptive Behavior* in 1984.

Hull's interests ranged far and wide—he could have become the Freud, Jung or Rorschach of his time. He conducted a Wednesday evening seminar that covered all kinds of topics in the social sciences. These seminars were later published in the journal *Perceptual and Motor Skills*. But when it came to learning, his approach was piecemeal, pedantic and rigidly experimental.

Hull was daunted by the *multiplicity of competing theories in psychology*. There are a number of competing theories of learning. The situation is worse in the study of personality. This is not how it is in the so-called "hard sciences." There are no competing atomic models or periodical charts. There are no competing theories of evolution.

Hull wrote in 1935 in *The Conflicting Psychologies of Learning—a Way Out*:

> "... among psychologists there is not only a bewilderingly large diversity of opinion, but that we are divided into sects ... this emotionalism and this inability to progress toward agreement obviously do not square with the ideals of objectivity ... somehow we have permitted ourselves to fall into essentially unscientific practices."

Hull's solution to this chaotic situation was the *hypothetical-deductive method*. He developed a set of explicit statements based on established research. These statements were called *postulates*. Postulates described relationships among carefully defined variables. Ideally, postulates were to be stated in formulas. Ideally, the variables were to be quantified. The purpose in stating formulas and in quantifying variables was to remove the surplus meaning of terms that bedevils operationism in psychology.

Hull believed that we must be as objective and precise as possible. The best way to achieve these goals was through mathematics. It was essential to measure and quantify everything and to state relationships of variables in formulas. He wrote in *Principles* that "... a clear formulation, even if later found to be incorrect, will ultimately lead more quickly and easily to a correct formulation."

Testable statements called *theorems* were to be deduced from the postulates. (The rest of psychology calls these deductions "hypotheses.") If the theorems were supported in original research, the postulates would gain support. If the theorems were not supported in original research, the postulates would lose support. Postulates would be systematically modified or rejected through such a corrective process.

The idea to modify or eliminate postulates on the basis of empirical research accords with Popper's fallibilism. However, the hypothetical-deductive method clashes with Popper's view that positive results fail to strengthen the truth of postulates. In Popper's view only negative results are decisive in evaluating theories.

Hull's formulaic approach was novel and intriguing. Ultimately, it did not prove successful. The failure may lie in the drive to create formulas. It may be that it is impossible to capture the complexity of learning in any formula. Or it may be that the formulaic approach is valid, but that Hull's formulas were wrong. Like Tolman, he had the task of deciding which variables to include in his system. Maybe he didn't include the right variables. Maybe he failed to include all the relevant variables.

Hull viewed organisms as living machines. (He was fascinated by machines and created a precursor to computers.) We collect the variables that go into the organism. We collect the variables that come out of the organism. And we state intervening variables to conceptualize what goes on inside the organism. Unlike Tolman's vaporous set, Hull's set of intervening variables was to be solidly physiological.

Hull's program was to start with simple, nonsocial, behavior in rats and other lower organisms and to progress to mammalian social behavior. Unfortunately, progress was interrupted rather permanently by his death. Kenneth Spence, Hull's crown prince, kept the formulas churning for a few more years, but this attempt was also terminated by the Grim Reaper.

Principles of Behavior is one of the most influential books in the history of psychology. It's an exquisitely organized book—a hull of a book—that offers a nearly Euclidean progression of postulates and theorems. Halfway through, we realize that the book has nothing to do with the world, as we know it, or with our lives, but we keep reading. The architecture of the book grips us. The fog of theory engulfs us. It's like driving into a pileup on the highway—we know we should stop, but we can't help ourselves. We keep going.

Kean University has a connection with Clark Hull. Adella Youtz, a former professor and dean, and her husband, Richard, both received doctorates in psychology from Yale while Hull was there. Hull cited a Youtz study in *Principles*—it appears to be by Richard. Adella died in 2004 at the grand age of 96. I remember her vaguely as inhabiting a corner office on the third floor in the Hutchinson Building. Students who take this course should relish the fact that our psychology department has an association with Hull. Granted, it's distant, but it's still an association.

I'm going to outline some of the postulates in *Principles*. (I'm not going to cover them in order.) The postulates are not the final version, but they are the most famous and they're as good as any other. *A Behavior System*, published the year of Hull's death, offered a revised postulate system. Critics charged that the postulates changed between books, but that's not a valid criticism. The whole point of the hypothetical-deductive system was the refinement of the postulates. I suppose this starts us on a never-ending journey and it keeps us out of gin mills and other disreputable places on the waterfront.

As with Skinner's concept of the *operant*, Hull believed that organisms did not learn a single or discrete response. As they go about their business, organisms do not perform exactly the same behavior. Rather, organisms learn a group of responses that achieve a particular effect or outcome. Hull referred to such groups of responses as *habit-family hierarchies.*

Hull suggested that the behaviors in habit-family hierarchies can be rank ordered from most likely to occur to least likely to occur. For example, when it comes to snacks, my hierarchy is chips, pretzels, popcorn. Hull further suggested that all responses in the hierarchy share in whatever reinforcements occur. When I buy chips, both pretzels and popcorn share in the reinforcement. Similarly, all responses in the hierarchy share in extinction trials. The chip slot in the machine is empty. So is the pretzel slot. I may not bother to try the popcorn slot. The interesting thing is that responses do not have to be performed to be strengthened or weakened. I'm not sure how this could be tested—maybe by resistance to extinction.

Hull's main dependent variable was *reaction potential*, abbreviated as $_sE_R$. (As you'll see, Hull had a thing for abbreviations and for subscripts.) Reaction potential is *the likelihood of a learned response occurring at any one moment.* As we build the formula, we're trying to predict the emission of a response in a particular habit-family hierarchy.

Reaction potential is a kind of high level or abstract dependent variable. It is operationalized by four true dependent variables. They are:

- *likelihood* (probability) that a response will occur;

- *latency* of a response;

- *amplitude* (strength) of a response;

- *resistance to extinction.*

Dependent variables make and break theories. Skinner's dependent variable—rate of response—is, we might say, first rate. In comparison, reaction potential is problematical. Critics pointed out that different predictions resulted from different choices of dependent variables. We may get different outcomes if we chose likelihood than if we chose amplitude. To quote that fellow stranded in the Rockies in a blizzard, "This is not a good situation."

In any event, onto the 1943 postulates.

Postulate One states that external stimuli (S) result in sensory neuronal impulses called stimulus traces. The stimulus trace is abbreviated with a small-case "s," since it's within the organism. In the case of Pavlovian trace conditioning the stimulus trace outlasts the external stimulus, which has concluded before the unconditioned stimulus turns on. A strict view of the principle of contiguity suggests that the association is not between the external stimulus (which is no longer present), but between the stimulus trace and the unconditioned stimulus. The association is not S – R, but s – R.

Postulate Two states that at any one moment numerous stimuli and stimuli traces impinge on the organism. Or in Hull's uptown language, numerous stimuli and stimuli traces *"impinge on the sensorium."*

Postulate Three states that the organism is born with a hierarchy of responses that are elicited under specific conditions. This postulate refers to the reflexes that underlie classical conditioning.

Postulate Six states that biological deficiencies within the organism result in drive states. Drive states are abbreviated D, sensibly enough. Biological deficiencies are entitled *needs*. Needs are *a function of deprivation* and they result in motivated behavior to restore satiated and non-deficient states. In a homeostatic manner, organisms are motivated to *reduce (eliminate) drive states.* Hunger arises as a function of the time since the last meal. Thirst arises as a function of the time since the last drink. Lust—to call sexuality by a quaint word—arises as a function of the time since the last roll in the sack.

Drive states are physiological or quasi-physiological intervening variables. Behaviorally, *they arouse and direct behavior toward specific goals.* And they give rise to internal feelings. The organism feels hungry. The organism feels thirsty. The organism feels ruttish. Hull assumed that the "feel" of each drive was different and independent. Raising the level of one drive does not raise the level of another drive—feeling hungry does not increase lust, for example. This assumption has not been entirely supported. Clever experiments in the study of emotions suggest that raising the level of one drive increases the level of another drive. In one experiment, frightening participants on a difficult nature hike made them more likely to ask another person on a date. This doesn't sound exactly right, but the moral of this experiment was that nothing fuels romance better than fear.

Postulate Four links drive states with learning. It is the mother of all postulates.

Postulate Four states that if a response occurs in the presence of stimuli or drive stimuli and if this connection occurs when there is a reduction in a drive, an association between the stimuli and the response is established. More simply put, reinforcement depends on drive reduction.

In Hull's formal language:

> "Whenever an effector activity and a receptor activity occur in close temporal contiguity ... and this contiguity is closely associated with the diminution of a need ... or with a stimulus which has been closely and consistently associated with the diminution of a need ... there will result an increment in the tendency for that afferent impulse on that occasion to evoke that reaction."

For learning to occur, drive states must be present. Tolman differentiated learning from motivation. Hull went a step further and made learning dependent on motivation.

Learning does not occur in a single trial, but over *a number of pairings of stimuli and responses under conditions of drive reduction.* Hull referred to this kind of pairing as *habit strength,* which he abbreviated as $_SH_R$. Growth in habit strength is greater in early pairings of stimuli and responses than in later pairings. At some point repetition adds little or nothing to the association.

Postulate Seven introduces the formula Hull intends to build. The formula reads $_SE_R = D \times {_SH_R}$. Reaction potential equals (or amounts to) drive times habit strength, both as defined previously. The key point is that the relationship is *multiplicative*—both variables must be present. Without a drive, there is no learning. If a drive state is not reduced, there is no learning.

Hull made *drive reduction the glue that binds stimuli and responses*. This is, in Popper's view, a bold and *risky conjecture* that originated in controlled laboratory experiments with rats satisfying basic needs and extended, at least in theory, to uncontrolled social behaviors involving humans. As a seminal explanatory principle, drive reduction as the source of reinforcement set off a firestorm of discussion and criticism. Like many seminal explanatory principles in the social sciences, it was found to be in need of correction.

To challenge (or refute) drive reduction we need to find behaviors that do not increase when a drive is reduced. And we need to find behaviors that increase without a reduction in a drive.

With respect to the former, Harry Harlow pointed out that the consummatory behaviors that occur when a drive is reduced interfere with the learning process. On the human level, note how difficult it would be to memorize today's lecture for a quiz while preoccupied with hunger, thirst or lust. If drive reduction serves only to explain how an organism gets to engage in consummatory behavior, it would be an important principle in the sense of survival, but it would hardly be an all-explanatory principle, since most of the things we learn have little to do with survival.

Harlow also pointed out that people can ignore strong drives and forestall reducing drives. There are people who fast for religious purposes and there are people who suffer the torments of diets. And there are people who, for religious purposes, remain celibate.

With respect to the latter, there are important "drives" like creativity and curiosity that are not linked to any physiologically deficient states. These drives never seem to satiate. People will spend years writing books and painting canvases. People will take course-after-course semester-after-semester to earn a piece of paper. People will go broke traveling. People will go broke seeking unique sensations. None of these behaviors resemble the manner in which hunger, thirst or lust are reduced. Even with these basic drives, people will engage in elaborate preparatory behaviors and rituals.

In the context of learning theories, the concept of latent learning was advanced as a refutation of drive reduction—learning occurs without finding food at the conclusion of a maze.

The concept of partial reinforcement was advanced as a refutation of habit strength. Partial reinforcement (schedules, in today's parlance) results in superior responding—greater resistance to extinction—than continuous reinforcement. That is, lower habit strength—fewer pairings of stimuli and responses—results in superior learning than greater habit strength.

Kenneth Spence cleverly suggested that the efficacy of partial reinforcement actually supports Hull's theory. The trials in which physiological drives are reduced result in reinforcement, obviously. The trials in which physiological drives are not reduced result in *frustration*. Frustration builds up and becomes a drive. When a physiological drive is reduced in a future trial, *the drive of frustration is simultaneously reduced.* The trials in which reinforcement occur perform double duty, reducing both physiological drives and frustration. We eat our reinforcement and have it, too.

The concept of drive reduction in its original state died shortly after it was born. At the least, it became highly qualified. Research in social psychology and in other learning theories (Hebb's) found that the reinforcing power of drive depends on the state of the person's arousal. That is, the efficacy of reinforcement depends on context. Every person has an *optimum level of arousal (or stimulation)* beyond which *increases or decreases* in arousal are experienced as aversive. When drive increases above the optimum level, it is reinforcing to lower the drive. *And when drive decreases below the optimum level, it is reinforcing to increase the drive.* In this material world of multi-tasking we know how stressful and frazzling our lives become. We are motivated to eliminate the stressors, simplify matters and clear the decks. But when we are bored—"bored to death," as we say—or when we are stuck indoors for too long, as in bad weather or on account of illness, we are motivated to break out and shake things up and make things happen. When we suffer "cabin fever," we are motivated to add stressors. The last thing we want is peace and quiet. We want to become frazzled.

Postulate Eight states that repetition results in fatigue. Fatigue is called *reactive inhibition* and is abbreviated I_R. Fatigue occurs within a medley of aversive states, such as boredom, agitation and antsyness, for want of a better term. These states interfere with learning. The unpleasant sensations dissipate over time as the organism leaves the learning situation and refreshes itself by doing something different. The formula now reads $_SE_R = D \times _SH_R - (I_R)$.

It is not productive to engage in long study sessions. Students live busy lives that sometimes force them to set aside chunks of time—often late at night—in which to study. This practice is called cramming or *massed practice* and it is an inferior way to study. By cramming, students get overloaded with poorly processed information. Students get stressed out. Students get tired and irritable. After a while, students are unable to concentrate. And students do not get sufficient sleep. Information is processed during sleep. When they wake up unrefreshed, they find much of the information has disappeared from memory. Maybe the sandman stole it.

A superior way to study is to engage in *distributed practice*. This is a style in which we study in short temporal segments separated by intervals in which we do something different and nonintellectual. Maybe in these intervals we can watch television or listen to music or exercise or cook or do housework. Distributed practice avoids the buildup of reactive inhibition. It's a pleasant way to study and it results in better retention. Distributed practice keeps us fresh and motivated and it results in the right kind of repetition—repetition without fatigue and other aversive sensations.

Postulate Nine states that the fatigue built up as a result of repetition serves as a drive state. Hull called this drive *conditioned inhibition*, abbreviated $_SI_R$. Behaviors that reduce conditioned inhibition get associated with the situation that created the drive. These behaviors recur in the learning situation and interfere with whatever motivation instigated the situation.

I believe the preeminent example of conditioned inhibition involves doing homework with young children. It's important that homework be a pleasant and uplifting experience. We want children to look forward to doing homework. Unfortunately, homework frequently becomes an aversive experience. It's anything but pleasant and uplifting—it's unpleasant and downlifting, to coin a term. The session goes on for too long. Parents put too much pressure on the children. The children can't get the answer. They can't concentrate on the question. They get cranky. They start to whine and fidget. They start to cry. Parents grow agitated and impatient. And they terminate the session. They'll try again later when everyone is calm. The children are sent to their rooms, where they promptly perk up.

The length of the session results in reactive inhibition. The drive builds. The whining and fidgeting and crankiness serve as behaviors that terminate the aversive situation. The drive is reduced. These behaviors become associated with homework. The next time reactive inhibition starts to build while doing homework, the children don't waste time trying to answer questions. They immediately perform the behaviors that worked previously to end the session.

The formula is now $_sE_R = D \times {_sH_R} - (I_R + {_sI_R})$. Drive and habit strength represent learning variables. Reactive inhibition and conditioned inhibition represent performance variables, in this case inhibitory variables that work against learning.

Before we move onto Hull's analysis of maze learning, I'll like to introduce two additional concepts. They are reaction threshold and response oscillation. And I'll like to describe a 1951 expansion of the formula.

The concept of *reaction threshold* is presented in *Postulates Eleven* and *Twelve*. The idea is that reaction potential must exceed a minimum value before learning is demonstrated. Several reinforced trials—practice trials involving drive reduction—are required before we see successful performance. The necessary number of reinforced trials depends on the complexity of the task. In our homework example, parents expect a number of repetitions in which their children do not get the right answers. After a period of practice, parents expect the children to get the right answers reliably.

Response oscillation is described in *Postulate Ten* and is abbreviated O_R. There is an inherent *unpredictability* in reaction potential. This unpredictability is greater *earlier in the learning process than later in the learning process*. We can expect greater unpredictability in getting the right answers when our children first learn a behavior—say, learning the multiplication table or learning to throw a curve ball. We expect greater predictability as children advance in grade levels and as they become seasoned veterans on the mound. But anything can happen in the long run. There are no certainties in life. Even an honors student fails a quiz on occasion. And even the ace of the staff has a bad outing.

Our formula is now $_sE_R = D \times {_s}H_R - (I_R + {_s}I_R) - O_R$.

Independent variables in Hull's system included the number of pairings of stimuli and responses, deprivation schedules of appetitive needs, the presence of aversive states (operationalized as electric shock), and the magnitude and quality of reinforcers (incentives).

The *dependent variable* was reaction potential, operationalized as latency of response, likelihood of response, amplitude of response and resistance to extinction.

Unlike Tolman's, Hull's *intervening variables* were rooted in physiology. The drive of hunger, for example, is related to deprivation. However, hunger is a complicated state. In humans hunger involves numerous social and cultural factors beyond the physiological components of brain, liver, fat cells, hormones and the bacteria in our guts. To be fair, Hull was not dealing with human hunger. Maybe at the level of lab rats all we need are schedules of deprivation.

In 1951 three additional variables were added to the formula. Each can be exactly defined. They were *stimulus intensity*, abbreviated V, *incentive*, abbreviated K in honor of Kenneth Spence, and *delay of reinforcement*, abbreviated J. The formula now reads:

$$_sE_R = D \times {_s}H_R \times V \times K \times J - (I_R + {_s}I_R) - O_R$$

We noted in the lecture on Pavlov that the more salient conditioned and unconditioned stimuli are, the more efficient the conditioning is. And we've seen the importance of incentive in shift in reward experiments— the difference between preferred and less preferred reinforcers. (Not all reinforcers are created equal.) Delay of reinforcement has been advanced in recent years as a concept in attention-deficit hyperactivity disorder. It was conjectured that some children handle delays in reinforcement very poorly and that there are narrow temporal windows with these children in which reinforcement is effective. Immediate reinforcers are held to be especially effective in these children. Delaying reinforcers result in these children failing to regulate and control behavior.

Here's an example of how the postulate system might work in explaining behavior. The referent experiment we'll use is Thorndike's puzzle box.

With success in the box, one response (R+) becomes more likely to occur. With lack of success, other responses (R-) become less likely to occur. Why does R+ become more likely? Because it leads to drive reduction (escaping from the box and obtaining milk)—Postulate Four. Why do R- gradually decrease? Because of extinction in the sense of reactive inhibition—Postulate Eight.

Responses that occur in the puzzle box originate in a number of sources. These sources are the particular drives activated as a result of deprivation—Postulate Six; unlearned behaviors—Postulate Three; the similarity of the current situation to past situations—Postulate Five, which we didn't cover, concerns stimulus generalization; and the number of pairings of stimuli and responses (habit strength)—Postulate Four.

Response oscillation—Postulate Ten—states that it is impossible to predict the behavior of cats in the confining box on any one trial. Greater experience in the box and greater success in escape increase predictability over the course of many trials.

We've seen how Tolman provided a frankly cognitive explanation of maze learning. Hull, an ardent behaviorist, was offended by the inclusion of cognitive concepts. He provided a peripheral and noncognitive explanation of maze learning and he believed that his explanation could be applied to other—all?—cognitive processes.

Hull suggested that *mazes are learned backward via classical conditioning*. Consummatory behavior amounts to an unconditioned stimulus (food) eliciting unconditioned responses (salivating and eating). The walls, floor, lighting, and smells of the maze serve as conditioned stimuli that eventually get attached to the consummatory behavior. However, running the maze cannot simply be a case of stimulus generalization. There's nothing to eat at the outset of the maze. There's nothing to eat in the middle of the maze. If the rats displayed consummatory responses outside the presence of the food, they would require counseling at a murine version of a psychiatric clinic.

Hull conjectured, as we covered with Pavlov, that the conditioned response moves forward in the process—away from the goal and backward toward the middle of the maze and then toward the start of the maze. Hull's insight was that the entire conditioned response does not move forward. *Only a portion or fraction of the conditioned response moves forward.* Hull entitled this component of the conditioned response the *fractional antedating goal response.* The component was abbreviated "r_G"—pronounced famously as "r-gee." (A lower case "r" is used, since the response occurs inside the organism.) Hull believed that the *fractional antedating goal response served as a momentary reward that increases as the organism nears the goal and keeps the organism going from start to finish.* The closer the organism is to the goal, the greater the component of the conditioned response. The component recedes the farther the organism is from the goal, but there is some slight amount of the component at the start of the maze. If we could measure it, we would expect a steady increase in saliva as the organism progressed in the maze.

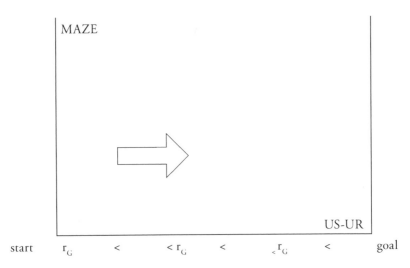

Hull believed that "r-gee" was an important contribution. He wrote in 1952 that the r_G "... mechanism leads in a strictly logical manner into what was formally regarded as the very heart of the psychic: interest, planning, foresight, foreknowledge, expectancy, and so on." He believed that by using r_G he was able to discuss cognitive concepts without delving into cognitive psychology.

The fractional antedating goal response may resolve the philosophical issue we left hanging at the end of lecture four. I pointed out that the effect of effect (reinforcement) seems to work backwards, which violates the scientific canon that causes must precede their effects. (The factor that increases rate of response occurs after the response is concluded.) We can use the r_G concept to fill in the temporal gap between responses and reinforcements. Because of practice and experience, the organism experiences a component of the reinforcer as the response is made. With further practice and experience, *the component comes to precede the response.* At this point, we're "good" with scientific canons.

The lines represent time:

response $\qquad\qquad\qquad\qquad\qquad\qquad\qquad\qquad$ reinforcer

response $\quad$ r_G $\qquad$ r_G $\qquad$ r_G $\qquad$ r_G $\qquad$ reinforcer

There's another concept Hull used to explain maze learning. This is the concept of the *goal gradient* described in a 1934 paper. *Behavior becomes more goal-like the nearer organisms are to the goal. Motivation becomes stronger to get to the goal the nearer we are to the goal.* Rats run faster the nearer they are to the goal. They make fewer errors the nearer they are to the goal. Errors that are made close to the goal are corrected before errors that are made farther away from the goal. Similarly, we drive faster the closer we are to the beach on our day trip. (Or we become less tolerant of traffic delays.) We make fewer wrong turns near the beach than we do at the outset of our trip.

I'm ordinarily a fast walker. I notice that I walk very fast as I approach the turnstile at the Fourteenth St. train station. This is true even if the train is not in the station. If the train were in the station, I'd break into a sprint and leap over the turnstile.

You might recollect my example of consuming nine strawberry ice cream cones to get the tenth cone free in the lecture on schedules of reinforcement. The goal gradient predicts that the closer I get to number ten, the faster I purchase cones. That is, there will be shorter intervals between purchases the closer I am to the tenth cone.

What's true in mazes and in ice cream shops is also true of romance. In the movie *King of the Gypsies* the hero and his date start to kiss on the first landing of the apartment building where he lives. They start to grope and fondle one another on the second landing. They start to strip on the third landing. By the time they arrive on the fourth landing where the bed is located, they're down to their unmentionables. They open the door—and Shelley Winters, the hero's stern mother, is waiting for them. Consummation of the drive of lust will have to wait.

Before we conclude, I have to bring up a topic I rarely see or hear mentioned. I don't recall students asking about it. I don't recall seeing it in textbooks or in journal articles. It's a factor that's under our noses—it's a factor that's in our noses. I'm referring to the sense of smell—I presume rats have this sense. I would think that the sense of smell has to be considered an alternative explanation of the goal gradient in particular and of maze learning in general. It may be that the rats run faster and make fewer errors at the conclusion of the maze because they can better smell the food. Similarly, we drive faster to the beach and make fewer wrong turns because we can smell the water. In addition, we see the sand and the resort amusements.

As I mentioned at the outset, Hull's theory generated an enormous amount of research and discussion. It was the elephant mid-twentieth century psychologists hunted. The theory was highly organized and the attempt to quantify variables and to state concepts precisely was laudable. So was the attempt to develop postulates that would clearly derive from established research. Huge chunks of personality and clinical psychology can benefit from this kind of laconic approach to theory and practice.

Hull's attempt to derive a single theory of learning was not successful. It wasn't successful with lowly rats. The attempt may not even be possible when it comes to humans. The theory suffered from its severe anti-cognitive orientation. The theory was not internally consistent, which is a fatal flaw in a theory professing precision and quantification. Despite the idea that experiments would clearly support or refute the postulates they were deduced from, experiments often had a tenuous connection to the postulates. That is, it took a lot of long-winded verbal formulations to describe the relationships between experimental outcomes and the postulates. And long-winded verbal formulations were the very things the theory was supposed to avoid.

Thank you.

LECTURE TWELVE

The Uses and Abuses of Punishment

Punishment is the situation in *which an unfavorable stimulus or event immediately follows a behavior.* The usual effect of punishment is to *decrease the rate of the behavior.*

We noted in the fourth lecture that Edward Thorndike reversed his initial view and suggested that punishment (negative effect) was not comparable to positive effect (reinforcement) in creating associations between stimuli and responses. He suggested that negative effect did not weaken connections in the same way that positive effect strengthened connections. In his view punishment results in response variation, that is, it gets the organism to do something different. The current consensus is that Thorndike had it right the first time. Punishment is as effective as reinforcement in changing behavior. However, there are so many side effects and issues with punishment that its use may be counterproductive.

There are two types of punishment. *Positive punishment is the immediate presentation of an unfavorable (aversive) stimulus or event following a behavior.* The aversive stimulus or event is not present until the behavior occurs. Positive punishment may involve stimuli that have biological effects, such as being slapped or spanked. Positive punishment may involve stimuli that have purely social effects, such as being insulted or humiliated.

Negative punishment is the immediate removal of a favorable or desired stimulus or event following a behavior. The favorable stimulus or event is present when the behavior occurs and is removed from the situation.

Negative punishment may involve the removal of stimuli that have biological value, such as the removal of food and water. Negative punishment may involve the removal of stimuli that have purely social value, such as being fined (*response cost*) or, in the case of teenagers, being "grounded."

There are occasions when it is difficult to distinguish positive punishment from negative punishment—is being insulted (nasty words) adding something to the situation or removing something (one's self-respect) from the situation?—but *all applications of punishment must be defined from the perspective of the person receiving it.* We may believe that we are punishing a person when, in fact, we are reinforcing a person. This happens when we "pay attention" to a person who engages in an act we find objectionable. We may believe the attention is punishing, but the person finds the attention satisfying. There may be social reinforcers that work against the implementation of punishment—for example, yelling at the class clown or incarcerating a gang member. In the former instance the class clown devours the attention and the laugher of his or her classmates. In the latter instance the gang member demonstrates fealty to the group by going to jail.

To be effective punishment must follow close in time and place to the behavior it intends to reduce in rate. Ideally, *punishment should immediately follow the behavior.* Obviously, this is not always the case. It cannot be the case in the legal justice system in which the due process of law often takes weeks or months. Behavior theory insists that the effect of punishment does not work backward in time. A behavior that occurred in the morning cannot be effectively reduced by punishment administered in the evening. A behavior that occurred early in the month cannot be effectively reduced by the administration of punishment later in the month. *Punishment affects only the behavior that immediately preceded it.*

There are high schools in our beautiful state that punish drug and alcohol use by suspending students and banning them from playing sports or participating in clubs and social activities. The intention is well-meaning, but the practice is misguided, since the punishment can be disconnected in time and place from the misbehavior. There's less of a problem if the drug or alcohol use occurred during the school year. There's more of a problem if the misbehavior occurred outside the school year. Students who get caught using drugs or alcohol at the start of summer may be thrown off teams and clubs once the school year starts in September. The delay between behavior and consequence violates the principle of immediacy. In addition, preventing students from participating in enjoyable activities is a hurtful (and unnecessary) consequence.

Punishment is widely used in child-rearing and in society in general. The title of a book published some years ago said it correctly—America is a "punitive society." (America may be *the* punitive society.) Punishment is the default response to everything and anything. Virtually every toddler in America has been spanked or grabbed in the attempt to control their behavior. Nineteen states, most of them in the former Confederacy, allow corporal punishment of grade school children. Corporal punishment persists in some homes into adolescence. Survey data indicate that 25% to 60% of high school males have been slapped or struck by their fathers. Most corporal punishment is engaged in by white middle-and-lower class families. The higher one's socioeconomic status, the less corporal punishment is used.

There are a number of *myths* concerning the use of punishment in raising children. People believe that punishers work more quickly than reinforcers. People believe that punishers are more effective than reinforcers. People believe that children will grow up "spoiled" without some punishment in their lives. People believe that punishment strengthens character. People believe that punishment enables children to "man up" to the trials and tribulations they will face in the adult world. People believe that punishment is the inevitable "next step" if reinforcement doesn't work. People believe that punishment is the proper response to a child's defiance. People believe that the use of reinforcers amounts to bribery. *These beliefs are all false.*

Punishment is effective in reducing behavior, but there are many problems in the use of punishment. These problems make the use of punishment counterproductive. I'm going to address a number of problems with the use of punishment. And I'll give what I believe are two examples of the failure of punishment to remediate societal ills (motor vehicle infractions and mass incarceration).

People who use punishment rarely use it consistently. Children may be punished on Monday for being disrespectful. The same disrespect may be overlooked on Tuesday. Children may have to wash their mouths out with soap for using profane language on Thursday, but not on Saturday. In addition, different individuals use punishment in different ways. Father may punish the children for a behavior that mother overlooks. One teacher may punish children for a behavior the teacher in the next classroom overlooks. In these cases, children learn to discriminate among individuals. They learn what they can "get away with."

Punishment decreases the rate of an undesirable response. *Punishment does not increase the rate of a desirable response.* Reinforcement does that. Punishing children for saying "7 x 7 = 48" does not make it more likely the children will next answer "49." They may answer "46" or "50." Punishment only makes it more likely the children will not respond with "48." Similarly, sending children to their rooms for being disrespectful at the dinner table makes the disrespectful behavior less likely (unless the children wanted to leave the dinner table). It does not make respectful behavior more likely.

Punishment teaches us what not to say and what not to do. Punishment teaches us who and what to avoid. It does not teach us what to say or what to do. Punishment does not teach us who and what to approach. To increase the occurrence of a particular behavior we need to use reinforcement.

Punishment can lead to an increase in undesirable behavior if no reinforcements are available for alternative desirable behavior. Children who are never praised for performing desirable behavior may perform undesirable behavior in order to receive attention. Class clowns may act up and do something silly in order to be noticed. The other students laugh at them and the teacher punishes them, but what they crave is the attention everyone gives. This, of course, is the idea that underlies the use of *time out* as a practice in the home and classroom. We don't pay attention to the class clowns, because attention is what they desire. We pay attention—we should pay attention—when class clowns act decorously.

Punishment leads to secretive behavior. I suppose there's nothing we can do about punishment when we're toddlers—we have to wobble and take it. When we get older, we learn ways to avoid punishment. We use bad language only when our parents are not around—you should hear us in the playground. We smoke only in the bleachers and we load up with mouthwash and cologne on the trip home. We're not performing admirably, we're getting better at concealing our misbehaviors.

People get better at avoiding punishment. I recall the story of a latch-key kid who was instructed by his father never to eat in the living room. He was to eat only at the kitchen table. When the boy was young, he ate only at the kitchen table. When he was older, he ate in the living room, watching the wide-screen television. Whenever he heard a car drive up, he ran to the window and peeked. If his father drove up, he shut the television off and hurriedly carried his plate into the kitchen. His father always caught him eating at the table, where he was supposed to. The father was never the wiser. Frequently, he gave his son a few extra dollars in his allowance for complying with the request to eat at the table. And he congratulated himself on raising so obedient a son.

Punishment works best if its delivery is guaranteed. If we suspect state troopers are lurking ahead, we obey the rules of the road. If we suspect the troopers are in the donut shop at the rest stop, we break every rule in the manual. Even in an age of surveillance cameras, it's impossible to observe every instance of an undesirable behavior. People will misbehave on the chance that they will not get caught. *"Getting away" with a misbehavior is highly reinforcing.*

People get used to punishment. Killer Kowalski, the great wrestler, was once asked if it hurt to wrestle. Killer answered that wrestling was like hitting oneself in the head with a hammer—"it hurts only when you stop." Used excessively, punishment no longer has an effect. Punishment becomes a routine part of one's life. It's there all the time and it happens regardless whether we behave for good or for ill. Punishment ceases to guide behavior. To that extent, it can be ignored.

Punishment leads to unpleasant situations. Parents get angry, children scream, observers are appalled. Punishment can make important interpersonal situations—homework, the family meal—aversive. No one looks forward to situations that should be ordinary and pleasant. Books and schoolbags, and plates and silverware, become aversive stimuli. Rather than looking forward to interacting with their parents, children look forward to aggravation and to vexation. Children start to act up ahead of time. *And parents start to look for things to punish.* Parents become overly sensitive to their children's behavior.

People learn to misbehave in order to end situations they do not want to be in. If children do not want to do their homework (because they have received a lot of punishment doing homework in the past), they may act up by whining and crying and by procrastinating and by making mistakes on purpose. The hope is that the parents will pay more attention to the acting up than to the homework. They will take the punishment—punishment is better than concentrating on homework. Homework becomes aversive to the parents as well. They may terminate it prematurely or they may let sloppy work "slide," just to be over and done with the aversive situation. Similarly, children who do not want to be at the dinner table may act up to get dismissed. Remember that punishment must be defined from the perspective of the person receiving it. Children who use punishment in this manner are reinforced through negative reinforcement. They are removed from situations they find aversive.

Punishment provides inadequate and inappropriate motives for engaging in desirable behavior. Children may do their homework only to get their parents "off their backs." This motive is not exactly conducive to a love of doing homework. Children may behave respectfully at the dinner table only to avoid punishment. Again, this motive is not conducive to developing manners.

Punishment can lead to the loss of motivation and to "giving up." Children who are punished during homework or at the dinner table may lose their motivation to perform well in those situations. They expect to receive punishment—and parents expect to dole out punishment. The entire relationship between children and their parents gets built around the inevitability of punishment.

Some years ago, Martin Seligman introduced a concept called *learned helplessness*. The idea was that organisms that were unable to terminate punishment in one situation transferred this failure to different situations in which they were able to terminate aversive stimuli. Being helpless in one situation prevented organisms from acting successfully in situations in which their behavior could be effective.

A 1967 experiment by Seligman and Maier is typical. There were three groups of dogs. In the first part of the experiment the dogs in Group One experienced escapable shock. The dogs in this group could terminate shock by pressing a panel with their snouts. The dogs in Group Two experienced inescapable shock. They could do nothing to stop the shock. There was a control group that received no shock. In the second part of the experiment the three groups were in a box in which they had to learn to jump over a barrier to escape shock. The dogs in Group One learned to jump. The dogs in the control group learned to jump. The dogs in Group Two failed to learn to jump. Having failed to escape shock previously, they were unable to learn to escape in a novel situation.

People can be punished for doing the best they can. For example, unathletic baseball players may be punished (humiliated) for doing the best they can—striking out. Students may be punished for failing to solve problems beyond their intellectual capacity—failing a quiz. These people are punished for trying to perform *the same behaviors we want them to perform.* By using punishment as a reaction to their failures, we reduce the likelihood that they learn the very behaviors we want to increase.

Punishment can serve as a signal that reward is coming. So Grandma punishes the child and then feels bad and regrets what she did. She may even feel as if she misbehaved in punishing the child. To make amends, Grandma gives the child a present—maybe extra cookies or a few extra dollars allowance. In this scenario the child learns to "take it" because the adult will eventually give in and repent the punishment. This scenario may underlie what happens in abusive homes. For example, alcoholic parents misbehave terribly in front of their children. When they sober up, they bestow rewards and affection on the same children they previously mistreated.

Punishment teaches aggression. The usual response to pain and humiliation is to get angry and hit back. If that's not possible, the next response is to feel resentment toward the people administering the punishment. *The more parents use corporal punishment, the more aggressive and less well behaved their children are.* The frequent use of corporal punishment leads to fighting among siblings. It also leads to the *displacement of punishment.* Older children who get punished hit young children or pets to release the anger and resentment.

Punishment models impatience and violence as the answers to interpersonal problems. Children learn that the response to any problem, obstacle or difficult situation is to lash out and hit someone.

Punishment can lead to crying, which is the usual response young children make to pain and to humiliation. The children can't help themselves. They cry and this often complicates the situation and worsens the punishment. The children get further humiliated for doing what they can't help doing.

Corporal punishment puts children at the risk of physical and psychological injuries. It's not a long step from punishment to accidental (or to intentional) abuse. Parents may not mean to, but they may physically hurt their children by hitting, spanking or grabbing them—not to speak of the injuries to self-esteem and to motivation. People who use one form of punishment (spanking and slapping) frequently and *simultaneously* use other forms of punishment (scolding and belittlement).

The use of corporal punishment in children has been linked to major depression in adulthood. There are correlations between recollections of corporal punishment in childhood and depressive symptoms in adulthood. However, we have to be cautious about cause-and-effect. These correlations are based on surveys and on retrospective recollections. When we are depressed, we tend to remember other instances in which we were depressed. This is called *mood-congruent retrieval,* an important concept in memory research. That is, when we are depressed, we may overestimate the number of past negative experiences.

The use of corporal punishment has been linked to spousal abuse. There are correlations between the corporal punishment of children and instances of spousal abuse. Spousal abuse may originate, in part, in the use of punishment as the default solution to interpersonal problems and frustrations. The same men who frequently hit their children may have few qualms about striking their wives.

Punishment works best for the people who need it least. People who are what developmental psychologists call "securely attached" to parents and authority figures need punishment the least. Often, these people receive a lot of unnecessary punishment. They worry about being punished and about behaving correctly to avoid possible punishment. These worries may interfere with performing properly assertive behaviors in their current lives. People who are "insecurely attached" also receive a lot of unnecessary punishment. Since they have less commitment to the punishing agents, they may or may not worry about being punished or about behaving correctly to avoid future punishment.

There are individuals for whom punishment does not work. Over the years I've collected newspaper articles about New Jersey and New York criminals who continue to drive despite astounding numbers of moving infractions. Because they continue to drive, innocent people come to bad ends. B. Uppal was charged ten times for driving without a license or insurance, three times for speeding, three times for unsafe operation of a vehicle, once for driving with a suspended license, once for reckless driving, once for fictitious license plates. His last offense was driving while drunk and causing an accident that killed three people. The license of P. Clayton was suspended 25 times in eight years. His last offense was striking and killing a pedestrian. The license of M. Parker was suspended 13 times. His last offense was running a red light and colliding with another vehicle, killing the driver. In a single month A. Sotomayor was arrested four times for drunk driving and one time for hitting a school bus and leaving the scene of that accident. His license has been suspended 23 times. J. Lawless was arrested eight times for drunk driving in a 13-year period. His last arrest occurred after an accident that resulted in a fatality. C. Grabowski had 24 license suspensions and three DWI convictions. His last arrest occurred after an accident that resulted in a fatality. P. Gonzales had 12 license suspensions, 19 moving violations and eight accidents. The last accident resulted in a fatality. I assure you that none of the names or the tallies of violations and accidents are made up.

There's a lot of lawlessness on the roads. Drunk driving and driving under the influence remain potent factors in claiming lives. Despite decades of bad publicity and widely-broadcast draconian penalties, on a yearly basis alcohol plays a role in around 30% of motor vehicle fatalities.

Texting and the use of hand-held cell phones continue to be serious problems. The National Safety Council reports that a quarter of all traffic accidents involve texting or using hand-held cell phones. This is more than a million crashes a year and nearly 400,000 injuries. To show how ineffective punishment is in curtailing what we now call "distracted driving," the *use of hand-held cell phones increased when penalties for their use increased.*

This is just not academic grousing about people who ignore the law. Individuals who ignore the law put us at grave risk. Approximately 20% of car crashes involve drivers without valid licenses. Our chances of being killed in an accident increase by six times involving a person driving without a valid license. Such unlicensed drivers are five times more likely to be involved in hit-and-run accidents. And such drivers are four times more likely to drive drunk or under the influence.

Observers have suggested that punishments for vehicular violations are too weak in the United States. We may not risk using a hand-held cell phone if the penalty for the first infraction was a thousand dollar fine. We may not risk speeding if the penalty was several thousand dollars. The country of Finland famously fines people depending on income. A wealthy man named R. Kuisla got a $58,000 speeding ticket (Finland currency—and I'm not making this number up). A wealthy man named A. Vanjoki was fined $148,000 when he was caught going 45-mph in a 30-mph zone. The fine was later reduced to $7,500. Another wealthy man named J. Salonoja was fined $216,900 for violating a 25-mph zone. I don't know if this fine was reduced and I don't know if this system would work in the United States, but the system now in place isn't working to reduce the carnage on our roads.

If punishment has so many side effects and leads to so many counterproductive outcomes, we can rightly ask why it continues to be widely used. There are a number of possible answers.

Many people are the product of a lifetime of punishment. They were punished as children and, as they keep telling us, they "turned out okay." They see nothing wrong with the use of punishment and they may not know any better. And they may not want to speak ill of their parents.

Punishment is often tied into a personal belief system about what works in the home and in society. Many people believe that punishment is normal and necessary. Many people believe that the disinclination to use punishment is abnormal and unusual.

People engage in selective recall. They remember the instances when punishment worked and forget instances when punishment failed to work.

People believe that a particular misbehavior persists because it has *not yet been punished*. They have faith in the belief that undesirable behaviors will change only when they are punished.

Punishment is easy to use—all we have to do is lash out and hit someone. It takes thought—forethought—to think how to discipline children without the use of punishment.

Punishment gives people a feeling of control and it seems to work. People fail to realize that the effects of punishment may be temporary and limited to specific situations. What works to stop behavior in the home may not work in the schoolhouse or playground.

Ironically, it's easier to identify undesirable behavior than desirable behavior. It's easy to identify examples of disrespect and punish them when they occur. It's more difficult to identify examples of respect and reinforce them when they occur. Or we may identify such examples, but not bother to reinforce them. It's easy to identify instances of defiance and punish them when they occur. It's more difficult to identify instances of compliance and reinforce them when they occur. Again, we may notice such examples, but not bother to reinforce them. In academia, teachers robotically encircle grammatical mistakes in red ink. Teachers do not ordinarily encircle correct use of grammar in green ink.

Finally, we have to admit that punishment may provide a sense of satisfaction to the user. (We don't like to think this, but punishment may also involve perverse and salacious motives.) The little brats "had it coming" and we gave it to them. We got even for all the mischief they caused and for all the disrespect they showed.

We always have options in changing the behavior of children. For example, if we want our children to run fast, we can reinforce them with praise whenever they run slightly faster. Or we can punish them for running slow. Or we can stop punishing them when they run slightly faster, which is the use of negative reinforcement. These three options carry entirely different situational and interpersonal implications. We need to ask which of the options is best to implement. We need to ask which of the three we would prefer if we were on the receiving end. And we need to remember that children need praise and reinforcement more than they need slaps and belittling.

If there is no alternative to the use of punishment, we need to ask a few questions. What behaviors are we punishing? What is our objective in punishing these behaviors? Will punishment allow us to reach this objective? How will punishment be received by the person? How will punishment be perceived by the people who view it? Will there be unintended consequences following the punishment?

We should use *punishment sparingly,* since people habituate to punishment. We should use punishment *consistently*—but this is a pipe dream. We should use punishment *close in time and place* to the misbehavior. We should try to apply punishment *early in the misbehavior sequence.* We should *pair punishment with immediate reinforcement of alternative desirable behavior.* And we should *start out with strong punishment,* to a point, of course. Weak levels of punishment immunize organisms to stronger levels. Stronger levels of punishment increase the effectiveness of weaker levels. Organisms will change behavior to weaker levels of punishment after experiencing stronger levels more than they will change behavior to stronger levels of punishment after experiencing weaker levels.

I previously tried to show that punishment has not been effective in correcting the vehicular madness that routinely occurs on our roads. I'll like to close by suggesting that the punishment of incarceration has not been effective in reducing crime in the United States.

The United States is entitled "the land of the free and the home of the brave." It is more aptly entitled "the land of the free and the homes of the brave and the incarcerated." Our nation can be called the "United Police States of America," as we choose to solve many misbehaviors by criminalizing them. The attitude among many in politics and law enforcement is "Arrest more people." "Build more prisons." Obviously, severe criminal acts occur all too frequently. There are other acts that may or may not be criminal but involve the criminal justice system. These acts include addictive behaviors, sexual behaviors, and behaviors that occur because of poverty, such as shoplifting, loitering and public intoxication.

The number of incarcerated individuals is staggering.

The United States has 5% of the world's population and 25% of the world's prison population. Our incarceration rate is five times the rate of the rest of the world. There are more people in jail in America than are in jail in Russia. There are more people in jail in America than are in jail in Communist China. There are more people in jail in America than in all the countries in the European Union.

In 2018 there were 102 Federal prisons, 1,719 state jails, 1,852 juvenile correctional centers, 3,161 city jails, 80 Native American jails, and an unknown number of military brigs. (Source: Prison Policy Initiative.)

Many of the state prisons are run by private corporations for profit—prisoners serve as sources of cheap labor. The number of city jails and correctional centers grows annually.

There are more than two million Americans "serving time" in these jails. This is a 300% increase since 1980. (In this time period the overall population rose by 40%.) There are 700,000 people on parole. There are more than four million people on probation. Twelve million people a year are arrested.

More than half of the individuals involved with the criminal justice system are minorities. African-American men are more likely than men of other racial categories to be convicted of crimes, to receive long sentences and to receive death sentences. One-in-twelve African-American men are incarcerated. By contrast, one-in-thirty-six Latino men are incarcerated. One-in-eighty-seven Caucasian men are incarcerated. African-Americans account for 12% of the overall population and 74% of incarcerated drug offenders. (An absurd implication is that Latino and Caucasian individuals do not use drugs. The truth is that African-Americans are more likely to be convicted.) Incarceration has had devastating effects on African-American communities. Compared to 2% of white children, 11% of black children have a parent currently in jail. Incarceration perpetuates many of the financial difficulties black families face. Before their incarceration, two-thirds of black men held jobs. Half were the primary support of their families. Even a short stay in prison can be financially catastrophic. The effects of loss of income are felt by family members who are innocent of wrongdoing.

Four times as many people are incarcerated for misdemeanor offenses, such as loitering, drinking in public and driving offenses, than are incarcerated for felonies. Half the people in prison are serving time for drug use or for the sale of drugs. More than half of this figure is for nonviolent possession of marijuana. Two-thirds of the prison population are incarcerated because they cannot meet cash bail or "court expenses" before trial. This number is approximately six million individuals annually. The failure to post bail is correlated with greater likelihood of conviction, with loss of employment and with future arrests.

It's estimated that 16% of incarcerated individuals are mentally disordered. This is over 300,000 individuals. Few receive more than cursory treatment. There are 80,000 inmates in "administrative segregation," which is an euphemism for solitary confinement. Confinement can last for days, weeks, months, years, decades. There are 500 inmates in solitary confinement in "the land of the free" for more than a decade. Half of prison suicides occur in solitary confinement.

More than 48,000 juveniles are confined nightly in correctional centers. About one third are held in long-term centers. More than 2,000 people are serving life sentences for crimes committed as juveniles.

For good measure, we can add that there are approximately 90,000 inmates serving time for wrongful convictions.

The cost of incarceration is enormous—70 billion dollars annually. New York City spends $112,665 per prisoner per year. Second only to New York state, the state of New Jersey spends $30,000 per prisoner per year. This is more than a year's tuition at most of the New Jersey state universities.

There is no reason to equivocate. *The punishment of incarceration has been a monumental failure.* It has not curbed drug use or gang violence. Often, prisons serve as "finishing schools" in which first-time offenders learn more effective ways to be criminals. Prisons do not deter crime. The ultimate deterrence of execution for capital crimes has no correlation with homicide rates. Incarceration has not made us safer as a nation. Every 15 minutes a person is shot to death in the United States. That's 95 people daily. An additional 300 people are shot and survive. American teens are 82 times more likely to be murdered than European teens. Incarceration has failed as rehabilitation—the recidivism rate of repeat offenders is 40%. And nothing appears to be corrected in what we call "the correctional system."

So much for the efficacy of punishment.

Thank you.

LECTURE THIRTEEN

Escape and Avoidance Learning

Punishment is the contingency in which an aversive stimulus follows a response and decreases the rate of the response. *Escape conditioning* is the situation in which a response terminates the occurrence of punishment. *Avoidance conditioning* is the situation in which a response prevents the occurrence of punishment. *Responses in both escape and avoidance conditioning increase in rate.* The operative principle behind both is negative reinforcement—whatever removes or prevents punishment is reinforcing.

The *two-factor theory of active avoidance* was associated with our old friend Hobart Mowrer, but it was an important research topic in which many people participated. It originated in a Hullian universe of discourse. Drives and drive states were fundamental concepts. The theory soon deserted the laboratories for the consulting rooms, as it offered a way to understand and to treat certain types of maladjustment.

Our first example derives from classical conditioning. It's called *discriminated* or *signaled avoidance.* A dog rests in a harness suspended off the floor. A tone sounds for five seconds. The tone ends and shock follows after a second or two interval. (The procedure involves trace conditioning.) If the dog's snout touches a panel located to the side, the shock immediately terminates. This is escape conditioning. If the dog's snout touches the panel in the inter-stimulus interval between the offset of the tone and the onset of the shock, the dog can avoid the shock. This is avoidance conditioning. As we might expect, dogs press the panel as soon as the tone comes on. Even poodles learn to avoid the shock. Well-trained dogs—probably, German shepherds—learn to touch the panel *before the tone comes on*. The dogs become ever more efficient at avoiding the shock.

Our second example takes us into the world of theory. The example involves a simple contraption called a *shuttle box*—or, as the procedure involves shock, a "shudder box." This is a box with two compartments separated by a divider that extends the width of the box. The divider is not as tall as the walls of the box. It can be climbed over to move from one compartment to the other. The floor of each compartment is a grid that can be electrified. We place a rat in one compartment. The rat has never been in a shuttle box—it will soon learn what happens in a shuttle box. We sound a tone for five seconds. The tone ends and shock follows after a second or two delay. If the rat climbs up and over the divider, it can escape shock. This is escape conditioning. In their lowly way, rats are as efficient as dogs. The rat learns to jump at the sound of the tone before the shock turns on. This is avoidance conditioning.

In a *one-way avoidance procedure* shock is applied only in one compartment of the box. The other compartment is always shock free. In a *two-way avoidance procedure* shock can be applied in both compartments. Both compartments can be dangerous. And both compartments can be safe.

The *first factor* in the theory of active avoidance is straightforward classical conditioning. The unconditioned stimulus of shock leads to the unconditioned response of pain. The tone serves as the conditioned stimulus. It's tone—shock—pain, tone—shock—pain. In Mowrer's terminology that we introduced in lecture two the conditioned stimulus is a *danger signal*. The tone indicates that the situation is turning bad and shock is on the way.

The *second factor* is straightforward operant conditioning. The rat performs a response that enables it to terminate the aversive stimulus of pain. In Hull's terminology the pain serves as a drive state. *Reducing the aversive drive state of pain by escaping over the divider is reinforcing.*

Because the tone is paired with shock, the rat comes to respond to the tone as it does to the shock. It jumps to the other compartment and escapes the shock. Notice that there is a subtle difference in the association of stimuli and responses in avoidance conditioning than there is in escape conditioning. In avoidance conditioning the tone is no longer paired with shock and with pain. The rat jumps over the divider at the sound of the tone *before the shock turns on.*

The question about avoidance conditioning that perplexed the great minds of New Haven was—if there is no shock and no pain, what drive is present when the rat climbs the divider? What drive is being reduced? Mowrer and others supplied the answer—fear. *The drive of fear is reduced in avoidance learning.*

Let's return to the structure of classical conditioning. The unconditioned stimulus of shock leads to the unconditioned response of pain. The conditioned stimulus of the tone leads to the conditioned response of fear.

To return to Mowrer's model, a different tone can sound when the rat lands in the safe compartment. This second tone serves as a *safety signal* that is paired with the absence of shock and with the *relief* obtained by successfully avoiding the shock. Safety signals facilitate avoidance learning. And safety signals can serve as reinforcers in different operant tasks.

The avoidance response is very difficult to reverse. It persists even if the conditioning changes and shock is no longer part of the situation. Fear outlasts the original pain. Fear outlasts pain that is no longer administered. The rat doesn't stay in the compartment long enough to find out that shock is no longer coming. The aversive state of fear is reduced by climbing the divider. Extinction is not given a chance to occur.

In 1987 Stampfl performed a clever experiment to demonstrate just how efficient the avoidance response becomes. Rats were shocked in a dark chamber at the end of a five-foot long track. They immediately fled the dark chamber to escape the shock. The floor of the track was actually a conveyor. It slowly moved the rats back toward the dark chamber. The rats were allowed to jump off the conveyor at any point. Stampfl found that, as the experiment continued, rats jumped off the conveyor farther and farther away from the dark chamber. They jumped sooner rather than later. The rats were becoming adept in avoiding the place where they had been shocked.

Human examples of escape and avoidance learning are not difficult to find. We can run to the cellar when the storm breaks out. Or we can walk to the cellar as the storm clouds gather. We can take puffs from our rescue inhaler when we start to wheeze with allergies. Or we can take an antihistamine pill before we grow short of breath. We can put winter coats on and huddle under the blankets when the temperature drops. Or we can turn the heat on before the temperature drops.

The learning psychologists of the 1940s and 1950s perceived the relation of avoidance learning to psychodynamic principles. In the experimental arrangements involving dogs and rats, the reduction of fear results in persistent responses. These responses can become maladaptive if the conditions of the experiment change and shock is no longer administered. That is, the persistent avoidance response results in unnecessary behavior and in restricted experiences. The rats never linger in the chamber long enough to learn whether continuing to jump is necessary.

In clinical examples, processes like defense mechanisms lead to the reduction of fear and anxiety—defense mechanisms are analogous to the rat's avoidant response of jumping. Defense mechanisms lead to unnecessary behaviors and to restricted experiences. Phobic individuals never stay in the elevators long enough to find out that nothing untoward happens. Obsessive-compulsive individuals never shake hands to find out whether they will become infected. As with rats in shuttle boxes, these individuals suffer a failure of extinction in altering behavior.

In olden days reference was made to the *neurotic paradox*—people performed self-defeating behaviors that never changed despite the personal dissatisfaction and discomfort such behaviors brought. The term neurotic paradox is no longer in vogue, but the concept remains current. People engage in foolish and unflattering behaviors that never change. These behaviors are discreditable and they never go away. "I know elevators are safe, but, to my chagrin, I can't step in one." "I know it's impolite, but, to my shame, I can't bring myself to shake hands."

Avoidance conditioning may provide an answer why people persist in performing behaviors that result in chagrin and shame. The person is overly successful in escaping and avoiding the frightening stimulus. And avoidance conditioning may provide a method to counteract this unwholesome situation. If we want the rat to learn that no shock is forthcoming, we have to make avoidance impossible—we have to put a lid on the shuttle box. The rat is terrified at first. After a few trials in which the tone is not followed by shock, the rat calms down and gets on with life, such as it is with rats. Similarly, clinicians need to put a lid on the escape and avoidant behaviors of their clients. Experiencing frightening situations must be allowed to occur. Extinction must be allowed to take its course.

Of course, there are differences between the origin of fear in rats and in humans. Avoidance experiments with rats involved real pain. Presumably, the pain that is squelched by defense mechanisms is not physical, but psychological. The views of Harry Stack Sullivan (1892 - 1949), the interpersonal psychiatrist, may help us here. Sullivan differentiated fear and anxiety. *Fear derives from threats to one's physical well-being.* We almost fall down a flight of stairs. We almost get struck by a car. A thief pulls out a pistol during a robbery in a crowded tavern. *Anxiety derives from threats to one's interpersonal well-being.* A manager publicly berates us. A coworker insults us. The thief instructs the men in the tavern to drop their pants so he can make a getaway and we're wearing pink polka dot boxer shorts.

There's another difference to consider about the origin of fear in rats and in humans. There may be no unconditioned stimuli in human maladjustment. Certainly, there's nothing comparable to electric shock in a shuttle box. A claustrophobic individual has never been trapped in an elevator. An obsessive-compulsive individual never took sick after shaking hands. These individuals *avoid things that never happened.* They are avoiding *the possibility of events* rather than the recall of actual events. "I never know when I'll get trapped, so I avoid elevators." "I never know when I'll take ill, so I avoid shaking hands." The supremely important ability *to think of possibilities*—to think of things that are not present to the senses—sabotages the happiness of certain people. The future events that loom large in imagination are seldom positive or pleasant. They always seem to be negative and unpleasant.

Millenia ago, the wonderful philosopher Epicurus perceived the relationship of foresight and fear. He wrote in reference to the unenlightened masses, "The fear of the future always presses on them ... and ... does not allow them to be happy or to be free from fear in the present." The infamous "man of honor" Joe Bonnano provided a superb definition of fear originating in foresight and imagination. "Fear," Bonnano wrote, "is when you think ahead about what may happen to you." Thomas "Stonewall" Jackson advised his soldiers, "Never take counsel of your fears." Unfortunately, taking counsel of their fears is precisely what certain people do. They live their lives around fear and around the avoidance of fear.

The clinical challenge to releasing the shackles of fear is to make escape and avoidance impossible. The person must stay in his or her psychological shuttle box and allow extinction to occur. The person may have little or no practice in particular situations. The person successfully left the situation before he or she learned what to say and do. In addition to the terrifying task of *avoiding avoidance, the person may need to learn how to behave.* To this extent, therapy includes an educative component. We have to be sure the person doesn't act ineptly when he or she bravely lingers in the formerly frightening situation.

The enormous edifice of behavior therapy aims to *get people to behave differently*. Psychologists have grown gray devising strategies to inspire changes in behavior. There are two well-developed strategies for getting people to encounter their fears and thereby enable extinction. The two are systematic desensitization and exposure therapy.

Systematic desensitization was fully developed by Joseph Wolpe (1915 - 1997) in the 1950s. Clients are taught to relax, since relaxation and fear are incompatible, and to imagine encountering the things that frighten them. They are instructed to think about handling these frightening situations differently—this is a productive use of imagination. The situations are rank ordered from least frightening to most frightening. We start with the minor fears and work our way up the psychic chains that bind us. I start by imagining standing in an elevator with the doors open. By the time I'm done treatment I'm imagining riding the elevator to the observation deck on the Freedom Tower in Lower Manhattan. I start by imagining touching a person's palm while wearing a glove. By the time I'm done treatment I'm imagining working as a masseur.

Exposure therapy has nothing to do with revealing what lies beneath the therapist's pink polka dot boxer shorts. The idea, which I associate with the British psychotherapist Isaac Marx, is that *to eliminate fears the person must physically encounter the frightening stimuli.* (Recall Mary Cover Jones and the case of Peter in the lecture on Watson.) Marx held that we can't eliminate fears strictly by relying on imagination. At some point we must go out in the world and face what frightens us. As in systematic desensitization, fears are rank ordered from least to most terrifying. So I'm frightened to cross bridges—the technical term for fear of bridges is *gephyrophobia*. I commence treatment by riding the shuttle bus that crosses the minuscule bridge that spans the Elizabeth River as it delivers students from the East Campus to the Main Campus. (The words "spans" and "river" are exaggerations.) By the time I'm done treatment I'm doing a soft-shoe routine across the Golden Gate Bridge that spans San Francisco Bay. (The word "spans" is entirely appropriate.)

Whether a person starts treatment with imagination or with real-life exposure to the frightening stimulus—*in vivo*, the term is—depends on the severity of the fear. Intense fears are better handled through imagination at the outset. And the nature of the stimulus determines whether it will be encountered in the mind or in reality. Some stimuli are impossible to bring inside the consulting room—bridges, for example. And other stimuli present ethical issues—it would be impossible to treat a fear of drowning by dropping a client off the deep end of the pool. In both systematic desensitization and exposure therapy clients may be taught new ways to behave—think of providing social skills training to a person with social anxieties.

There is a type of behavior called *counterphobic* in which a person skips progressing through the rank order of stimuli and intentionally encounters the most fearsome stimulus. The logic is—if I can face what most frightens me, I can face whatever frightens me less intensely. Counterphobic behavior is the inverse of avoidance. We've heard stories—maybe we've seen movies—in which a painfully shy and pimpled nerd asks the gorgeous captain of the cheerleaders to the prom or in which a cowardly soldier seeks out combat at its most ferocious. These are instances that cut to the chase. Actually, they forestall the chase. They may or may not work. We don't like to think ahead about what failure means in these two examples. Probably for most people, the safest course in eliminating fears is piecemeal, the proverbial baby step by baby step through the ranking from bottom to top.

Thank you.

LECTURE FOURTEEN

Donald Hebb

Donald Olding Hebb was born in July 1904 in Nova Scotia. We shouldn't hold the fact that he was Canadian against him. He died unexpectedly during surgery in August 1985.

Hebb had an unusual background, coming out of an intellectual nowhere to collaborate with highly influential people. He worked as a farmer, as a laborer and as the headmaster of a school before he entered academia. After his first wife died—he was married three times—he studied psychology, working with Karl Lashley at the University of Chicago and later at Harvard. At Harvard he completed a dissertation on the effects of light deprivation on the brain. He spent the majority of his career at McGill University in Montreal. His major work was *The Organization of Behavior*, published in 1949.

Karl Lashley (1890 - 1958) was an important figure in the history of experimental psychology. Like many important figures of the past, he's mostly unknown today. Whatever reputation lingers derives from his "search for the engram," which was the search for the sites of specific memories in the brain. Lashley trained rats to perform an avoidance task—they had to jump to avoid shock. He then destroyed different parts of their brains to see how this would affect conditioning. He concluded that it was not necessarily what sites he destroyed that disrupted learning as it was *how much of the brain he destroyed*. Lashley introduced the concept of *mass action*—the brain acts as an integrated whole. There is no specific site for an engram. Memories are dispersed or distributed throughout the association cortex of the brain. We now know that the concept of mass action has to be qualified. Despite neuronal plasticity, the brain is an exquisitely organized organ.

I have an odd detail to share about Lashley. In the 1990s I corresponded with Chauncey Holt, a rather interesting character who was an artist, writer and, likely, confidence man. (His autobiography is entitled *Self-Portrait of a Scoundrel.*) Holt, who is since deceased, presumably of natural causes, was featured in what we pretend to believe is a nonfiction book, *The Man on the Grassy Knoll.* Holt claimed to have delivered the gun to the grassy knoll assassin who shot President Kennedy—apparently, the assassin didn't have a gun of his own. This story may or may not be true, but Holt once worked for Lashley as a medical illustrator. He wrote that Lashley was a quiet man who liked to sit alone in parks. For some reason, I'm not sure why, I wanted you to know this.

Hebb went on to work with Wilbur Penfield (1891 - 1976), a famous surgeon and neuroscientist. Penfield was the surgeon in *Death Be Not Proud,* John Gunther's memoir of his son's struggle with cancer of the brain. Penfield mapped much of the cerebral cortex, but he is perhaps best known for a series of experiments (surgeries) that, incorrectly as it turned out, appeared to show that everything we experience is retained in memory. Penfield found that patients experienced vivid images when he electrically stimulated sites in the temporal lobes. These images were initially interpreted as memories. Further research indicated that these images were not memories in the sense of being based on real events. Rather, these images were like coherent visual constructions or confabulations experienced as if they were memories. In some cases people "remembered" events that did not occur. As I recall, one of these false memories was of a birthday party that never happened. Of course, interpreting these images as visual constructions is as amazing a finding as if they were found to be actual memories.

Like Thorndike, Hebb had an eclectic research career not limited to the psychology of learning. He studied the effects of brain damage on behavior and the effects of early experiences on later intelligence. He developed mazes and tests that might be considered intelligence tests. Later in his career he drifted into cognitive psychology. Perhaps his most notorious line of research involved sensory deprivation. This kind of research, which occurred in the early years of the Cold War, was intended to develop "brainwashing" techniques.

Hebb is unique among our theorists. He was convinced that there was considerable overlap between psychology and neuroscience. This is a truism today, but it was not a truism in the period he worked. Hebb believed that psychologists who studied learning needed to study the brain as well. The reverse was also true. Neuroscientists needed to rely on psychology to relate brain functioning to behavior and mental processes. We covered a number of theories that made no mention of the brain. It is possible to proceed in this manner. Note the influence of Skinner's brain (and mind) free theory in education, clinical psychology, and organization-industrial psychology. According to Hebb, it was a mistake for psychologists to disregard neuroscience. It was analogous to a physical trainer proceeding without any reference to the muscles or to a dietician proceeding without any reference to the digestive system.

Hebb believed that *thought processes should be the central topics in psychology*. He noted the fundamental importance of expectation and foresight in our human experience. He was certainly no Hull in this regard. Hebb insisted that expectation and foresight were cognitive concepts. Of course, they would be brain concepts as well, but our cognitive experiences are valid in and of themselves. Whether everything can be reduced to the brain is a topic for serious discussion, but our conscious experience exists at an independent level. However reductionistic our viewpoints, consciousness must be considered *sui generis*.

Hebb suggested *that responses are determined by more than immediate sensory stimuli*. If we keep to a behavioral language, we would have to include a lot of small-case "s's" in our descriptions. Think of visiting a house of worship. We can precisely define everything in the building. We can photograph and take movies of the place. But we respond to a lot that is not physically present. We respond to emotions and autobiographical memories. And we respond to the semantic memories that underlie the images and holy objects in the building.

Think of visiting the East Campus after graduation. The chairs and blackboards and haunted corridors are visible, but there's a lot more going on. As you walk past the classrooms, you recall your professors and classmates, none of whom are present. Maybe you recall some of the lectures and some of the assignments.

Hebb believed that neurological and cognitive constructs were avoided because of the domination of behaviorism and because of the dearth of knowledge about these topics. Hebb published his book at mid-century, but he worked in the dark ages when it came to knowledge of the brain. In that time period most of the knowledge of the brain came from studying cadavers and correlating anatomical damage with behavioral deficiencies in life. And consider that at mid-century there was a protracted conflict within neuroscience over the fundamental issue whether nervous transmission was strictly electrical or a combination of electrical impulses and the chemicals that became known as neurotransmitters. The latter view was correct, but it took a while and a lot of debate to find this out.

We can note Hebb's orientation in his fundamental principle (1949):

> "When an axon of cell A is near enough to excite a cell B
> and repeatedly or persistently takes part in firing it, some
> growth process or metabolic change takes place in one or
> both cells such that A's efficiency, as one of the cells firing
> B, is increased."

As the slogan has it, "Neurons that fire together wire together."

It's not difficult to relate this principle—called, sensibly enough, *Hebb's law*—to the current concept of *brain plasticity*. Yes, there is a structure to the brain, but the neurons continually reconfigure themselves based on experience. Whenever we learn something new, whenever we think of something new, new connections are formed among neurons and new pathways are laid down.

The majority of neurons do not divide like other cells through the process of mitosis. Neurons grow in two ways—through the process of proliferation of axons and dendrites and through the process of myelination. As we learn something new and as we think of something new, more and more axons and dendrites are "hooking up" at the synapses. Through myelination a fatty substance (myelin) grows on the axons. This process, which takes up to 20 years to complete, speeds up nervous transmission.

A third process of neuronal growth is called *neurogenesis*. This is the transformation of stem cells in the adult brain into neurons. Neurogenesis is a controversial topic and is generally discounted as an important source of brain growth.

There's also a process of culling neurons and paring them out of existence. At certain periods in infancy and adolescence neurons dissipate and disappear. Neurons that are not involved in the functions of our existence enter a physiological oblivion. We like to think they step into the abyss voluntarily. Metaphorically, the process is like cleaning clutter in our homes or cutting back the growth of weedy gardens.

There's a literature going back decades on the relationship between *brain growth and enriched and impoverished environments.* The experimental procedure was to randomly assign rats into enriched or impoverished environments. Enriched environments included a lot of social stimulation and a variety of toys and objects to explore. Impoverished environments included limited social stimulation and a minimal number of toys and objects. After residing in these environments for a period of time, the rats were sacrificed—sent to the murine afterlife. Their brains were dissected and analyzed. The brains of the rats that resided in enriched environments were heavier and had more proliferation of dendrites and axons than the brains of the rats that resided in impoverished environments.

These studies have been extrapolated to humans at both ends of the developmental spectrum. It's crucial that infants and children experience social stimulation and a diversity of experiences. And it's crucial for infants and children to consume proper nutrition. The brain requires a lot of calories to work. It's 2% of the weight of the body and it uses up 20% of the daily calories. The common expression is "food for thought." Another important, but uncommon, expression is "thought is food." *For proper brain growth infants and children need to* consume *both dietary calories and intellectual calories.*

So do elderly people. The nineteenth century Irish had a term in their civil records when it came to the elderly—"senile decay" was listed as the cause of many people's deaths. There are, of course, diseases of the brain and dementias based on cellular changes as the brain ages. But a primary cause of "senile decay" is lack of social stimulation and lack of proper nutrition. Gramps doesn't get out much. He has no living friends—his only friend is the television set. And he doesn't eat three meals a day. Gramps starts to deteriorate psychologically. He's living in an impoverished environment. Place Gramps in an enriched environment and we might see some reversal of the deterioration.

Hebb believed that there were different levels of learning or association. Infants and children learn through direct association of stimuli and responses. Adolescents and adults learn in a cognitive style. Infants and children acquire the rudiments. Adolescents and adults possess the rudiments. Children have to learn to throw a ball. Adults pitch a ball game. Children have to learn to read. Adults read for pleasure. Sometimes, adults read deeply for knowledge. Children have to learn to write. Adults write stories and sonnets.

Hebb suggested that there were different levels of neuronal association. The simplest level is called *cell assembly. This is a package of neurons that, following Hebb's law, fire together.* Cell A occurs, cell B also occurs. Cell A fires, cell B also fires. (Of course, with billions of neurons and trillions of synaptic connections, it's never a one neuron to one neuron association.) So lightning is followed by thunder. A pencil has a point at one end and an eraser at the other end. Tapping sounds that grow in volume are followed by the appearance of the mother's face over the crib.

Expectation is built into cell assemblies. I see lighting, I expect thunder. I see the pencil point, I expect to see an eraser—maybe a worried student bit the eraser off. I hear the tapping sounds, I expect to see Mom—if she doesn't appear, maybe it's time to call Ghost Busters.

A *phase sequence is a higher level of neuronal association* than cell assemblies. *A phase sequence is an integrated series or network of cell assemblies.* I see lightning, I hear thunder—and I think umbrella. Maybe I think shelter. I see a pencil point and an eraser—and I think of that line of iambic pentameter I'm trying to compose. I hear tapping sounds, I see Mom—and I think bottle and baby food.

Expectations are integral characteristics of phase sequences. I see lightning, I hear thunder—I expect that the ribs of the umbrella won't turn inside out. I see a pencil point and an eraser—I expect that the point will write English words. I hear tapping sounds and see Mom—I expect to be squeezed into a high chair.

Cell assemblies and phase sequences are based on experience. My experience with storms would differ if I watched the storm from inside a shelter or if I got struck by lightning while standing under a tree. My experience with the pencil would differ if I wrote a line of poetry with it or if I stuck it in my ear—by accident, of course. *And cell assemblies and phase sequences can occur without any relevant external stimulus being present.* I can daydream about Mom whether or not she's physically in the room.

Hebb (1946) performed a well-known experiment on fear in chimpanzees that we can use to assess the interactions of phase sequences and experiences.

Hebb operationalized fear in chimps in the following manner. They had to express nonverbal behavior commonly identified as fear. We've seen enough Tarzan movies to recognize when Cheetah made the "fear face." The fear face includes piloerection, screaming, and threatening gestures. Chimps had to maintain a distance from the stimulus that frightened them. The fear face and the physical adjustment had to commence abruptly with the introduction of the stimulus into the cage.

Hebb created two categories of stimuli—what he called "primate objects" and "non-primate objects." (To be honest, some of the objects were pretty odd.) Thirty chimps were studied, one at a time with a total of 29 stimulus objects. All of the items were novel, as the chimps were reared in the laboratory and had no experiences with them.

With respect to the "primate objects," the following stimuli produced the most fear:

- 24 chimps showed fear to the skull of a chimp with movable jaw,
- 16 chimps showed fear to a string-controlled spider monkey,
- 14 chimps showed fear to the unpainted case of a chimp head,
- 12 chimps showed fear to a life-sized dummy human head,
- 7 chimps showed fear to a 3/5ths life-sized papier-mâché chimp.

With respect to the "non-primate objects," the following stimuli produced the most fear:

- ～ 21 chimps showed fear to a wax replica of a 24-inch snake,
- ～ 10 chimps showed fear to a puppet of a dog's head,
- ～ 8 chimps showed fear to a toy turtle,
- ～ 8 chimps showed fear to a seven-inch cloth dog,
- ～ 5 chimps showed fear to a three-inch rubber dog.

There were wide individual differences in the fear response. Some chimps showed fear to many objects. Other chimps showed fear to a few objects. The fear response was instantaneous with the presentation of the object. Fear did not require conditioning, as with Little Albert in Watson and Rayner's experiment. The possibility exists that some fears were instinctual. Note that two-thirds of the sample showed immediate fear to the wax snake. None of the chimps had ever seen a snake previously, wax or otherwise.

Hebb conjectured that *fear results when familiar objects are encountered in unfamiliar ways.* That is, there is a discrepancy or clash between the object as experienced and the underlying phase sequence of the object. The chimps showed little fear to completely familiar objects and they showed little fear to completely unfamiliar objects. (If "fear" is too strong a word, we can say they showed no "vigilance" or no "surprise.") Completely familiar objects match their phase sequences. There is no discrepancy between the objects and the phase sequences, so there is no fear or surprise. Completely unfamiliar objects have no phase sequences, so there is no possibility of a discrepancy.

Familiar objects experienced in unfamiliar ways result in fear. There are clashes between the objects as experienced and the corresponding phase sequences. *There are discrepancies between what we expect and what we experience.* We expect to experience something and we don't. Or we experience an event in different ways than usual. We expect thunder to follow lightning and it doesn't. We expect an eraser to be at the head of a pencil and it isn't. We expect Mom's beautiful face to appear after hearing her footfalls and it doesn't.

Examples of discrepancies between experiences and phase sequences aren't hard to come by. Every day at 8:00 AM Connor's parents put him on the big yellow bus. They wish for him to have a good day at school and they blow air kisses as the bus rides off. Every day at 3:00 PM Connor's parents wait for the big yellow bus to return. The bus pulls up, the neighborhood kids get off and Connor is not among them. The scene is completely familiar—except for Connor. The scene is completely familiar—and the parents experience it in a new and unfamiliar way. This is not what they expect. The parents are frightened. They're more than frightened. They're terrified.

Every day Romeo waits for Juliet to leave the factory. He waits by the security booth, rose in hand. The whistle blows at the end of the shift and the workers charge through the gate. But Juliet is not among them. The scene is completely familiar—except for Juliet. The scene is completely familiar—and Romeo experiences it in a new and unfamiliar way. This is not what he expects. He's frightened. He's more than frightened. He's upset and worried.

Think of the creatures in horror movies. If horror movies portrayed creatures in completely familiar ways, they would not be frightening. The creatures would match our phase sequences. If horror movies portrayed creatures in completely unfamiliar ways, we wouldn't recognize them. We would have no phase sequences. The effects of creatures in horror movies depend on portraying familiar objects in unfamiliar ways. Birds attack. Dolls kill. The dead walk, funny. Puppets come to life. So do inanimate objects. Vampires look like us, although they have flaming red eyes and oversized teeth. Demons look like us, although they have black eye sockets and smell of sulfur cologne. Angels look like us, although they have wings on their shoulder blades. And aliens look like us, although they're smaller with large eyes, gray skin and the physique of an apostrophe.

It's interesting to note that comedians make the same argument for humor as Hebb made for fear. The effect of comedy depends on surprise. The audience expects one outcome to occur at the conclusion of a gag and something else occurs. The experience does not match the expectation. The audience expects one punch line at the conclusion of a joke and a different line occurs. The experience does not match the expectation. I suppose whether fear or laughter follows the clash between experience and expectation depends on the context in which the discrepancy occurs.

There's one more topic to cover. It is a topic that will lead us far afield to decidedly unpleasant places.

Hebb (and others) ran experiments involving *sensory deprivation*. Putatively, the purpose of the experiments was to challenge Hull's notion of drive reduction. If reducing stimulation is reinforcing, the absence of drives and drive states should be experienced as pleasant and desirable. In fact, the opposite was found. The absence of stimulation is often experienced as aversive and undesirable.

The organization that funded much of the research had a different objective than refuting drive reduction. The Central Intelligence Agency wanted to learn if sensory deprivation could result in "brainwashing." Brainwashing was a Korean War term involving a belief that forcible indoctrination of soldiers could result in the creation of spies and traitors. These traitors would unwittingly betray America and carry out sabotage at the enemy's bidding. The fear was that there would be a brainwashing gap with Communist China or the Soviet Union.

An experiment by Heron (1957) is prototypical. Heron paid students to do nothing. At Kean University, it sometimes works the other way around. Students pay us and then do nothing. The students in Heron's study sat and slept in a bare room. They wore gloves and experienced diffuse lighting and noise. The majority could endure this blank state for only two or three days. The longest lasted six days.

Heron may have inadvertently biased the results by instructing the students they could terminate the experience at any time by pressing a "panic button." Hearing this, students may have expected the experience to be unusual and unpleasant. The instructions they received at the outset may have predisposed them to cut the experience short. If they received less threatening instructions, they may not have perceived sensory deprivation as so aversive.

There was an unsavory side to sensory deprivation research. This involved the treatment, so-called, of schizophrenic individuals by Ewen Cameron (1901 - 1967). Cameron was an influential Canadian psychiatrist who was president—at different times—of the American Psychiatric

Association and the Canadian Psychiatric Association. Cameron had a theory that schizophrenics had to have their personalities broken down and rebuilt. He developed the idea of "psychic driving." This involved placing schizophrenics in sensory deprivation chambers and continuously playing the same audiotape. The message on the tape informed them that their fears were groundless and their hallucinations unreal. In the last stage of personality breakdown "the patient loses all recollection of the fact that he formerly possessed a space time image which served to explain the events of the day to him." If this sounds crazy, it is because it is crazy.

In the 1960s Cameron concluded that his work on psychic driving was a "ten-year trip down the wrong road." This was unfortunate for him. And it was unfortunate for the poor souls who endured this preposterous treatment. As you might anticipate, no one got better. Personalities were broken down. Personalities were never rebuilt. Cameron's work was described in a 1997 book, *In the Sleep Room* by Anne Collins.

Cameron's treatment was in a long line of pointless and barbaric treatments perpetrated on schizophrenic individuals. Elliot Valenstein, a prominent neuroscientist, described the history of these treatments in *Great and Terrible Cures*, published in 1986. His book is required reading by all psychologists. It serves as a cautionary tale and as a curb on our excessive enthusiasm for modern "treatments" of mental disorder.

Never mind the atrocities of Medieval history. Besides psychic driving, twentieth century treatments of schizophrenia included the following. Insulin-induced comas. Electroconvulsive shock. Fever therapy. Ice water therapy. Sleep therapy. Sweat cabinets. Surgeries of various sorts. Most famously, prefrontal lobotomy.

Lobotomy involves disconnecting the frontal lobes of the brain from the thalamus and from the rest of the brain. The modern treatment by lobotomy began with Egas Moniz in 1935. Moniz won a Nobel Prize for his efforts. The leading American practitioner of lobotomy was Walter Freeman (1895 - 1972). It is believed that Freeman performed as many as 3,000 lobotomies. All told, about 40,000 Americans were lobotomized. A comparable number of Europeans were lobotomized.

Initially, lobotomy was major surgery involving hospitalization. In 1946 Freeman developed the method that made him infamous. This was "transorbital lobotomy," a method that horrifies us to this day. The procedure involved thrusting what were essentially ice picks three inches into the brain from the inside corner of each eye. Freeman would give the ice picks a slight twist once he reached this depth to ensure that the frontal lobes were disconnected. The procedure took ten minutes. It could be done on the desk in this classroom. It could be done on a kitchen table. The only visible side effects were black eyes. Probably, many patients never knew what happened to them.

Freeman did none of this in secret. There are films of him doing the procedure—they make for graphic viewing. He kept meticulous records of his patients. He stayed in touch with many and sent them Christmas cards. He published papers, attended conferences and proselytized with religious zeal. Every neuroscientist and surgeon knew what he was doing. It was "normal science"—almost normal science. As you can tell from the numbers, he had a lot of imitators. Sadly, families allowed these physicians to slice the brains of their schizophrenic offspring and relatives. We can understand why families would reach for help. Anyone who has ever seen an unmedicated psychotic episode has seen something terrifying and something anyone would be desperate to remediate, however extreme the treatment.

President Kennedy's sister, Rosemary (1918 - 2005), was lobotomized by the surgical procedure in 1941. No living person is sure why. It may be that she was intellectually "slow." It may be that she had difficulties controlling her emotions or sexual impulses. There is no question that her father, Joe Kennedy, thought he was doing the right thing. In any event, something went wrong. The surgery may have been bungled or Rosemary may have had an unusual reaction to the assault on her brain. The result of the surgery was devastating. Rosemary was completely disabled by the surgery. She could not walk, talk or take care of herself. She spent the rest of her long life out of public view in a nunnery.

Rose Kennedy, her mother, dedicated her 1974 autobiography *Times to Remember* to Rosemary and to other "retarded" individuals. This was a misrepresentation. Whatever her situation was before the lobotomy, Rosemary was not born incapacitated. The surgery did that to her.

Harry Stack Sullivan, the interpersonal psychiatrist, may or may not have suffered a schizophrenic episode early in his life. No living person knows. But Sullivan made a remark that he was glad he was schizophrenic before the time when therapists like Walter Freeman treated mentally ill people by turning them into "morons." Sullivan's choice of words is unfortunate, but the idea is accurate.

In a 1942 textbook coauthored with James Watts and Thelma Hunt, Freeman made extravagant claims for lobotomy:

> "Most of the patients are able to live fairly active, constructive lives, free from the harassing doubts and fears that characterized their illnesses, with their intelligence intact ... Many of them are better adjusted than they have ever been in their adult period ... some of them are taking on new responsibilities ... Almost all of them find existence more pleasurable ..."

Unfortunately for everyone, this passage was bunkum. Lobotomy did not work. It quieted schizophrenics and stilled the psychotic fireworks. To that extent, it made patients manageable. And that's about all it did. Lobotomy changed people for the worse and it did not cure anything. The death rate for transorbital lobotomy was greater than 10%. The medical profession at the time did not condone lobotomy. The *Journal of the American Medical Association* advised in 1941 that, "... this operation should not be considered ... there is ample evidence of the serious defects produced."

Freeman continued to perform lobotomies into the 1950s. He bought a van, entitled it the "lobotomobile," and hit the road. He became the travelling lobotomist. There's an expression, "Pick your brain." Freeman ice picked brains.

A lesser known, but equally barbaric, surgical cure of mental disorders commenced at our own Trenton State Mental Hospital (formerly the New Jersey State Lunatic Asylum). Like lobotomy, it spread throughout the land. This was the brain child of Henry Cotton (1876 - 1933), superintendent of the hospital for a quarter century. (This sordid episode is detailed in the 2005 book *Madhouse* by Andrew Scull). Cotton got the idea that mental disorder was caused by infection. Sepsis lurked somewhere in the bodies of mental patients. Remove the infected organs and the patients will recover.

Even if infection was not found anywhere in the body, it was there in hiding. Some organ had to be removed.

In 1916 surgeons in Trenton started removing parts of patients' bodies. They began with teeth—this is why institutionalized patients were toothless. The surgeons promptly moved onto the tonsils and then onto other organs—the gall bladder, the spleen, the thyroid, the testicles, the ovaries, the colon, pieces of the stomach. In 1919 surgeons performed 57 laparotomies—this is removal of portions of the abdominal wall. Seven patients died. In 1922 - 1924 surgeons performed 133 colectomies. Forty-four patients died. In a 1922 paper Cotton reported on 250 colon resections. Twenty five percent fully recovered psychologically, 15% improved, 30% showed no improvement and 30% died.

None of these surgeries was done in secret. Cotton was candid about what they were doing. He published papers, attended conferences and carried on professionally. Like Freeman with lobotomy, he continued to schedule surgeries despite the appalling death rate and clear evidence that the ablations of body parts did not heal mental disorder. In an experiment conducted in New York in 1923 by Kopeloff and Kirby a group of hospitalized mental patients was randomly selected to undergo surgery. Their recovery rate was no different than a control group of patients who were not operated on. (Yes, this experiment was actually performed.) The authors concluded that there was "No cause and effect between specific bacterial toxins ... and functional psychosis."

As with Freeman, we're not dealing with an isolated individual doing macabre things behind locked doors. These surgeries were "normal science"—almost normal science. Other psychiatrists started to search for sepsis in the bodies of patients in their clinics. Desperate for help, families heard about the surgeries. Unfortunately, families heard the misrepresentation of their outcome. A New York *Times* review of a lecture by Cotton concluded:

> "... under the brilliant leadership of the medical director, Dr. Henry A. Cotton, there is in fact the most searching, aggressive and profound scientific investigation that has yet been made of the whole field of mental and nervous disorders."

Voltaire wrote that *"If we believe absurdities, we shall commit atrocities."* Treatment by sensory deprivation, treatment by lobotomy, treatment by surgical removal of uninfected organs—we recognize that the beliefs behind these practices were absurdities. Unfortunately, these beliefs were not recognized as absurdities at the time. Rather, these beliefs were recognized as "advances." Without question, these beliefs led to atrocities.

It's usually said that men like Cameron, Freeman and Cotton started out with the "best intentions." They wanted to treat—to cure—mental disorders. I'm not sure that these men had any motives over than hubris. They were influential men in positions where their absurd views could work great harm. I'm not sure there were any "best intentions" at the outset of these barbaric practices. Contrary to being healers in the forefront of their profession, these men appear from our perspective as deranged. Their efforts appear cruel and sadistic. Isolating schizophrenics and bombarding them with recycled messages? Thrusting ice picks in the corners of their eyes? Removing healthy organs? Continuing these practices for years despite the accumulation of negative evidence clearly showing such treatments did not succeed? How on earth can any of this have been seen as benevolent or as curative?

Consider that Henry Cotton believed that *organ removal would prevent future mental disorders.* He recommended surgery as a prophylactic measure in children who were undisciplined or unruly. He had the teeth of his own sons removed to keep them from developing mental disorder as adults. He suggested that constipation led to insanity and to criminal behavior. This wasn't chronic constipation over the course of weeks, but over the course of twenty-four hours. If people didn't have a bowel movement on a daily basis, they risked becoming "pathological." A clean colon led to a clean body and a sound mind. An unclean colon led to the opposite—and to a surgeon's scalpel. These were the views, not of a delusional patient in a padded room, but of a man who, supposedly sane, ran a huge mental hospital for a quarter century.

I'll like to close by suggesting that there's a profoundly simple belief at the core of these savage practices. This belief is—*the mind is the brain.* If something goes wrong with the mind, we have to fix the brain. To restore the mind to health, we have to tamper with the brain. (Cotton tampered with the entire body.) We need to bombard the brain with

LECTURE FIFTEEN

B. F. Skinner

B. F. Skinner was born in Pennsylvania in March 1904. He died in August 1990—specifically on August 18. I know the date because I was watching late night television when the news ribbon came on the screen announcing that Skinner had died. The ribbon was testimony to the fame Skinner acquired.

Skinner earned a B.A. in English from Hamilton College in Clinton, New York. He intended to become a writer and actually lived for a while in a place called Greenwich Village in Manhattan. Living the Bohemian life style in Greenwich Village is supposed to inspire creativity, but Skinner found that the Muse bypassed his neighborhood. Of course, he later wrote a novel *Walden Two*, which is a fictionalized account of an utopian community organized on the principles of operant conditioning.

He obtained a Ph.D. from Harvard in 1931. He taught at the University of Minnesota and at Indiana University before returning to Harvard in 1948. He remained an active researcher, teacher and polemicist till the week before he died.

Skinner is ranked at the top or nearly at the top in terms of influence in American psychology. Duane Schultz, the textbook author, wrote that "American psychology in general has been shaped and influenced more by his work than by the work of any other individual." Skinner may be the only psychologist to have a division of the American Psychological Association—#25, founded in 1965—to promulgate his work. Two journals focus on his behavioral orientation, the *Journal of the Experimental Analysis of Behavior* and the *Journal of Applied Behavior Analysis*.

His influence derived in part from his longevity. He was a contemporary of Thorndike and Pavlov and remained active till August 1990. His influence also derived from his behavioral stance. There are two sides to his career—the experimental and the polemical (behaviorist). We can appreciate one without the other or we can appreciate both together. It is difficult to ignore the two.

His influence also derived from his visibility and accessibility. He wrote best-selling books. He was frequently on television. He made the rounds of university psychology departments. He was one of the most famous scientists in America from the 1960s forward. He was a lifelong teacher as well as an experimenter. He was responsive to students at all levels. A student here at Kean wrote him a letter—and received a reply. Probably, it was the highlight of the student's career.

Skinner's popularity derived from his orientation. It was empirical, pragmatic, optimistic and, compared to many areas in psychology, practical. His orientation toward the subject matter of psychology was unique and different from most other orientations. Even if we disagree with it, his orientation is refreshing. He offered simple solutions to complex problems, solutions invariably based on the application of reinforcement. Who can argue against the fact that reinforcement is preferable to punishment? And who can argue against the fact that we need more reinforcement in our daily lives? I know I can't.

Finally, Skinner's influence derived from his methodology. We can argue against a behaviorist worldview, but we can't argue with the fact that Skinner had a very rigorous and very applicable methodology. Skinner's methodological approach involved the following—an emphasis on experimentation in controlled laboratory settings; use of lower organisms; a non-statistical and small-N analysis of data; a disinclination to use intervening variables; and a disinclination to fashion large theories.

Skinner always emphasized *experimentation* as the fundamental method in psychology. He bemoaned what he called "the flight from the laboratory." In this, he was the guru of basic science. He was the guru of Baconian science, as defined in the second lecture.

One time, I was in a room with Skinner—along with 500 other people. The event, held at the 1987 convention, was called "An Evening with B. F. Skinner." The concept was that he would be on stage and field questions. The problem was Skinner was hard of hearing. He couldn't hear the questions members of the audience threw at him—adulators lobbed soft balls, critics hurled hard balls. Rather than repeat the word "What?' all evening, he gave an impromptu talk about books he was reading. Strangely, all the books referenced him.

He heard one question, however. Someone asked what psychologists could do in a world of nuclear arsenals. Skinner's answer was the same to this as to every question—go to the laboratory and do research. I thought about the advice and came up with an example. In avoidance conditioning experiments rats quickly learn to escape and avoid shock. If we place two well-trained rats in the shuttle box and turn shock on, they do not try to escape. Instead, they fight. By analogy, this is what occurred between America and the former Soviet Union. We didn't attempt to escape the annihilation of nuclear destruction. Instead, we fought.

In previous lectures we covered the rationale for using *lower organisms* in learning experiments. There will always be unaccounted variance amid the data with the use of humans. There will always be unknown factors that complicate our analysis. We can't control the genetic history of human participants. We can't control their learning history—keeping humans in cages went out with Tamerlane in the fourteenth century. We can't control what the participants think of the procedure. Are they guessing what the hypothesis might be? Are they trying to please the experimenter? Or are they trying to subvert the experimenter?

Skinner's approach to data was *non-statistical*. One of the greatest methodologists in our field never computed a single analysis of variance. I doubt whether Skinner computed as much as a puny Pearson correlation. The only statistical analyses in Skinner's work were the use of graphs defining rates of response as assessed by cumulative recorders.

The thrust of research today involves large sample sizes, sometimes very large sample sizes. This is made possible by computers. In the old days we were handicapped by the limitations of calculators. Sample sizes were small, of the order of 30 – 50 participants. Anything larger would cause the lights to go out in the Bronx. Today, Excel on our home computers can provide any statistic on any number of participants in a matter of seconds. Skinner, of course, is the contrarian in this large-N strategy. He demonstrates *small-N* research. *The Behavior of Organisms* (1938), his major work, involved a small number of pigeons and rats. Ever the thrifty researcher, Skinner used the same organisms under a number of experimental conditions.

Skinner *refused to enter the organism and posit intervening variables, whether psychological or physiological.* Like Watson, he saw no place for "mental life" in the study of behavior. And he didn't see his role as elucidating physiological or brain processes. In this, his orientation contradicts the current melding of psychology and neuroscience.

Hebb wrote in 1951 (*The Role of Neurological Ideas in Psychology*) that "We have no choice but to physiologize in psychology." Skinner disagreed, heartily. He viewed behavior, pure and simple, as the subject matter of psychology. His attitude was—if you want to study the brain, visit a neuroscientist. If you want to study the mind, visit a psychodynamic psychologist. If you want to study behavior, make an appointment to visit me.

Finally, Skinner's approach was *anti-theoretical.* He once wrote an influential paper (1950) *Are Theories of Learning Necessary?* (We can guess the answer.) For Skinner, we stay at the level of behavior. Note that his book is *The Behavior of Organisms*. By contrast, Hull's book is *Principles of Behavior*. He believed that adding additional levels of discourse—levels invariably tied to intervening variables—contributed little, if anything, to the observation of behavior. He didn't need theories because he didn't posit intervening variables. There were no gaps to fill in with formulas or excessive verbiage.

For Skinner, description of behavior is our goal. *Description is explanation.* Of course, psychologists from Thorndike to Hebb disagreed. In our time description comes with brain scans and brain imaging. These techniques were not available in Skinner's career. I doubt he would have availed himself of them, if they were.

Despite his anti-theoretical position, Skinner's approach comes off solidly in our criteria of what makes theories useful. His approach is communicable, clear, extremely test-able (and tested), and eminently parsimonious. Not bad, for not being a theory.

Like Watson, Skinner preferred to place psychology within the natural sciences rather than within the social sciences. He believed that psychology is most closely allied with biology, specifically with evolutionary biology, as it focuses on the relationship between organisms and their environments. Ironically, psychology has moved close to biology in the twenty first century, but to a different, anatomically-oriented, biology than the one Skinner gravitated to.

Like Watson, Skinner believed that the objectives of psychology are the *prediction and control of behavior.* These objectives have served as the buzzwords of behaviorism for a century. I suppose in their way they are laudable. They are also problematical.

With respect to control, Skinner pointed out that behavior has always been controlled. Parents control their children. Teachers control their students. Managers control their employees. The police control the streets. Big Brother controls everyone. Skinner suggested that the issue of control has been one of the two most strenuously critiqued elements of behaviorism. (We'll get to the second, unless something bad happens in the interim.) Skinner contended that this critique originated in the success behaviorists have had in changing behavior—or so they keep telling everyone.

There are additional factors that complicate the behaviorist emphasis on control. Behaviorists place the onus of control not on the recipients of consequences, but on the parents, teachers and managers who serve as the agents of control. It's easier to blame children, students and employees when things go awry. In addition, the notion of control runs counter to our desire to do whatever we want. We dislike feeling that we're controlled. We don't mind if the other fellow is controlled, especially if he annoys us. But when it comes to our own impetus to do whatever we want—well, leave us alone, or else.

Skinner suggested that there are two kinds of control in the behavioral world. The first is *control by punishment.* We perform a behavior to avoid being punished. The second is *control by reinforcement.* We perform a behavior to obtain a particular reward. Skinner suggested that most people have difficulty with the second rather than with the first kind of control. Controlling people by dangling reinforcers in front of them appears manipulative and it places the element of control on the environment rather than on personality. Avoiding punishment appears to place the element of control on the personality—I choose to comply or I choose to suffer the consequences. No one likes the idea that they are being coerced by bribes to comply. And no one from toddlers to great-grandparents can argue with the attempt to avoid punishment.

The question Skinner puts before us is—*what is the subject matter of psychology to be?*

Skinner pointed out that since ancient times the answer to this question is—the subject matter of psychology is mental life, observed through introspection and revealed through self-report. This orientation—called *mentalism*—can be found in ancient Greek, Indian and Chinese philosophies. This orientation can be found in nearly all religions. In the Hebrew Testament Joshua exhorts us (24: 1-3) to "choose thou this day whom ye will serve." It is explicitly stated in the Roman Catholic *Act of Contrition* that we "choose to do wrong" and "fail to do good." This orientation is also found in the legal system. Citizens bear the responsibility to obey or break the law. Whichever option we choose, the responsibility is on us.

This orientation is found throughout the history of psychology. It's found in the psychodynamic theories of personality (Freud and company), in Wundt's structuralism and in McDougall's hormic psychology. Whether the focus is religious, legal or psychological, in mentalism "to know thyself" means to know one's thoughts and feelings.

In mentalism thoughts and feelings are held to be *the causes of behavior.* Thoughts and feelings are given primacy because they appear to *precede and direct behavior.* (Interestingly, we rarely consider the opposite, that behaviors and external conditions determine thoughts and feelings.) "I want an orange," I think before walking to the refrigerator. "I want a linzer cookie," I think before driving to the bakery. In *Social Interest: A Challenge to Mankind* (1938), Alfred Adler was explicit—"I am convinced a person's behavior springs from his ideas." C.S. Lewis wrote that we seem to have "inside information" when it comes to our behavior. Our minds appear to look out over our behavior, as a captain looks out over the bow of his vessel. The mind is on the bridge and steering. Behavior is on the poop deck and rowing.

Skinner delighted in pointing out that mentalism was pretty much a dead end. Plato would have no trouble understanding the non-neuroscience chapters of a twenty first century textbook in psychology. The atomists

Democritus and Epicurus wouldn't understand a word in a twenty first century textbook on physics, even if it was translated into ancient Greek.

Skinner believed that there has been little progress in psychology (other than in his branch of behaviorism) because *psychologists have been looking in the wrong direction for the causes of behavior.* Psychologists have been looking inside the organism for the causes of behavior. They should be looking outside the organism for the causes of behavior. They should be looking toward the environment, specifically toward the *environment as it selects behavior.*

Skinner didn't use the term, but we can understand this issue using the social psychological concept of the *fundamental attribution error* (Fritz Heider). This is the idea that in attributing causation we can focus on the person or on the situation (environment). We can say a person did such-and-such on account of his or her personality. Or we can say a person did such-and-such because the environment made him or her do so. Like Skinner, social psychologists believe that most people, psychologists included, *overestimate the importance of personality and underestimate the importance of the situation.*

Skinner must have wallowed in the glory days of behaviorism in America. This was the period 1920 – 1960. Unfortunately for him, he lived long enough to witness the return of mentalism into mainstream psychology. Since the 1970s mentalism has been called "cognitive science." Even the term "mentalism" resurfaced from the netherworld. Roger Sperry, the eminent neuroscientist, wrote in *American Psychologist* (1988), "I renounced my earlier views ... in favor of a new mentalist position."

Skinner's writings on the "cognitive revolution" are bitter and despairing. He must have been deeply distressed by developments in psychology. In *The Shame of American Education* (1984) Skinner called the cognitive "revolt" a "retreat." In *Can the Experimental Analysis of Behavior Rescue Psychology?* (1983) Skinner wrote that "psychology has lost its hold on reality by following the Pied Piper of cognitive science." In the same paper he wrote that psychology has returned to a "hypothetical inner world" and in so doing has become a "shambles."

The last paper he wrote, delivered at the 1990 convention a week before he died, is entitled *Can Psychology Be a Science of Mind?* The paper is a nostalgic walk through the history of learning, referencing Thorndike, Hull and Tolman. (A polemicist to the end, Skinner chides them for failing to relate the study of behavior to evolutionary selection and variability.) The paper restates the answer Skinner supplied for a half century to the question in the title—psychology cannot be a science of the mind. Psychology can only be a science of behavior.

The science of behaviorism is the study of the *relationship between behavior and the environment*. The emphasis is on the *selecting environment* more than it is on the *responding organism*. This emphasis favors a selectionist orientation rather than an essentialist orientation. A *selectionist orientation* focuses on the acquisition and change of behavior. The environment selects the responses that are to continue. An *essentialist orientation* focuses on personality and on the possession of traits. The organism possesses traits and responses that it carries inside itself and demonstrates as the occasion demands.

As far back as 1953, Skinner conjectured that behavior is a function of three kinds of selection—natural selection, operant selection, and cultural selection.

Natural selection occurs across the life of a species. The term "organism" is appropriate at this level. Organisms are not born *tabula rasa*—this is a caricature of the behaviorist position—and not all responses are equally conditionable. Natural selection bestows physiological and anatomical limits on the behavior of organisms. The principles of natural selection work to the advantage of species when environmental conditions are stable and when a limited number of response options are successful. Organisms do not fare well when conditions change or when the repertoire of responses are no longer successful.

Operant selection occurs across the life of an individual organism. When it comes to *Homo sapiens* the term "person" is appropriate. Operant conditioning provides greater opportunity for survival, as it enables a larger and more flexible repertoire of responses. *To survive, organisms can learn new behaviors*. Perhaps you remember my example in a previous lecture of gulls that have learned to rip open garbage bags in dumpsters to find sources of food. Gulls are scavengers. They're called "sea gulls," but they will eat whatever they find, regardless whether it comes from the sea. Leftovers may be no more nutritious than crabs or pencil fish, but they provide another source of food—a source that has to be learned based on practice and experience. I suppose the source is also learned via observation, considering the savage fights that break out on the driveways over last night's dinner.

Cultural selection is unique to humans. The appropriate term at this level is "self."

There are several aspects to cultural selection. An obvious aspect involves *language*. Language allows for the transmission of information. Language short-circuits the learning process. That is, I can learn what other people have experienced without myself experiencing the conditions that went into learning. This is something gulls cannot do. They cannot pass the information about dumpster diving to their offspring. I profit from my experiences, or so I like to think. I also profit from the experiences of other people. When I'm hungry and broke I can ask around how to find food. A kindly neighbor may advise me to dumpster dive. Or maybe I read about dumpster diving in a book. I don't have to learn the technique myself. I can apply what other people have discovered.

This trove of verbalized past experience is passed on as directions, instructions, rules, proverbs, prescriptions, commandments and guidebooks. Certainly, science and literature transmit information. And so do street signs. "Slippery when wet." "Bridge ices before road surface." "Deer crossing." These signs tell us how to behave based on accumulated knowledge. They're based on what happened to people who drove too fast on particular roads or who didn't stay alert to the presence of deer.

Skinner called this verbalized trove of collective experience *rule-governed behavior*. Presumably, we get reinforced for following the rules and punished for not following the rules. We make it home safely and don't go into skids on wet surfaces or into the flanks of deer. The Moken (Morgan) sea gypsies are a small Indonesian tribe of fishers. They survived the horrendous 2005 tsunami that killed so many because they followed tribal lore that instructed them to find high ground if the sea receded. The people who didn't possess this lore perished when they went to the beaches to see where the ocean went.

Rule-governed behavior short-circuits acculturation—we profit from the experiences of the people of the past—but it is not as powerful as behavior learned from actual consequences. It is the difference between *explanation*—being told to slow down when the road is wet—and *experience*—crashing into the pine trees for driving too fast when the road is wet. It is the difference between being told not to touch the hot stove and touching the hot stove.

Language creates culture by transmitting information from one generation to the next. *Language also creates selves.* I have the words and I attribute characteristics to myself. "I am such-and-such—handsome, smart, tall, good-natured, generous and so on through the list of positive attributes." "I am not such-and-such—appearance-and intellect-challenged, mean-spirited, miserly and so on through the list of negative attributes." I am told what I am by other people, who have the words to describe me. I then apply the words to myself. If I lack a word for good or ill—well, it's difficult to call myself by a descriptor I don't have.

Another aspect of cultural selection lies in this—*the culture establishes the reinforcers and punishers that follow particular behaviors.* A behavior that earned punishment in one place and time may no longer be punished. The behavior may now be reinforced. Similarly, a behavior that once was reinforced may no longer be reinforced. The behavior may now be punished.

Consider spousal abuse. In former times this was not a crime. Police looked the other way. In our time spousal abuse is a crime and no one looks the other way. Consider the use of seat belts in cars. In former years it was not a crime to go headfirst through the windshield. In our time, if you don't "click it," you risk "a ticket." Consider drunk driving and driving under the influence. In former times many people never had a second thought about driving after consuming alcoholic beverages. In our time we have "zero tolerance" for driving under the influence. (Unfortunately, too many people disregard zero tolerance. About a third of vehicular fatalities nationwide involve alcohol.) And consider behavior that was once judged aberrant. Homosexuality, lesbianism, unspecified "loose behavior' by women—these behaviors could result in ostracism, jail time and worse. The mental health profession considered these behaviors as mental disorders—gays, lesbians and loose women earned diagnoses declaring them "abnormal" and "disordered." In our time we recognize that such orientations are acceptable and appropriate. We no longer experience panic attacks when we see two people of the same sex kiss.

Skinner's focus was on the selecting environment rather than on the responding organism. For Skinner *causal control of behavior lies outside the organism*. Along with the issue of control, this is the second bone of contention people have with his behaviorism.

Skinner's focus on the environment as the causative agent and his extreme anti-mentalism is nothing new in psychology. It goes back to the time of Watson and the founding of behaviorism. E. B. Holt (1873 – 1946) wrote in the oddly named but prescient book *The Freudian Wish* (1915) that "It is the most precious achievement of the physical sciences that the 'secrets behind' phenomena lie in the phenomena and are to be found out by observing the phenomena ... the 'mental sciences' have not yet learned the lesson." For Holt "the study of what men do ... how they behave ... comprises the entire field of psychology."

Holt pointed out that astronomy and chemistry advanced only when they dropped the notion that there were presences or personalities within phenomena. The god Helios was dropped and the sun became a star, pure and simple. And the god Hermes Trismegistus was dropped and mercury became an element, pure and simple. Psychology has yet to apply this purely naturalistic approach. We still look inside personalities for the causes of behavior.

Skinner may have been flattering himself, but he saw behaviorism contesting the same reactionary issues evolutionary biologists faced in their battles with creationists. In the same way evolutionary biologists reject the notion of a creative deity, behaviorists reject the notion of an indwelling being originating and directing behavior. If this sounds odd that we're dismissing such items as personality and consciousness, consider that our focus is on the *causes of behavior*.

Skinner became an admired, maybe even a revered, figure by the end of his life. For better or worse, he was a prominent part of the history of psychology. He was, as the saying goes, "living history." The cognitive revolution overthrew many of the behaviorist proscriptions, but Skinner kept up the fight to the last week of his life. We have to admire someone who keeps fighting in a losing cause.

Skinner was not particularly admired and certainly not revered earlier in his career. He was never president of the American Psychological Association. He was an overly eager polemicist and he was arrogant. He was right. Everyone else was wrong. Even many of his fellow travelers in the field of learning were wrong. Throughout his career Skinner never hesitated to offer criticisms of psychology understood as "the study of the mind." I'm no behaviorist, but I believe these criticisms are "spot on," as they say in the land of tea and scones. These criticisms bear examining.

Skinner believed psychology cannot be the study of the mind because *the mind is private*. We can never be sure we reinforce thoughts and feelings—the right thoughts and feelings. We can reinforce a child to differentiate between colors and to answer factual questions, such as "What's seven times seven?" We cannot be sure we consistently reinforce a child to differentiate among emotions or to verbalize subtle internal states. We hear a child's self-report of thoughts and feelings, but we cannot be sure the child accurately reports what he or she thinks and feels and we cannot be sure we share the child's meaning.

Never mind the subtleties of feeling fear, anxiety, dread, despair, angst and so on. Never mind the complexities of feeling self-esteem and self-worth. Basic biological states such as hunger and pain may not be reported accurately or accurately understood. The child insists, "I'm hungry," and the parent answers, "No, you're not." Or the parent says "Eat your dinner," and the child protests, "I'm not hungry." People of all ages are notoriously poor at localizing pain. I say my shoulder hurts, but my lungs are the cause of my pain. I say the tooth on the upper right side hurts, but the tooth on the lower left side is infected.

Skinner suggested that cognitive and personality psychologists engaged in an *incomplete causal analysis*. They stop at the level of intervening variables and they confuse intervening variables with independent variables. Remember that Skinner is looking for the causes of behavior. He locates these causes in the physical environment rather than inside the organism.

So a teen sulks in her room. We say she sulks because she feels resentment. We interpret the resentment as the cause of the sulking. We stop at resentment. We don't take the additional step to identify what causes the resentment. In this case we'll conjecture that it's inconsistent punishment.

So a child acts aggressively. We say this child acts aggressively because he's frustrated. We interpret the frustration as the cause of the aggression. We stop at frustration. We don't take the additional step to identify what causes the frustration. In this case we'll conjecture that it's facing arithmetic problems he can't solve.

As a third and final example, we meet a person who exhibits phobic behavior about using escalators. We say this person is phobic because of anxiety. We interpret the anxiety as the cause of the phobia. We stop at anxiety. We don't take the additional step to identify what causes the anxiety. In this case we'll conjecture that it was a social blunder of some sort made on an escalator that caused the anxiety.

Skinner suggested that most psychologists saw the relationship among variables as linear—independent variables result in intervening variables that result in dependent variables. Skinner believed the relationship was different. In his view *independent variables simultaneously result in both intervening variables and dependent variables.* The relationship of intervening variables and dependent variables is *concomitant.* They occur together, but intervening variables are not the causes of dependent variables. Both are caused by independent variables.

So inconsistent punishment causes both resentment and sulking. Impossible academic challenges cause both frustration and aggression. And a social blunder causes both anxiety and an aversion to escalators.

The relationship among these variables may be bidirectional. Intervening variables and dependent variables may exacerbate each other. Resentment intensifies the sulking and sulking intensifies the resentment. Frustration intensifies the aggression and aggression intensifies the frustration. And anxiety intensifies the phobic behavior and phobic behavior intensifies the anxiety. But in all cases the variables result from environmental independent variables.

Skinner suggested that the preoccupation with intervening variables detracts from searching for environmental factors that can effectively change behaviors. There's precious little we can do when we focus on resentment or on frustration or on anxiety. Our focus on such internal states may well intensify them. More can be done by focusing on the environmental events that create troublesome feelings and behaviors. Parents can strive to be more consistent in punishing their overly-sensitive teenage children. Educators can strive to better match the level of arithmetic problems and the intellectual capabilities of students. Adults can strive to master social skills in order to avoid interpersonal blunders.

In a 1988 paper entitled *The Operant Side of Behavior Therapy* Skinner wrote:

> "By rejecting feelings and states of mind as the initiating causes of behavior, and turning instead to the environmental conditions responsible both for what people do and feel while doing it, behavior analysts, and with them behavior therapists, can approach the larger problems of human behavior in a much more effective way."

We move away from what can be accomplished when we concentrate on intervening variables. The solution to changing behavior lies in changing behavior, which is a function of changing the consequences of the behavior. This, of course, is easier said than done. Many undesirable behaviors carry potent and pleasurable consequences that people are loath to give up.

Throughout his career, Skinner viewed behavior as a topic of study in its own right, *sui generis*. To the contrary, many people view behavior as trivial and as superficial. Behavior is devalued and seen as less important than cognition. Behavior is viewed as a signpost directing us to intervening states. This is common practice in trait psychology. Raymond Cattell defined a trait as a "mental structure" that is inferred from observable behavior and, what is more often the case, from surveys. So I view a child sobbing. I immediately posit the trait of sadness. I view another child laughing. I immediately posit the trait of humor. I view another child solving arithmetic problems. I immediately posit the trait of intelligence.

These traits are said to cause behavior, but they are unexplained. It's rarely specified how these traits originate. And these traits are often redundant. They don't offer anything beyond what we discover by observing behavior. To this extent, traits are *examples of circular reasoning*. Frequently, they are *alternate descriptions serving as explanations*.

We say he drinks too much rum because he has an oral complex. Positing an oral complex doesn't add anything to what we already know— he drinks too much rum. We say she's fastidious because of an anal complex. The "complex" doesn't clarify matters—we already know her house is so clean we can eat off the floorboards. We see a child throwing chapter books in the preschool. We say the child demonstrates the trait of aggressiveness. But we already know that—we had to duck as a Berenstain Bear hardcover sailed towards our heads.

Even biological urges can be expressed in a redundant manner. He's eating because he's "hungry." How do we know he's hungry? Because we see him eat (and assume falsely that only hungry people eat). It's difficult to define the internal state of hunger without recourse to environmental events—we see him eat and we know he's fasted since break of day. Usually, however, we don't go this far in our analysis. We make an incomplete causal analysis and stop at the feeling of hunger.

There are innumerable traits posited as responsible for behavior. What's worse, there are a number of "partial people" or "psychological entities" that are considered as the causes of behavior. Famously, we have the conflict between the id and the superego mediated by the ego. I'm on edge tonight—my anima must be ovulating. I'm mischievous tonight—my persona is acting up. I'm striving to better myself—I'm on the yellow brick road to selfhood. The psychologists who devised these concepts claimed that they were *explanatory fictions*. Somehow or other, the word "fictions" gets dropped and oracle-worshipping students reify these imaginary concepts.

Traits are characteristics drawn from observing behavior—they are, if we're lucky. More frequently, traits are based on surveys. Skinner was a critic of the vast field of tests and measurements. He viewed survey research as, at best, a secondary method. (Weirdly, Skinner once developed a projective test—the verbal summator—in which people would interpret partially audible words.) Survey research substitutes verbal descriptions of memories and judgments about the incidence of behavior for the direct observation of behavior. We can ask people what they do. Or we can observe what people do.

Skinner's focus was on the effect of the environment on behavior. He was not particularly interested in cognitive factors. But over the course of his career he offered a behaviorist interpretation of intervening variables. Some of these interpretations seem on the money. Others seem to have a cash flow problem.

He viewed *thoughts and feelings as collateral to behavior.* They occur at the same time as behavior and, through conditioning, may come to precede behavior, but they are not the causes of behavior. It's like being on a train. I took a long train ride once. Peter Ustinov was on the train. So was Anne Bancroft. So were Christopher Plummer and Shelley Winters. Oh, wait, that was a movie I saw about a long train ride. Anyway, the analogy goes like this. The thoughts and feelings I possess are the scenery. The scenery is enjoyable. Sometimes it's scary. But the scenery doesn't move the train. The third rails that run alongside the tracks move the train. The third rails are the consequences of reinforcements and punishments that move people through life.

Skinner had a *functional view of knowledge.* Teachers often say of students that they "have it." Or that they "got it." This makes knowledge to be a kind of possession, like giving students loaves of challah bread. We talk as if we hand students actual "bodies" of knowledge. (Sometimes the bodies are living and sometimes they're corpses.) Skinner viewed knowledge—say mastery of the theories of learning course—not as a body of knowledge but as a *body of action.* We know what to do and when to do it, if only to answer questions on a quiz. For Skinner, knowledge is not an entity, but a process. Knowledge is not a noun, "thoughts," but a verb, "thinking."

Skinner was opposed to the idea that we *store thoughts and memories* or that we carry copies of responses that we consult when needed. He viewed memory storage less like a computer than like a light bulb. Light is not stored in the bulb. Light occurs when electricity heats the filament inside the bulb. Behavior occurs not because of copies stored inside us, but because behavior has been selected by environmental consequences. *We do not store changes—we are changed.*

The concept of stored copies or representations of events fractures the unity of behavior (or of personality). And it leaves serious questions unanswered. We have a copy of an event in our mind—who's viewing the copy? How is the copy different from the viewer of the copy? Philosophically, this leads to what was called "infinite regression." We explain things by going back a step—we view a copy of an event. But we do not explain or account for the step. Skinner pointed out that we view the "stream of consciousness," but we cannot view how the stream is created.

Monty Python illuminated infinite regression in a comedy skit. Explorers in a jungle come across a film crew filming them. They turn around and there's another film crew filming them. This crew turns around—you can guess what they see.

These criticisms of Skinner are intriguing, but they overlook the fact that memories can be viewed in the theater of the mind. We appear to possess mental copies of events and we do, at times, review these copies. I can review while seated in this room the trip I took last summer to Orange Park, Florida. I can review the trip in a chronological manner and I can judge what I liked and didn't like about the trip. Similarly, I can recount in a courtroom the car accident I witnessed at the corner of Morris and North Avenues last April. Given the problematic nature of eyewitness testimony, it's an open question whether my review accurately matches the accident. The point is I can cognitively review my recollection of the accident.

When it comes to *feelings* Skinner supported the James-Lange theory of emotions. This theory starts with an authentic independent variable—something environmental produces changes in the body. The original James-Lange theory erroneously focused on changes in the viscera. The revised James-Lange theory focuses on the face. We have an emotion as we become aware of changes in facial expression.

When it comes to feelings Skinner avoids making an incomplete causal analysis. He always proceeds from the organism to the causative environment. (Of course, feelings involve more than events in the environment.) Experiencing favorable consequences results in *eagerness*. Experiencing unfavorable consequences results in *doubt and a disinclination to act*. Aversive events result in *frustration*. Dangerous events result in *fear*. Escaping from aversive stimuli results in *freedom*. Claiming credit for our achievements results in *dignity*.

When it comes to *choice* Skinner supported the *matching law* developed by his Harvard colleague Richard Herrnstein. (Shortly before he died in 1994, Herrnstein became notorious for coauthoring a book—*The Bell Curve*—that suggested that there were racial differences in intelligence.) The matching law, developed in the context of behavioral economics, is solid behaviorism in that it centers on behavioral, rather than on cognitive, factors in making decisions.

The matching law states that there is a positive correlation between the rate of response and the number of reinforcements an organism received. *When given choices, organisms will do what they have been most often reinforced to do.* The assumption is that organisms want to maximize the number of reinforcements they receive.

We can see how the matching law plays out in this "real world" example. Many parents face the situation in which their children are "good in sports and poor at study." Parents attribute this difference to "laziness" and bemoan the fact that their children do not apply the same diligence at homework as they do on the ballfield. Behaviorists would contradict the parents and suggest that the behavior of their children follows the matching law. In choosing whether to study or to hurl a football, children choose the behavior that has provided the most reinforcements. In this case, it's hurling a football.

There are additional factors that enter into decision making. One factor is the *immediacy or delay in receiving reinforcement.* Once again, hurling a football has the advantage. Compared to academics, there are immediate payoffs in sports. Teammates carry the quarterback off the field on their shoulder pads. The coaches high five the quarterback. The athletic director lights a victory cigar. The crowd erupts in applause. In academia payoffs are often delayed. The student has to wait till the following week to get the quiz results back. Report cards come out a few times a year. The honor roll is printed once a year.

In making choices we also have to consider the concept of *melioration,* that is, the *perceived value of a reinforcer.* The idea is that the choices that are available have different values. These values may not correspond to the number of reinforcers a person received. In fact, sometimes *the choices we prefer derived from fewer rather than from a greater number of reinforcers.* The quarterback may be on the field every practice, but he really prefers acting in the plays of Shakespeare. And a student majoring in chemistry may really prefer to sing arias on the concert stage.

Julian Rotter (1916 – 2014) developed a similar concept in his social learning theories. (Interestingly, Rotter tried to devise formulas in his theory.) Rotter suggested that the prediction of behavior is a function both of the expectation that a particular behavior will result in reinforcement and the *value placed on the reinforcer*.

Skinner's influence was enormous in American psychology in the second half of the twentieth century. This influence derived from the ease and seeming simplicity in applying the principles of operant conditioning. The application of positive reinforcement (and the avoidance of punishment) permeated the worlds of education and business. A massive shift—a paradigm shift?—occurred in the clinical setting with the rise of behavior therapy and behavior modification as alternatives to traditional psychodynamic therapies. The shift continued with the development of cognitive-behavioral therapy in the treatment of depression. In some clinical populations—the autistic spectrum and learning disabilities—conditioning techniques offered the only treatment strategies.

Skinner experimented exclusively with lower organisms, but he was never shy about generalizing behavioral principles developed in the operant conditioning chamber to human populations. For example, he once suggested (1977) that we could replace revenue from taxation with revenue from gambling. To do this, we would have to create a nation of gamblers by conditioning gambling. Conditioning games of chance would commence in grade school and carry into adulthood. Of course, Skinner was far behind the times in making this suggestion, since we're already a nation of gamblers.

Skinner wrote about creating an utopian society based on operant conditioning. The guiding idea, which we found many lectures ago in Thorndike, was that the principles of science can engineer a better world than the one that now exists. In *The Steep and Thorny Way to a Science of Behavior* (1975) Skinner called on us to:

"... forsake the primrose path of total individualism, of self-actualization, self-adoration and self-love and turn

instead to the construction of that heaven on earth which
is within reach of the methods of science."

Alas, Skinner's utopia hasn't come about. I don't know about you,
but when I picture utopia I imagine scantily clad models lounging beside
waterfalls in a setting that looks like Tahiti. Skinner's utopia is nothing like
that. It's rather a bland place in which we refrain from war, consume only
what we need, and have only enough children to replace ourselves. That
would be one of me, unless I was beside myself, in which case that would
be two of me. And Skinner's utopia is a world where people earn rewards
only for performing productive behavior. There would be no dole to keep
the poor poor and there would be no hedge funds to keep the rich rich.

Skinner suggested that the movement toward utopia hasn't occurred
because there are too many vested interests in maintaining the status quo
and because future punishing consequences for failing to produce utopia
have little effect on current behavior. The latter concept is particularly
cogent when it comes to global warming. Unless Antarctica collapses
into the sea during the semester break, the punishing effects of global
warming won't be seen for twenty-five or fifty years. We won't be around
to experience them, but our children and grandchildren will. Even if
the negative implications of global warming are overstated by fifty or
ninety percent, it seems we have a responsibility to see that the world
our descendants inhabit is a safe place. (It may be that one of the reasons
people don't take global warming seriously is because the term "greenhouse
effect" is used. The image of a greenhouse is not particularly alarming.
Scientists may have inspired greater alarm if they used a different term—
"death house effect" or "Your grandchildren are going to suffocate to death
effect.")

A point about Skinner's utopia is politically relevant. In his utopia
lawmakers live under the same contingencies as the rest of society. This is
often not the case in our current system. Lawmakers live very different lives
from the unwashed hordes over whom they legislate. Consider that until
recently members of Congress were exempt from insider trader regulations.
Members of Congress could get rich for doing what would send private
citizens to the gray-bar hotel.

Skinner's theory has been widely applied and broadly appreciated—if not the behaviorist drapery, then the conditioning floorboards. But like every theory, it is open to criticism. In closing, I'll like to consider a few criticisms.

There is excessive generalization from lower organisms to human beings. There is no question that reinforcers and punishers are effective at the human level. Anyone with children or pets knows this. However, there may be additional factors that we need to take into consideration at the human level. To name two, there's creativity and there's love. I suppose there's also hate, but that would be three factors. And there's an interpersonal dimension we need to consider. Unlike events in the operant conditioning chamber, where it doesn't make a bit of difference who feeds in pellets of rat food, on the human level the people who provide reinforcers and punishers matter a great deal. Praise and condemnation are not received impersonally. It makes a great deal of difference who regales us with praise and who chucks dornicks of condemnation.

Like Watson's, Skinner's behaviorism works by ignoring vast swaths of human existence—swaths like emotion, personality, and social psychology. There's a nod to account for such factors, but the nods often seem half measures at best. Freedom, for example, seems to be more than escaping aversive consequences and dignity seems to be more than taking credit for one's achievements. To be fair, behaviorists weren't the only psychologists who ignored vast swaths of human existence. Carlson (1966) examined topics in the *Psychological Abstracts* from 1954 - 1960. He found 801 references to anxiety (it was the middle of the twentieth century, after all), 124 references to fear, and a paltry 69 to love and 49 to humor.

There's a nearly irrefutable use of reinforcement to cover all behavior from muscle twitches to language to creativity. (Skinner once suggested that creativity results from being reinforced for making different responses from trial to trial. This definition hardly matches what creative writers and artists and musicians do on a daily basis.) And the concept of reinforcement covers a vast spread of time. I take a shot of whiskey and immediately feel the effect. But I am also working on getting a graduate degree, which takes years. This time period is incompatible with immediate effects. And this time period includes quite a bit of punishment, as well—driving on New Jersey roads to the East Campus, finding a parking spot, listening to lectures, writing essays and memorizing chunks of difficult material. The goal toward which we laboriously struggle is strewn with as many annoyances as pleasantries.

There's a blind faith in the efficacy of reinforcers and punishers. At the human level we can resist reinforcers because of morals and values— or we may resist reinforcers simply because we're on a diet. People act in defiant ways despite the possibility of reinforcement. And people will not change their behavior despite the possibility of punishment. We see this in individual lives—people can resist temptations and receive punishments in the place of reinforcements. And we see this in the course of history. During the Cold War thousands upon thousands of East Europeans resisted joining the communist state. In place of the positive reinforcement of inclusion in the ruling party and the negative reinforcement of being left alone, free from abuse and torture, these people preferred punishment to conformity.

This resistance demonstrates *reactance*, which is the tendency *not to comply with behavioral contingencies when we perceive we are being manipulated*. I believe reactance is seriously underestimated by behaviorists who assume that reinforcements and punishments will automatically work. We tell children to eat their spinach to get extra lumps of ice cream. The children refuse. For that matter, we tell children to be quiet. They shriek louder. Drivers tailgate to get slow cars out of the fast lane. Slow drivers drive slower. As is frequently the case, when we tell people to do something, they refuse. And when we tell them not to do something, they do it. The latter "reverse psychology" is a frequent technique in a parent's toolbox.

Despite the reliance on observable behavior, behaviorists have not solved the issue of *duplicity*. You may remember a previous example—a boy eats at the kitchen table only when he believes his father will see him eating in the living room. *We comply with contingencies only when we have to. We comply with contingencies only when we are being observed.* This is a serious issue, not only in suburban homes, but in prisons and treatment centers. People will comply with contingencies because courts require that they do. Life becomes easier inside prisons and treatment centers and the stay inside such facilities shortens. Once the inmates are released from such places, the new behaviors shed like dead skin after a sunburn and it's back to the same old style of misbehavior.

Finally, the requirements of *prediction and control* focus our attention on trivial behaviors. I'm a creature of habit—I admitted that previously. I get up at the same time, I retire at the same time, I eat the same meals, I drive the same routes, I listen to the same radio stations, can you believe I watch the same reruns on television?—this is all drearily well and good. *Unless something different happens* while I conduct my daily business, my behavior is eminently predictable. And my behavior is eminently uninteresting. The predictable aspects of our lives are the least interesting aspects of our lives. For better or worse, *the most interesting aspects of our lives are the unpredictable aspects of our lives.* As they are unpredictable, they can't be under our control or under anyone's control. And they are the aspects of our lives that are usually not repeatable. Think about falling in love—this is rather important and it's not predictable. Think about getting in a car accident—this is rather important and it's not predictable. Think about the next time we buy a scratch off lottery ticket—most of the time we tear the ticket up and drop it in the nearest trash bin, but the day may come when we don't throw the ticket away and start singing hallelujahs instead. Like falling in love and like getting into a crash, hitting the jackpot *decisively changes our lives.* Such infrequent events are what we put in our autobiographies. We exclude the trivial events. The truly important events are not included in Skinner's (or anyone's) behaviorism—they can't be. The unimportant events are included, as they are predictable and controllable. They are also repeated, countless times.

To use a Biblical analogy in closing, by focusing on the predictable and controllable events in our lives, behaviorists study specks and miss the logs.

Thank you.

ADDENDUM

Essay Questions

Essay One ~ Thorndike

Late in his career Thorndike revised his "laws of learning." The most important revision concerned the law of effect. Contrary to his first view, Thorndike suggested that an annoying state of affairs does not stamp out stimulus - response connections in the same fundamental way that a satisfying state of affairs stamp in stimulus - response connections. In modern terms Thorndike suggested that punishment does not affect learning in the same fundamental way that reinforcement does.

Many psychologists believe that Thorndike had it right the first time and that he made a mistake rejecting the negative half of the law of effect.

What is your view on this issue? Please explain why you think Thorndike was right to reject the negative half of the law of effect. Or do you believe that Thorndike made a mistake revising the law of effect?

Essay Two ~ Operant Conditioning

B. F. Skinner conducted experiments using pigeons and rats, but he was never shy about generalizing the data from such organisms to the human situation. Skinner once suggested that we could use the principles of operant conditioning to create a nation of gamblers. Revenue from gambling would replace revenue from taxation.

Let's take Skinner seriously. Describe specific principles of operant conditioning that, if applied, would increase the rate of gambling. (You can choose any game of chance the state of New Jersey currently permits.) How could you employ the principles you describe to increase gambling? Some of these principles may be in current use—how could you improve the principles in order to increase revenue from gambling?

Please keep the focus of the answer on operant conditioning rather than on the games of chance. Use the behavior of gambling to demonstrate your understanding of operant conditioning.

Essay Three ~ the Garcia Effect

The Garcia Effect refers to the fact that animals form taste aversions easily and in contradiction to two principles of classical conditioning (the inter-stimulus interval and contiguity). So coyotes avoid attacking sheep and chickens after consuming carcasses tainted with substances that make them sick.

It is an open question whether the Garcia Effect exists in humans. Many people continue to drink and to use drugs after becoming sick with their use. People continue to eat the same meals that make them sick.

Please address the factors that may cause people to continue to ingest substances that make them sick. Why don't humans respond in the avoidant way coyotes respond to substances that induce sickness?

Essay Four ~ Guthrie

If you're like me, you don't have bad habits. Maybe you know a person who has a bad habit you'd like to change. Please describe the habit and how you'd go about changing the habit through the application of the three methods of behavior change outlined by Guthrie. These methods are the incompatible response method, the threshold method and the fatigue method.

You may want to decrease the occurrence of an undesirable habit. Alternately, you may want to increase the occurrence of a desirable habit. Keep in mind that all three methods may not apply in the case of the habit you described.

The habit cannot be smoking, nail biting or procrastination. And the habit cannot be any of the habits described in class or in the textbook.

Essay Five ~ Tolman

Edward Tolman was eclectic in his approach to psychology. He was intrigued by philosophy, by Gestalt psychology, even by psychoanalysis. Purposive behaviorism, his theory of learning, was a blend of classic behaviorist elements, such as we saw in the theories of Thorndike and Pavlov, and unique cognitive elements not often seen in the learning theories of his generation. Tolman was both a behaviorist and a pioneer in what became cognitive psychology.

Describe what elements in purposive behaviorism reflected a behaviorist orientation.

Describe what elements in purposive behaviorism reflected a cognitive orientation.

And address the issue of an eclectic approach to psychological topics. Was Tolman right to be eclectic? Or would it have been better if he restricted his approach to either behaviorism or to cognitive psychology?

Essay Six ~ Hull

Clark Hull's approach to theory was to define and quantify a number of variables. These variables would then be inserted in a formula. The purpose of the formula was to account for the various elements that we need to predict behavior. This formulaic conceptualization of behavior was unique among the theorists we cover in this course.

Please address the following.

What do you see as the strengths of this formulaic approach? What advantages does this approach provide Hull in comparison to the other theorists we covered?

What do you see as the weaknesses of this formulaic approach? What impediments does this approach raise in developing a useful theory of behavior?

Essay Seven ~ Hebb

We've encountered two contradictory attitudes in this course about the inclusion of physiological intervening variables into theories of learning. B. F. Skinner believed that neuroscientific concepts were not necessary in theories of learning. Donald Hebb believed, to the contrary, that theories of learning had to incorporate neuroscientific concepts.

Which approach do you prefer? Can we formulate theories of learning without including elements of neuroscience? Or do we need to include elements of neuroscience in the formulation of theories of learning? What is the strongest argument you can make in support of your position on this issue?

Printed in the United States
By Bookmasters